FVL
+ 1.00
(14 online)

52 Great Weekend Escapes

in Southern California

Ray Bangs and Chris Becker

INSIDERS'GUIDE®

GUILFORD, CONNECTICUT
AN IMPRINT OF THE GLOBE PEQUOT PRESS

For my brother, Peter, who has always been a better fisherman.

Ray Bangs

To Danielle and Mom for giving me my first great camera, and to Northland Publishing for giving us our first big chance.

Chris Becker

INSIDERS'GUIDE®

Text design and spot photography: Peter Friedrich
Maps created by Danielle Becker

ISSN 1549-5957
ISBN 0-7627-3083-8

Manufactured in the United States of America
First Edition/First Printing

Contents

Spring

Easy

Medium

Difficult

Summer

Easy

Fall

Winter

Easy

Medium

Difficult

Acknowledgments

Southern California overflows with terrific people and companies dedicated to showing residents and visitors alike a great time. You'll find many of them mentioned in these pages. We apologize to any we've missed the first time around—though we look forward to including you in the second edition!

Several folks deserve special mention. Claude Fiset at Uptimal stayed in touch throughout the long writing process, and was a huge help all the way. Chad Bastian at Fly Above All Airsports, and all the folks at High Adventure were also indispensable. (Must be something about paragliding that gives these people such sunny dispositions.) Tom and Mary Clare Mulhall at the Terra Cotta Inn were a joy to work with; they single-handedly gave us all the "in" we needed in the Palm Springs adventure/tourism community. The good people working in California's national and state parks and other natural areas were a tremendous asset as well; in fact, not one request or favor we asked of them went unfulfilled. Finally, we'd like to say a big thanks to all the organizations, outfitters, and photographers who contributed many beautiful images when our own photos just weren't good enough. Everybody's help has been greatly appreciated.

One thing we've tried to keep in mind while writing these books is that nothing exists in a vacuum—weekend adventure must coexist with the impulse to preserve what we're enjoying during these excursions. Organizations like the Bolsa Chica Conservancy, the

Salton Sea Authority, and the docent network volunteering across California's park system are all dedicated to protecting the state's natural heritage; we have them (and a multitude of others) to thank for preserving the natural beauty Southern California offers. Being outdoors on the West Coast would be a far different and much less rewarding experience without their tireless, earth-moving efforts. Thank you, thank you, thank you.

We'd also like to say thanks to the various tourism organizations and professionals, from the California Division of Tourism all the way down to the local chambers of commerce. We received great supplemental information from officials around the state. As the preservationists keep California beautiful, these tourism experts provide vacationers all the information they might need to ensure people get out there to see the beauty and enjoy their visit.

We'd like to thank all our family members and friends whose support and encouragement made this book possible. A few went well beyond the call of duty. First, a big thanks to officers Kristin Koskelin and Amy Bonner for their "armed escort" to Catalina Island —that was truly a great weekend escape. Thanks to Erik Hoffman for his help and some of the best chapter ideas, and for leading the way on several trips. Special thanks also to the Schiesser family and the Garriguses, Don and Frannie, for coming through with some much needed last-minute assistance. Thank you to Darcy Jo Brandt and Dave Newlin, who were always there for encouragement and positive outlook. Much appreciation goes to Peter Taylor, Megan Finnerty, and Jenn Lafferty who were always ready to roll. Thanks to Joel Klandrud for his unrivaled and continued technical expertise, and for tagging along on more than a couple "let's go now" last-minute escapes. Thanks to Karoline Strigl, who came all the way from Germany to "help with research" and spend a month on the road— *nicky schlect*. A special thanks goes to Jeff Gourley, Mike Watson, and the rest of the *Divers Ocean Planet Magazine* crew. Finally, we'd especially like to tip our hats to Scott Adams at Globe Pequot Press and Tammy Gales at Northland Publishing—no writers have ever worked with more honest and helpful editors.

Thank you all very much. Many safe travels.

Introduction

Life seems to get busier all the time. School, work, family, relationships—obligations seem to pile up, leading to lots of stress. It's often not until later in life, when things finally settle down a bit, retirement comes around, and hours pass like a calm breeze, that we seem to have the time for fun. But doesn't it make more sense to enjoy life as you're living it today?

Weekend escapes can help you to deal with that stress, recharge your spirit and refresh your soul, to have some *fun*. This book provides plenty of quick escape options to help you do just that. Having fun is what Southern California is all about.

First, however, before anyone from the central coast gets too excited, we wholeheartedly admit that portions of this book cover weekend destinations north of what most would consider Southern California. This book reaches from the Mexico border north roughly half the length of California, from Big Sur on the coast to King's Canyon National Park in the east. (Be sure to pick up a copy of the upcoming *52 Great Weekend Escapes in Northern California,* which covers adventures in the northern reaches of the state.)

Don't worry about missing out because your weekend doesn't happen to begin on a Friday. In fact, most midweek "weekends" save you money and often help you avoid the Saturday and Sunday crowds. Additionally, while this book focuses on short trips spanning one, two, or three days, keep in mind that many of these weekends are easy to stretch into four- or five-day excursions, or even two-week adventures, if you wish.

Most importantly, this book is designed to show you a great escape from the routine. While every weekend of your life certainly doesn't need to be some elaborate adventure or ultra vacation, there are few better things than a short trip away to recharge yourself and beat back some of that stress. Here, most of the homework has already been done for you, and as a result, it's that much easier to drag yourself off the sofa and cut loose for a couple of days. You'll be amazed what's out there. With this book in hand, you hold a prime opportunity to discover a new side to yourself, to establish a new hobby or take part in a pursuit you absolutely love, to find a little peace and quiet, to enjoy a few days of R&R, or to do whatever it is you need to do. So read through the book and pick out a few choices, dial a few phone numbers, and make plans for a great weekend escape. It doesn't get any easier than this!

How to Use This Guide

This book is written for you and offers a year's worth of options for great recreation in Southern California. We strive to get you out the door, trying something new and exciting. We feel it's good practice to make the great weekend escape as often as possible because you'll always find yourself returning to the routine recharged and refreshed. If you're feeling adventurous, try some activities you may not have done before. Go skydiving if it suits you. We'd like to remind you of all the incredible landscapes just out there waiting, beautiful scenery sure to inspire just as it has inspired millions for generations. This book also strives to get you involved with some of the organizations that protect these valuable resources and phenomenal places. Read through the wealth of exciting options, and pick out a couple of adventures to explore further. Get involved. Have fun, and have a great trip.

Description

Each escape is broken down into six sections: The chapters describe what the weekends entail, what to know before you go, and how to prepare for the experience. We also provide inside info whenever possible or necessary—ideas, suggestions, even warnings to keep you informed on the aspects of the adventure that are hard to know about without some on-the-ground experience. So choose the adventures that sound appealing to you, make a few phone calls, prepare yourself, and follow our advice (and your outfitter's) about what to do once you are there.

Maps and Directions

The maps and directions lead you to the start of your adventure, whether it is a national park entrance, trailhead, parking lot, or harbor. Some outfitters mentioned will meet you at your resort or hotel or arrange a meeting point. Use the maps in the book to get a general idea of where your escape is located, then follow the written directions to the start of the adventure. Detailed maps such as topography or recreation maps are also a good acquisition for certain types of adventures. For example, you may survive the Mount Whitney trail without toting along a whole slew of wilderness topo maps, but it's a good idea to do further research whenever heading off the beaten path or into backcountry areas. For this type of escape, detailed maps may be a necessity, and if a map is required, do what it takes to get the map you need. It's also a good idea to have a quality road map in the car, especially when driving around bigger cities such as Los Angeles and San Diego. Of course, for many of these great weekend escape destinations, it's easy to find a map when you arrive. You might find a great Catalina Island map on a restaurant placemat or perhaps at a postcard shop. Don't forget to ask your outfitter. Finally, a map is not worth much if you can't read it—if you don't know how, take some time to learn.

Season

The activities and destinations are organized by their optimal season. Keep in mind that you may enjoy many of these adventures any time of the year. Heed warnings about temperature extremes though, especially in the summer and winter, and always remember to take plenty of water. Be especially cautious when heading to mountainous regions, as temperature and weather can turn treacherous in an instant. Keep in mind that the off-season or shoulder-season visit may save a few bucks or keep you away from crowds. Be sure to check with the respective management agencies and outfitters for weather updates, forecasts, and current conditions.

Difficulty

Please be advised that the levels of difficulty assigned to these escapes are based only on our opinions and those of the outfitters. We try to be fair and even conservative, but the difficulty levels should not be taken as an indication that everyone may be able to perform each activity. It is your responsibility, as the weekend warrior, to decide what kind of adventure you are physically and mentally able to undertake. Be aware that it's a good idea to prepare your body and mind for all the adventures offered in this book, and that some activities clearly require more effort and training. A few require months of preparation.

The ratings can vary greatly, depending on how you choose to pursue the activity. For example, riding a mountain bike around a local park path may be easy, but taking your bike up on the chairlift at Big Bear, then cruising technical downhill singletrack requires an entirely different level of fitness and expertise. Likewise, whitewater kayaking, paragliding, and various other sports take training. We provide contact information for outfitters or guides that can help you learn the basics of an activity; it is up to you to decide if you need more preparation. Just make sure your weekend of choice suits your skills and abilities, then practice and physically prepare yourself in order to make the experience more rewarding. Train up to challenge yourself.

As far as the ratings go, an easy adventure is one that most average people can do, with less regard to age or fitness level. Many are family-oriented activities and often involve guided tours or seminars, tourist pursuits, or relaxing leisure destinations. Some require moderate amounts of easy hiking or walking, but nothing that will bother most people with an average level of fitness. Minimal technical skills may also be required. For example, playing around in the surf, Jet Skiing, or even taking a weekend rafting trip on the Kern River do not require gold medalist swimming skills, but if an emergency arises, you'll need to keep a clear head and at least tread water to stay afloat. Similarly, driving a big RV may not be appealing to some folks. Though a weekend at a Palm Springs naturist spa is rated easy, not everyone has the guts to "let it all hang out," so to speak. While you should certainly not try to do anything you cannot handle, the simple fact is that because these are all active vacations, under the worst circumstances, things can go wrong. The easy rating signifies that the probability of things going wrong is lower.

A medium rating means there is either some prior skill required to perform the activity or a higher level of fitness is necessary, or both. Renting a Harley is a medium-difficulty adventure because no one will rent you a $15,000+ motorcycle if you've never ridden anything bigger than a ten-speed. On the other hand, mountain biking is a medium-level activity because it requires some fitness and endurance, as does backpacking Kings Canyon. Some of these more difficult weekends are suitable as family activities, though there are fewer here than in the easy category. Of course, it depends on what your kids can handle. In general, expect to spend more time planning and preparing for medium-level weekend escapes. Physical training may be required. You may also need to purchase or rent the required equipment, and you'll often need practice with the gear.

Great weekend escapes rated as difficult are tests of skill, endurance, and courage. This type of demanding weekend isn't suited to everyone, but these challenges will reward those who seek them out. Difficult weekends require a top level of fitness, as well as previous active, outdoor experience. They are meant for those who feel proficient and at home in the wild outdoors and want to push themselves even further against more extreme conditions. Some are just plain tough, like running marathons and mountaineering, while others, such as scuba diving and rock climbing, can be dangerous if you don't pay attention to what you're doing. Several escapes combine demanding activities with weather extremes, which generally increases risk of injury. Waterskiing and surfing are strenuous enough, but just being in the water also presents its own issues, factors that combine for a difficult rating. Some of these difficult activities may be experienced on a limited basis to whet your appetite and entice you to further pursue the sport. Remember that, although just about every weekend escape in this book (in every difficulty rating) can be taken to the nth, most extreme, degree, you should never attempt an activity clearly exceeding your capabilities, especially without proper training and preparation. Most of these difficult weekend adventures take commitment, and the greater the challenge in getting there, the greater the weekend will reward you when you've finally seen it through. As our mothers always say, please be careful.

We mentioned physical conditioning before, but it bears repeating. With any of these weekend escapes, your adventure will be more rewarding if you are physically prepared for it. It's no fun to be sore all week after a demanding adventure, and you're less likely to look back at the experience with fond memories if you are, making you hesitant to take a similar challenge in the future. Working with a health professional to prepare a proper regimen of aerobic exercise and strength training is a great way to both get in shape for your trip and generally improve the quality of your life. You can also simulate your adventure on a smaller scale by practicing near your home; your local hiking trail may not be quite as rugged as the Whitney trail, but it can certainly help train your legs. It comes down to this: The healthier your body is, the less of a factor physical work becomes in your escape, and the more you can enjoy your surroundings.

While you're preparing your body, don't neglect your mental plan, especially for the most challenging of our escapes. Although your goal is to relax and have fun, intense concentration is often necessary while whitewater kayaking, rock climbing, paragliding, and in any other endeavor demanding close attention to detail. Prepare your mind for problems that may arise. We all hope for the best situation, but the possibility of the worst is something you should be ready for, especially when the activity takes on an element of danger due to treacherous conditions. By being mentally alert and prepared when you go, you'll be better equipped to handle whatever your adventure might throw at you. First aid, CPR, and other medical training courses are not a bad idea either.

Finally, don't be discouraged by the risks of these activities. The better prepared you are to accept and deal with the inherent risks, often in an unfamiliar environment, the more you'll gain from your adventures. Fun trips are safe trips.

Price

Prices for many weekend escapes will vary across a somewhat broad range, allowing for your individual preferences especially when it comes to lodging. From quaint seaside bungalows to average hotels to luxury resorts, Southern California has plenty of overnight options. The local chambers of commerce or visitor bureaus listed in each escape will help you find your dream digs. Remember, some weekends are al fresco only, meaning you might be able to stay in an RV, or there may be cabins, but there's a good chance you'll be snoring in your tent. Although several chapters include lodging as part of the escape, such as a stay at the Terra Cotta Inn or a weekend spent snow camping, other itineraries allow much flexibility to fit your budget and personal preferences. For most chapters, there are major hotel chains nearby along with a host of other options ranging from high-rise hotels to cozy bed-and-breakfasts by the ocean to luxury condos. To help keep the cost of your weekend getaway to a minimum, we've also included a Sleep Cheap section at the end of each chapter. Since you won't be spending all day in the hotel room anyway, there often isn't a need to go overboard on luxury accommodations, unless of course you prefer a posh pad and don't mind paying for it. In each Sleep Cheap section we've picked out some of the best and most conveniently located campgrounds, hostels, inexpensive hotels, and other low-price lodging options.

The cost for your weekend will also depend on what level of adventure you're looking to take. Some of the weekend escapes offer a variety of options at different prices. Adding options such as the supplemental Ocean Experience at the Aquarium of the Pacific can increase the value of your experience. While this educational boat trip out into the harbor may cost more than just an entrance ticket, it's only a tiny additional price for an exceptional value. We offer suggestions, but the choices are up to you based on your budget. Finally, the price range does not include the cost of travel. With these destinations scattered all over the southern half of California, we've left it up to you to factor in the travel costs.

Outfitters and Contact Information, Recommended Reading

We know one of the hardest parts about getting away for the weekend is the planning, so to make it easier we've listed tour operators, outfitters, and their contact information. All those mentioned in this book are listed simply because they are considered among the best in what they offer. No listing fees were charged, so no company bought their way in. These providers have proven themselves to hundreds, even thousands, of active travelers, and each offers an enjoyable experience complete with excitement, education, relaxation, discovery, and fun. They have great safety records and excellent customer service. The guides and trip leaders are pleasant and polite, as well as technically skilled, in order to ensure a safe and stress-free outdoor experience. The outfitters will inform you of any special equipment, training, or skills necessary. They will let you know what it takes to be adequately prepared, both physically and mentally.

When choosing outfitters and tour operators for this book, cost was taken into account, but not as heavily as actual value. Other companies may be less expensive or less experienced than some of the ones included here; however, you may be sacrificing a fun vacation, a lifetime of memories, or maybe even your safety, all for the sake of saving a few dollars. We've included the best in the business, the folks sure to deliver the most bang for the buck, rather than a cut-rate experience at a cut-rate price.

Just in case you want to read up on your chosen escape before you go, we've also included a list of good books to follow up with. It's quite understandable if your first skydive takes just a little extra convincing!

Make Your Adventure Memorable

So you've taken the plunge—you've scheduled a weekend of hiking, or skiing, or camping, and now you're anxiously waiting for the minute you can be on your way. As this will be something new and special, you'll want to make sure that your adventure stays fresh in your mind for a long time to come. Here are a few suggestions to make the memories last well into your future.

Take Lots of Pictures—We can't stress this enough. Photos are the best way to tote one-of-a-kind Southern California weekends back home with you. You may want to invest in a 35 mm or, preferably, a digital camera to record your adventures. Digital cameras eliminate the monetary and environmental costs of developing film, plus you print out only the photos you want. The more pictures you take, the better you'll get at it, and soon you'll be a pro at capturing the splendor and sights. Eventually, glancing back over all the great pictures becomes as much a part of your adventuring as the weekend itself. Best yet, showing your kids and even your grandkids that photo of you hang gliding or those shots of you at surf camp will likely, as they get older, help convince them to try some fun adventures for themselves.

Keep a Journal—Especially on hikes and drives, this method of capturing the moment is easy and intensely personal. Southern California offers many inspirational landscapes, from the rugged and beautiful Big Sur coast south to San Diego's sandy sun-soaked beaches. Writing about the incredible sights, describing your feelings, and detailing your thoughts will allow you to appreciate the experience even more. Keep an ongoing travel journal, and you'll have interesting reading for the rest of your life.

Take Family and Friends Along—All of these activities can easily be enjoyed by groups of people and, in most cases, are more fun with family and friends. Learning to kayak or scuba dive alone is not nearly as enjoyable as learning with someone else, preferably one with whom you can share the activity after the initial training is completed. Moreover, if you find that you want to pursue the adventure further by becoming more proficient or turning it into a regular pastime, you'll have a partner who will enjoy traveling that road with you. The more, the merrier.

Join a Club—There are clubs and organizations for every kind of outdoor activity, from skydiving to skiing to spelunking. They're by no means limited to Southern California or only parts of the state either—if you happen to take up rock climbing one weekend at Joshua Tree, you're likely to find an interested community back in San Diego, or Saskatchewan, or just about anywhere. In our Internet-connected world, it's not hard to hook up with one of these clubs. Attend a meeting and check it out. At the very least, these organizations can direct you toward your next adventure, but more likely, you'll find a new group of great friends.

Buy Equipment—As you start your weekend adventures, you'll find that most outfitters are able to provide the major equipment needed for the weekend. Nevertheless, if you find an activity that you plan to pursue regularly, the best way to improve your skills is to invest in your own set of gear, personalized to your specific body type, skill level, and so on. Ask an expert you trust to know what you're looking for. Gearing up can get expensive, but if you talk to some folks already involved in the activity (try the clubs or the outfitters), they may be able to direct you to the best stores and perhaps used equipment networks. Flea markets, yard sales, and Internet auction Web sites are great places to find inexpensive, quality gear. Just by making the commitment and purchasing gear, you're more likely to pursue the activity.

Get to Know Your Outfitter—Any person who makes a living playing outdoors is worth keeping in touch with, especially if you're planning to stay involved. If you've had a great experience, tell them so, and use them again the next time you're planning a similar escape. Many of Southern California's outfitters even cross-specialize in multiple activities, and the company that took you kayaking may be the same one to give you a screaming deal on a fantastic hiking adventure. At the very least, guides are likely to have good ideas for where to buy crucial gear.

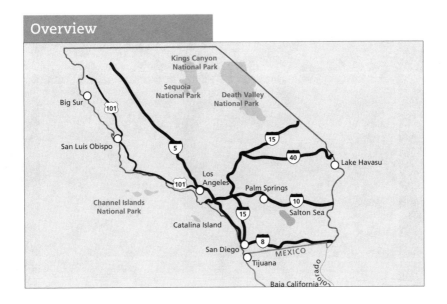

All in all, Southern California boasts enough adventure to satisfy everyone. It's truly a shame to visit, or worse yet, to live here and not search out these great experiences. *52 Great Weekend Escapes in Southern California* is designed to set you well on your way to being a modern-day weekend explorer, toward better appreciating our amazing natural surroundings, and toward discovering exactly what fun and adventure are all about. Use this guide as your starting point, and soon you'll be forging your own path, taking back your weekends, and sharing them with people who, like you, are looking to get out and play. So pick a great weekend escape and go have fun exploring Southern California. Many safe travels!

The prices and rates listed in this guidebook were confirmed at press time. We recommend, however, that you call establishments to obtain current information before traveling.

Spring

Mission Touring El Camino Real

Hello, Southern California!

Welcome to California. From the moment you step off the plane, jump from your car, or wander out your front door, adventures beckon from every direction. Even if you're the type to tack a state map on the wall and toss darts to pick your weekend destination, chances are you've got more opportunity for fun within a hundred-mile radius of that dart's tip than most could ever imagine. Again, welcome to Southern California!

The perfect way to begin your adventures in the southern half of the state is to spend a weekend or two taking a basic history, geography, and scenery lesson, best accomplished in a car following one of the state's oldest paths. In the earliest days, forging a route north from San Diego toward Monterey Bay, connecting the infrequent outposts of civilization along the way, Captain Gaspar de Portolá established the first leg of El Camino Real (The King's Highway). Portolá, who served as governor of Las Californias (Baja California, now part of Mexico, and Alta, or present-day California), also provided the military backing for Padre Junípero Serra, president of the missions. Although the roadways today are not as dusty as they once were, you can still sample part of the exploration experience as the early colonists, soldiers, and missionaries did.

Your exact weekend itinerary is up to you, and it mostly depends on how long you want to spend at each mission and how much driving you want to do. Basically, you can see as many or as

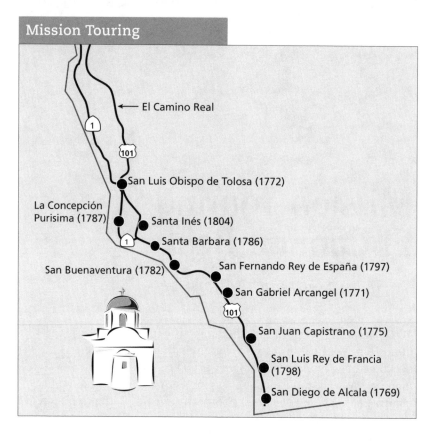

El Camino Real

San Luis Obispo de Tolosa (1772)

La Concepción Purisima (1787)

Santa Inés (1804)

Santa Barbara (1786)

San Buenaventura (1782)

San Fernando Rey de España (1797)

San Gabriel Arcangel (1771)

San Juan Capistrano (1775)

San Luis Rey de Francia (1798)

San Diego de Alcala (1769)

few of the twelve missions in the southern half of the state as you want to in one weekend; there are numerous options for exploring the 550 miles of roads connecting them, and there are certainly plenty of distractions at each stop and along the way. Of course, since that distance is one-way, it's a much better idea to split your mission tour into two or more trips. If you live somewhere along the middle of the route, just set out south one weekend and head north another. For those highly motivated, over-the-road types who just want to cruise and see plenty of countryside, making only rather short stops at each of the missions, three days can be enough, barely, to see it all there and back.

California's Historic Mission Trail links twenty-one missions from San Diego to Sonoma, the modern highways roughly tracing the original El Camino Real. The last mission was founded in 1823; however, improvement and reconstruction throughout the years, undertaken to counter the effects of uprisings, coastal weather, earthquakes, and neglect, have left the grand adobes we see today in their best condition ever. For an interesting sampling, start at the first mission founded, San Diego de Alcala, and head north to the Old Mission of Santa Barbara. This road trip will let you discover a storied chapter in California's early history and provides a weekend well worth remembering.

On July 16, 1769, Padre Junípero Serra officially founded San Diego de Alcala on a coastal overlook near the mouth of the San Diego River, the first of twenty-one missions to be established along the California coast. Originally just a brushwood shack, the mission today is gleaming white adobe, adorned with lush and colorful bougainvillea. As you stroll through the grounds, keep in mind that some of the trees in the gardens are hundreds of years old—it's possible even Padre Serra himself may have eaten an orange, olive, or avocado picked from the same plant you see.

Be sure to listen for the bells here; the large bottom bell rings daily at noon and 6:00 P.M., though all five bells ring in unison only once a year—on the anniversary of the mission's founding. Bells were extremely important in mission life, acting as clocks and schedule keepers. The various rings, tones, and sequences told when it was time to work, eat, pray, and play. If you have a little extra time and want to learn more about Padre Serra, who founded a total of nine missions in California, be sure to stop at the Junípero Serra Museum, which commemorates the site of the first San Diego de Alcala (the current site is not the original one, as the mission was moved).

Continuing north, your next stop will be just east of Oceanside at San Luis Rey de Francia. On the Feast of St. Anthony in 1798, Padre Lasuen, who also founded nine missions in California, dedicated this cross-shaped church in the name of France's king Louis IX. Known as the "King of the Missions," it is the largest of California's missions and was once the biggest building in the state. The gardens feature California's first pepper tree, as well as a bountiful fruit orchard. Today San Luis Rey de Francia, the eighteenth mission completed, is fully restored and widely considered the most architecturally graceful in California.

Approaching Los Angeles, just past Camp Pendleton Marine Corps Base, you'll find the rebuilt San Juan Capistrano mission (most of the structures were devastated by a major earthquake in 1812). While you're at this mission, be sure to check out the Serra Chapel of 1777, the only original church remaining where Padre Serra said Mass and the oldest building still in use in California.

The incredible handiwork on this fountain at the Santa Barbara Old Mission is just one example of the mission founders' attention to detail. ROBERT HOLMES/CALTOUR

Keep a lookout for orange birds of paradise in the gardens, and if you need an excuse to celebrate, a traditional Mexican fiesta is held every St. Joseph's Day (March 19) to commemorate the return migration of the cliff swallows from Argentina.

San Gabriel Arcangel, just south of Pasadena, was the fourth mission built and was founded in 1771 by Junípero Serra. At one time, the mission covered several hundred thousand acres; nearly a quarter of the California missions' livestock and grain came from San Gabriel. The thick-walled design is unique and many of the original structures remain intact thanks to it. In the San Fernando Valley, just north of Los Angeles, is San Fernando Rey de España, the seventeenth mission created in the California chain and named in honor of King Ferdinand III of Spain in 1797. Among the buildings here is an enormous *convento;* this wing, once a place where monks would congregate and travelers could stay, is one of the largest adobe structures of the California missions. Heading back to the coast, on the main street of Ventura, 3 blocks from the ocean, is San Buenaventura, the ninth mission. Dedicated to St. Bonaventure, this mission was founded on Easter Sunday in 1782, the last church christened by Padre Serra. The two wooden bells, the only bells of this type in California, along with numerous other artifacts, are displayed in the nearby museum.

Heading north and into the central coast region, you'll find one of the best ocean views in Santa Barbara atop the Old Mission. Founded in 1786, the Santa Barbara Old Mission, known as the "Queen of the Missions," was the tenth built in the sequence. A mighty earthquake crumbled the church in 1925, but extensive restorations have rebuilt the structure to its previous grandeur.

This 250-mile segment of El Camino Real from San Diego to Santa Barbara passes by seven missions. If you want to extend your weekend, twice as many more await if you follow the rest of the Mission Trail all the way to Sonoma. The entrance fee for each mission is usually under $10, and you should feel good about chipping in—your money goes toward restoration and helping to preserve this treasured trail of California history for generations to come. As you return from exploring and are looking back at all the ground you covered, keep this in mind: These missions were originally situated to be one day's walk apart. Who knows? Maybe next year, you'll tackle the Mission Trail on foot.

Price: $50–$250

(Spring, Easy)

DRIVING DIRECTIONS

(1) From the San Diego de Alcala mission, head north on I–5 toward Oceanside and exit on Highway 76, driving east approximately 4 miles to the Rancho del Oro exit; San Luis Rey de Francia mission will be on the left. (2) San Juan Capistrano is located just north of San Clemente, 3 blocks west of I–5 on the Ortega Highway. (3) To reach San Gabriel Arcangel, follow I–5 North to I–710 North, then turn east on I–10; exit and go north on New Avenue to Mission Drive. (4) Retrace your route by heading west on I–10; however, continue past I–710, and instead turn north on I–5 toward San Fernando. Exit on Brand Boulevard and follow the signs to San Fernando Rey de España. (5) To reach San Buenaventura, head south briefly on I–405 to Highway 101; in Ventura, exit and turn right on California Street, then turn left onto Main Street. (6) Continue driving north on Highway 101 into Santa Barbara; exit on Mission Street and turn right. Turn left on Laguna Street; the Old Mission is straight ahead 2 blocks.

FOR MORE INFORMATION

SAN DIEGO DE ALCALA
San Diego
(619) 281–8449
www.missionsandiego.com

JUNÍPERO SERRA MUSEUM
San Diego
(619) 297–3258
www.sandiegohistory.org

SAN LUIS REY DE FRANCIA
San Luis Rey
(760) 757–3651
www.sanluisrey.org

SAN JUAN CAPISTRANO
San Juan Capistrano
(949) 234–1300
www.missionsjc.com

SAN GABRIEL ARCANGEL
San Gabriel
(626) 457–3048
www.sangabrielcity.com

SAN FERNANDO REY DE ESPAÑA
Mission Hills
(818) 361–0186
www.californiamissions.com

SAN BUENAVENTURA
Ventura
(805) 643–4318
www.sanbuenaventura
mission.org

SANTA BARBARA OLD MISSION
Santa Barbara
(805) 682–4149
www.sbmission.org

RECOMMENDED READING

Couve de Murville, M. N. L. *The Man Who Founded California: The Life of Blessed Junipero Serra.* Fort Collins, Colo.: Ignatius Press, 2000.

Kurillo, Max, and Erline M. Tuttle. *California's El Camino Real and Its Historic Bells.* San Diego: Sunbelt Publications, 2000.

Levick, Melba, Stanley Young, and Sally B. Woodbridge. *The Missions of California.* San Francisco: Chronicle Books, 1998.

SLEEP CHEAP

Three options for lodging location on this great escape fit around the two ends and somewhere close to the halfway point, allowing you to spend your weekend as you wish. In San Diego, try Sweetwater Regional Park, located only 10 miles southeast of downtown San Diego, east of I–805, just off Highway 54. All fifty-three campsites have water and electricity, while restroom facilities include hot showers. Standing at the Summit Site, you can see San Diego Bay and the Pacific Ocean to the west, the Sweetwater Reservoir to the east, and Tijuana, Mexico, to the south. Campsites may be reserved up to three months in advance. Other San Diego camping parks are available. For more information, call San Diego County Parks and Recreation (858–694–3049). Near Santa Barbara on the northern end of the mission tour, and less than 10 miles from the Old Mission Santa Inés, is the Flying Flags RV Park. This comfortably modern-enough park features 260 grassy, pull-through sites with utilities, as well as numerous tent campsites, a heated outdoor pool, two spas, clean showers and restrooms, laundry facilities, convenience arcade games, and even cable TV. There's even a nine-hole golf course next door if you have time for a quick round. Call (805) 688–3716 for more information as well as current rates, which vary according to amenities. Prices start at just over $10 per night—not bad for a place that makes camping almost too easy. For the middle stop on this weekend, few would believe such serenity exists so close to the crazy business of Los Angeles, but the San Gabriels Campground in Angeles National Forest is truly angelic. From Highway 210, drive north on Angeles Crest Highway (SR2) for 34 miles to find $12-per-night camping from April to November. Close retreats like this have a tendency to fill up fast, so reservations are highly recommended (805–736–6316).

Jeep and Hummer Tours

*Rollin' and Rumblin' through the
Golden State*

You've just flown into L.A., and already the city life is getting
you down. The inescapable traffic, persistent smog, and crush of
people are making you wonder what the heck you were thinking,
coming to vacation in this crazy blacktop jungle. While you were
planning your getaway, all you could think about was fleeing
your daily grind; now, here you are fresh off the plane, on the
first day of your escape, and you've got all the same pollution,
traffic, and crowding you had before you left Phoenix, or
Chicago, or Seattle. "Some freakin' vacation!" you snarl, snared
up in Route 5's ridiculous rush hour.

Not to worry—it gets better, we promise. Once you get out of the
city, you'll find that California is the capital of America's outdoor
adventure industry for good reason. The countryside offers every
kind of wilderness adventure you can think of, from long, leisurely
hikes through protected sequoia forests to punishing scrambles up
faces of sheer rock. No matter who you are, Southern California has
something to offer, and you'll soon find that braving L.A. traffic
was a small price to pay for a destination so perfect.

You don't even have to give up auto-based transportation to
enjoy the California wilderness. If you like the feel of four heavy-
duty wheels underneath you, try California's antitraffic adventure:
Jeep and Hummer touring in the state's wilder regions. Each tour
offers its own special qualities: the thrill of riding in the Hummer,

the most powerful four-wheeled vehicle on Earth; straddling the San Andreas Fault in a feat of geological Russian roulette; nighttime dune running near Pismo Beach. Whatever tour you decide to go with, you're sure to get a new appreciation for the vehicles that drive you even as you forget the teeming traffic swarms that greeted you.

Although the scenery is always the star in any outdoor driving adventure, the gearheads among you should look into taking a Hummer tour just to gawk at the vehicle. Hummers are not just something movie stars drive (though you may have seen some if you passed through Beverly Hills); the vehicle's original mission when it was built for the U.S. military was to go anywhere, under any conditions. It can scale 22-inch vertical rock ledges like a mountain goat, or climb up a 60 percent grade as if trucking up a speed bump. It can plow through 30 inches of water, mud, snow, or any other muck you can find. Thanks to 37-inch tires and almost a foot and a half of ground clearance, the Hummer makes a whole new kind of off-roading possible—and the California landscape you'll be traveling over demands just that kind of vehicular athleticism.

Take Pacific Adventure Tours, for example. The company operates Hummer tours in Pismo Beach and the surrounding areas, and prides itself on taking tourists for rides only a Hummer could handle. They mush these super trucks up unconquerable slopes, sideways inside dune bowls, and through deep sand that would stymie a lesser vehicle. You'll find yourself saying, "How're we going to get up *that?*" a few times, usually right before your Hummer conquers its next obstacle. For those of us with a mellower disposition or young children in tow, Pacific offers a milder tour, complete with explanations of the area's geological, natural, and human history. They also conduct nighttime tours along the beach, cruising over 7 miles of dark sand armed with brighter-than-bright off-roading lights.

If you're a little farther inland, you may want to take a walk on the wild side, geologically speaking, and visit the infamous San Andreas Fault with Desert Adventures out of Palm Springs. This outfitter prides itself on ecological friendliness and goes to great lengths to "tread lightly" through California's fragile desert. It offers several different tours, capitalizing on the region's Native American heritage, its recent cowboy past, and the geological wonder of the Colorado Sonoran Desert. Drive slowly for a while through this arid place, and you will find it is not the wasted, featureless land you see when you're looking at it from a plane or speeding past it on the freeway; it is a dynamic, living region, covered in spots by boulders and buttes and cut by Technicolor canyons in others. The rocks are by no means dead or static, either, however they may look as you're driving past, and Desert Adventures' guides are more than happy to tell you about the region's history. The San Andreas Fault's tortured geology is responsible for California's earthquake mystique, and just driving through the region feels somehow dangerous.

Best of the Best Tours also operates out of Palm Springs and covers much of the same terrain as Desert Adventures. Their draw is the White Water Wonderland tour, which takes you to an artesian well and natural oasis formed by the snow melting from Big Bear Mountain. This rare combination of water and desert has spawned a veritable paradise, complete with huge trees and river plants. You'll even have the chance to fish for your lunch; don't worry about fish cleaning and preparation, though, as your guides will handle the dirty work.

Traffic is certainly a reason to flee the big city, but don't throw the Hummer out with the bathwater. It's not the vehicles that are bad, just the sheer number of them; once you've got the road to yourself, or rather miles and miles of open space, being in the car doesn't seem like quite the chore it once did. And you don't even need to drive—think of it as a chauffeured hike. So sit back, expect some bumps, and enjoy the ride.

Price: $50–$100
(Spring, Easy)

DRIVING DIRECTIONS

The tour provider you decide to go with will give you directions to either their offices or the place you need to rendezvous before your ride. Just ask where to go when you're making your reservations.

FOR MORE INFORMATION

Outfitters

BEST OF THE BEST TOURS
Palm Springs
(760) 320–1365
www.bestofthebesttours.com

DESERT ADVENTURES JEEP ECO TOURS
Cathedral City
(760) 324–5337
www.red-jeep.com

PACIFIC ADVENTURE TOURS
Oceano
(805) 481–9330
www.pacificadventuretours.com

Other

OFFICIAL HUMMER WEB SITE
www.hummer.com

RECOMMENDED READING

Churchwell, Mary Jo. *Palm Springs: The Landscape, the History, the Lore.* Palm Springs, Calif.: Ironwood Editions, 2001.

Crowell, David. *Exploring Southern California Beaches.* Helena, Mont.: Falcon Publishing, 2000.

Green, Michael. *Hummer: The Next Generation.* Osceola, Wisc.: Motorbooks International, 1995.

SLEEP CHEAP

Pacific Adventure Tours is located close to the only beach in the state that allows vehicles on its sands. You may want to throw a mattress in the back of your pickup and sleep out under the stars. You can pitch a tent there as well, and you're paying only $6.00 per night per vehicle for oceanfront camping. There are drawbacks, though: Your campsite is inside Oceano Dunes State Vehicular Recreation Area, and you may find yourself waking up to revving engines throughout the night. Give it a try; sleeping on the beach is too good to pass up for a little racket, and the crashing surf will probably create enough white noise to keep you comfy. Call (800) 444-7275 for reservations (highly recommended, especially during holiday weekends), or (805) 473-7223 for recorded information about the Oceano Dunes Recreation Area.

Magic Mountain and Hurricane Harbor

Coaster Thrills and Waterslide Spills

As the winter chill leaves the air and reminds us that spring has indeed sprung, the outdoor folk among us take to the hills on foot or wheel, ditching city life for another world full of excitement, exhilaration, and challenge. They ride and hike to their heart's content, all the while enjoying both the outdoors' challenges and the quiet solitude nature offers its patrons.

But what if it's the humming purr of roller-coaster wheels that gets you going? What if you prefer shaking things up, your body getting whipped around and upside down? What if you're looking for something a little faster, a little scarier? Then perhaps you should greet the springtime with a thrilling speed fix at Southern California's roller-coaster capital: Six Flags Magic Mountain.

In 1977, a disaster movie called *Rollercoaster* opened nationwide. Yet another terrible '70s disaster flick is not very interesting by itself; however, Magic Mountain's Revolution roller coaster, opened in 1976, served as one of the centerpieces of that film, and the park itself has starred in a number of movies and TV shows since. Among these movies is the band Kiss's *Phantom of the Park,* one of the tackiest, weirdest film spectacles you'll ever sit through. (For some postadventure laughs, see both it and *Rollercoaster* after your trip, and pick out the attractions still standing. Don't forget to throw on your best bell-bottoms first.)

Magic Mountain

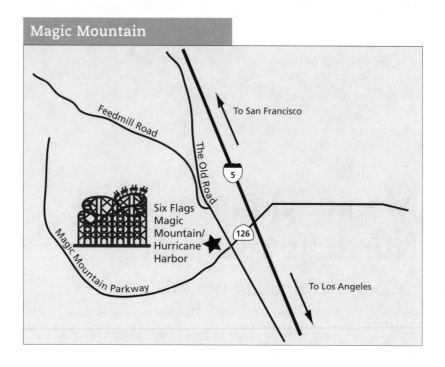

In the years that followed, coasters got bigger and faster, capitalizing on stronger metal frames rather than traditional wooden ones. Huge metal-frame coasters are the norm today, and, as a result, designers are capable of swinging, dropping, and hurling riders in almost any direction at any given time. Simple loops aren't enough anymore; today, coasters run backwards, do corkscrews, hang from their tracks rather than glide over them, and spin around as they careen forward. Magic Mountain boasts over fifteen giant coasters today, each of them capable of some dizzying combination that will leave you either begging for more or begging the ground to stop moving.

Since Magic Mountain opens a major new attraction nearly every year, it's easy to get overwhelmed by the sheer number of giant metal beasts towering around you. The craziest addition to the stable opened in 2003, and it is a true doozy: Scream is a floorless roller coaster, meaning riders are strapped into so-called flying chairs and launched around the track with no floor below, no track above, and no car around them. From the get-go, Scream attacks; the first drop throws riders down 150 sheer feet, and no less than seven 360-degree inversions (that's loops, to the uninitiated) await after that. You'll reach speeds pushing 65 mph as you race through a whole gauntlet of stomach-turning loops, drops, and turns.

However, Scream barely compares in sheer brutal size to Goliath, the longest coaster in the park. This behemoth provides a 255-foot vertical drop at one point and races over 4,500 feet of track at 80 mph. You'll see its orange track outlined in the sky above the park and hear its victims from a long way off. Of course, Goliath doesn't fly as high as Superman—the "ride" known as Superman: The Escape accelerates from 0 to 100 mph in less than seven seconds and drops riders over forty stories (that's 415 feet or so).

Here's the best part: There are over a dozen more extreme coasters, each boasting its own method for making you scream. Depending on when you go (weekend or weekday), it may take you two days just to ride them all. And we haven't even mentioned the other rides, or nearby Hurricane Harbor, the Six Flags water park next door.

This park is a lot like its scream-inducing counterpart, except a whole lot wetter. You'll find a bunch of nirvana-inducing waterslides that parallel the coasters: some are crazier than others, but all will make you holler with delight or terror. There are a number of beach and pool areas to relax in as well, most notably the Forgotten Sea Wave Pool (sans sharks, in case you were wondering), Lizard Lagoon (a tropical beach area), and Castaway Cove (a kids-only play zone).

Keep in mind that Hurricane Harbor doesn't open until May, when the mercury starts to bubble a bit higher. If you are in the area for the heat, though, be sure to keep open one day for splashing around. For one thing, it is a lot less expensive than Magic Mountain; tickets are nearly $20 less, though your best deal is to buy a combo ticket for both parks (a little over $50), start early, and stay late. You'll get the most for your money that way and enjoy yourself knowing you've got a couple extra bucks for souvenirs and snacks.

If you've got children in tow, have no fear. Magic Mountain has worked hard to satisfy the kiddies in recent years, and today the park boasts dozens of attractions for the little 'uns. Bugs Bunny and his pals bounce around the park spreading good cheer, and the Looney Tunes Lodge offers a million adventures for little loonies. You may even want to break the tykes in on a roller-coaster odyssey of their own: Goliath Jr. is a miniature version of the park's biggest coaster and a good starting point for future speed addicts.

Trekking through California's backcountry may be the wildest way to experience the state, but riding the coasters at Magic Mountain is

The massive Déjà Vu coaster, just waiting to pitch you down its ninety-degree first drop. SIX FLAGS INC.

certainly the woolliest. It's big game hunting without the guns, bungee jumping without the bridge. Some people may not see amusement parks as challenging adventure destinations, but when one boasts the distinctive variety of death-defying steel that Magic Mountain does, you better believe you're living dangerously.

Price: $50–$100

($45 for one-day tickets to Magic Mountain, $55 for combo tickets to both Magic Mountain and Hurricane Harbor. Contact the park to ask about specials.)

(Spring, Easy)

DRIVING DIRECTIONS

Six Flags Magic Mountain and Hurricane Harbor are located one hour south of Bakersfield, just minutes north of Hollywood at the

Magic Mountain Parkway exit off Interstate 5 in Valencia. Exit on Magic Mountain Parkway, then turn left at the bottom of the exit ramp going under the freeway overpass. Proceed along Magic Mountain Parkway to parking and the entrance to the parks.

FOR MORE INFORMATION

HURRICANE HARBOR LOS ANGELES
Valencia
(661) 255–4100
www.sixflags.com/parks/
hurricaneharborla

SIX FLAGS MAGIC MOUNTAIN
Valencia
(661) 255–4100
www.sixflags.com/parks/magic
mountain

AMERICAN COASTER ENTHUSIASTS
www.aceonline.org

ROLLER COASTER DATABASE
www.rcdb.com

RECOMMENDED READING

Rutherford, Scott. *The American Roller Coaster*. St. Paul, Minn.: MBI Publishing, 2000.

Samuelson, Dale, and Wendy Yegoiants. *The American Amusement Park*. St. Paul, Minn.: MBI Publishing, 2001.

SLEEP CHEAP

Angeles National Forest is only a short trip on I–5, in the San Gabriel Mountains. In the spring and early summer, when L.A. is shrouded in gloom and clouds, the cobalt skies still stretch across the horizon here, making the forest a perfect place to unwind after your high-speed roller-coaster adventures. Fees run under $12 for the forest's over one hundred campgrounds, allowing smart travelers to save some bucks for their next day's ride ticket. Call (626) 574–1613 for more information, or visit the forest's Web site at www.r5.fs.fed.us/angeles.

The San Luis Obispo Life

Escaping the Phone

It's okay. Put this book down for a moment, and answer the phone. Been ringing off the hook recently, hasn't it?

You really want to stay in touch with friends and family—get that call from Uncle Joe out in Kalamazoo, or maybe from the friends you left back home. But no matter what you do, short of unplugging and losing all commo, the telemarketers are coming to get ya, usually right when you're expecting the next big communiqué. Anyone daring enough to pick up that evening phone call has undoubtedly enjoyed some semi-smooth pitch for everything from state-of-the-art home security systems, to super-duper all-digital movie-on-demand, to a monstrous magnitude of minutes on a cell phone smaller than your watch, one that guarantees pin-drop reception on the snowy summit of Mount Kilimanjaro (note: roaming charges still apply). When these calls finally get the best of you, just when you are about to scream at friendly Kim from Bob's Windshield Repair to take you off their list in so many four-letter words, thank her kindly, then tell her all about your next great weekend escape.

You've packed little more than the bare essentials: hat and sunglasses, walking shoes and sandals, a couple of T-shirts, comfortable shorts, and a sweatshirt for misty mornings and cool evenings. You are focusing on cheap, clean, and easy telemarketer-free fun, and what better place to find it than San Luis Obispo County? After all, as Ferris Bueller almost said, life moves pretty fast—if you don't SLO down once in a while, you could miss it.

That being said, it's best to arrive early Thursday to take full advantage of the festive, phone-free fun. After you've settled in at your choice from the hundreds of hotels, resorts, and campsites in the area, it's time to clear your head and recharge your chakras. First stop: Avila Beach, the perfect spot for frolicking and flirting with the ocean. Take off your shoes and get your feet wet, fly a kite or toss around a Frisbee, walk your dog if you have one, but whatever you do (or don't do), be sure to let the relaxing cadence of the breakers wash away all the rigors of routine. A little play-time usually works like magic; however, if you need serious destressing, stop for a soak at the nearby hot springs. If golf is your way to unwind, check out Avila Beach Golf Resort—the Titleist-gobbling tidal estuary on the back nine adds a whole new dimension to water hazards, but the wildlife is abundant and the scenery superb.

After you treat yourself to some scenic solitude, head to down-town San Luis Obispo in the late afternoon, and be sure to go with a hearty appetite. As businesses close shop around 6:00 P.M., Higuera Street bustles with activity: Local farmers display colorful fresh-picked produce, street performers and musicians position on various corners, and area restaurants fire up barbecue wagons. Follow your nose and the crowds to the best local offerings of tri-tip steak sandwiches, smoked salmon, ribs, and chicken. The grilled garlic bread is about as good as it gets. Wash it all down with pressed cider or a local brew.

The next morning, it's time to burn off a few of those delicious street fair calories. If you didn't overindulge, take a leisurely stroll along any of the county's numerous beaches. If you need a good suggestion, head to Pismo Beach; the laidback surfer-town feel radi-ates in the early morning hours, preparing you for a great day of laying back. In addition to over 20 miles of sand between your toes, Pismo Beach boasts pristine playgrounds for surfing, boogie board-ing, horseback riding, or even just pier fishing.

On the other hand, if you stuffed yourself a smorgasbord at the farmers' market, or simply aren't scared of a good sweat, take a quad-burning mountain biking tour. Departing Meadow Park, bikers pedal to the base of Madonna Mountain, stopping for one last chance to limber up and stretch before tackling the vigorous uphill section. Don't despair, though; it may be a lung-busting climb if

The San Luis Obispo Life

you've let your fitness slide, but the incredible views of the area and the downhill zoom are well worth the effort. The three-hour trip finishes up with an easy cruise around town, where your guides will point out some of their favorite haunts. Hiking and custom biking itineraries are also available.

Hopefully by now, you are fully forgetful of that all-too-familiar phone (unless, of course, it just rang again—okay, suppose you should get it . . .), and your stomach will probably be calling for more fuel. A good way to spend the afternoon is to explore San Luis Obispo, one of California's oldest communities, founded by Padre Junípero Serra in 1772 along the historic Mission Trail. Stop by the visitor center for gads of info on the whole gamut of great activities and events in the area. Then, with a stroll along San Luis Obispo Creek, you'll discover numerous restaurants with outdoor patios, the perfect places to unwind and rejuvenate the spirit over a light lunch. Browse through the visitor center info and brochures that perked your interest—you'll be hard pressed not to find some fun. Before you embark on your afternoon, however, make a quick stop at Cafe Mondeo Pronto, and sample their homemade ginger ale to kickstart the next part of your adventure.

There are so many options in every direction and for every preference that San Luis Obispo County can wear you out even as you're unwinding. But if your idea of relaxing is minimal exertion, and your SLO escape happens to fall between November and February, cruise over to the North Campground at Pismo State Beach. Every Friday, Saturday, and Sunday throughout the season, docent-led walks through the area feature tens of thousands of regal monarch butterflies flittering through the air and clustering as densely as leaves on the trees. Nearby Morro Bay State Park and Montana de Oro State Park are also popular stops on the butterfly circuit.

Another good option for those seeking less-demanding adventures is to enlist the services of the Environmental Center of San Luis Obispo County (EcoSLO). Be sure to call ahead, or check their Web site for upcoming events; guided hikes to local favorites like Bishop Peak, Irish Hills, Pismo Dunes, Cuesta Ridge Botanical Area, and Stenner Canyon are always popular excursions. Visitors can stop by the downtown office for literature and information on personal and environmental responsibility. It's difficult not to commend and support this nonprofit organization dedicated to protecting and enhancing human health and lifestyle, as well as the environment.

California has long been a place of forward thinking. For the most part, good forward thinking involves good work today to promote a better life for all. That being said, all that forward thinking can get the phone ringing off the hook and bog you down in the details. San Luis Obispo presents the perfect spot to exit the fast lane and spend your weekend exactly the way you want to. Vast and ranging from super-relaxing to extra-invigorating, your adventure options wait only for you to give the go-ahead. Best yet, the next time good old Uncle Joe calls, you'll have plenty to talk about.

Price: $50–$250

(Spring, Easy)

DRIVING DIRECTIONS

San Luis Obispo is located 200 miles north of Los Angeles and 230 miles south of San Francisco on U.S. Highway 101 and State Highway 1. For an extra dose of scenery, take Highway 1 south from the Bay Area. From the east, follow Highway 46 or Highway 166 east to U.S. 101, and follow the signs to San Luis Obispo.

Morro Bay. DAVE GARTH/SAN LUIS OBISPO CHAMBER OF COMMERCE

FOR MORE INFORMATION

Outfitters

AVILA BEACH GOLF RESORT
(805) 595–4000
www.avilabeachresort.com

AVILA VALLEY HOT SPRINGS
San Luis Obispo
(805) 595–2359
www.avilahotsprings.com

CAFE MONDEO PRONTO
San Luis Obispo
(805) 544–2956

Other

ENVIRONMENTAL CENTER OF SLO COUNTY
San Luis Obispo
(805) 544–1777
www.ecoslo.org

MONTANA DE ORO STATE PARK
(805) 528–0513

MUSEUM OF NATURAL HISTORY
Morro Bay State Park
(805) 772–2694
www.mbspmuseum.org

PISMO STATE BEACH
(805) 489–2684

SAN LUIS OBISPO CHAMBER VISITOR CENTER
San Luis Obispo
(805) 781–2777
www.visitslo.com

RECOMMENDED READING

Dickerson, Sharon Lewis. *An Informative Guide for Leisurely Motoring or Bicycling San Luis Obispo County.* San Luis Obispo, Calif.: EZ Nature Books, 1988.

Leon, Vicki. *San Luis Obispo County Coast and Castle.* San Luis Obispo, Calif.: Blake Publishing, Inc., 1989.

Stone, Robert. *Day Hikes in San Luis Obispo County, California.* Red Lodge, Mont.: Day Hike Books, 2000.

SLEEP CHEAP

San Luis Obispo County offers plenty of inexpensive options and dozens of great campgrounds, but for a unique camping experience, head over to the Oceano Dunes State Vehicular Recreation Area (formerly Pismo Dunes SVRA). This is the only place in California where you can drive right out onto the beach, but keep in mind a 4WD vehicle is recommended. Camping is permitted south of Post 2 and in the open dune area. There are no hookups; however, toilets are available. You also must bring your own water. The one drawback is that this area is zoned for ATV and motorcycle use, which is fun during the day but can be noisy at night. The ocean breakers, however, drown out most of the ruckus. Best yet, a delicious dinner is easy—dig a few of the famous Pismo clams to steam over the campfire. Campsites are available by reservation year-round and can be made from ten days to six months in advance. Reservations are highly recommended (800–444–7275), especially for summer weekends and any holiday periods.

Sequoias and Caves

From Mighty Heights to Marble Depths

Immortality. Imagine living forever while other plants and animals grow and die around you, one generation rolling into the next for thousands of years. Rather than join in this cycle, you only grow larger and taller, until you tower above it all, the undisputed king (or queen) of your realm. Droughts, wars, and fires come, but they leave you only slightly scathed; you stand watch over all of it, above chaos and havoc, living and growing ever higher. You are wilderness without the cycle of life and death: the giant sequoia, living proof that nature can be, in fact, bigger than life.

Giant sequoias are incredible to behold. Standing over 200 feet tall in many cases, these breathtaking trees boast girths seemingly as wide as city blocks and produce 40 cubic feet of wood each year as they grow. They are also ancient beyond human conception; larger specimens are estimated at over 2,000 years old. There is nothing in the natural world that compares with the trees in sheer size, and moving through an immense forest of sequoias is one of the most memorable hikes you could imagine.

Sequoia National Park, founded in 1891 and the nation's second-oldest national park, is the place to be if you want to spend some time among these giants. It is right next door to Kings Canyon National Park, and the two are managed as one even though they both offer their own set of fascinating sites. On a weekend escape in Sequoia, you'll want to spend much of your time marveling at the massive trees, and the National Park Service has made doing so quite easy for everyone. To get an impression of how big the trees are, just drive through the Tunnel Log, or drive *on* the Auto Log, a fallen behemoth with a roadway cut into its top.

But don't stop there; the best way to see the park is on foot, walking one of the short paths through the sequoias. The Giant Forest and Lodgepole areas are probably your best bet for pure tree gawking, as four of the five largest sequoias in the world grow there. One of these, the General Sherman Tree, has earned the title "World's Largest Living Thing": It stands 275 feet tall and measures over 100 feet in circumference at its base (and growing). If that sounds impressive, think about how long it took to get that way—there is a very good chance that this tree first sprouted 1,500 years before Columbus hit the New World.

The park offers excellent educational exhibits, too. The Lodgepole Visitor Center is a good place to get acquainted with the area's natural and human history, and the new Giant Forest Museum tells the sequoias' story, as well as how to protect them. (Logging has been a problem in the past, and the sequoia population, despite its seeming invincibility, still requires stewardship and protection.) The rest of the park is certainly worth seeing, but for sheer size and sights (the Auto and Tunnel logs are also in this section), Giant Forest and Lodgepole are the way to go.

Sequoia National Park has more to offer than immense trees, however. Strangely enough, more of Southern California's natural treasures await you under the park: Crystal Cave and Boyden Cavern. These underground warrens provide a beautiful diversion after your hike through the redwoods, and they are easy on the wallet, too. Although you can take basic tours of both caves, your best bet is to take the two-hour special tour in Crystal. Starting at the cave's parking lot, you head down into Cascade Creek Canyon and through Crystal Cave, learning along the way about the geology and biology that created the underground world beneath the sequoias. Small group size and extended time limits give you an intimate, relaxed, and informative atmosphere that allows for in-depth discussion and lots of questions. You will learn a ton about California's geological past, and the tour costs less than $20 per person—not bad for such a great diversion. There's also a wild cave tour that lets you scramble through tight crevasses and through breathtaking formations off-trail, for a trip through subterranean natural history you won't soon forget.

One word of caution if you'll be camping in Sequoia: Beware of black bears! Though they are usually shy, the bears do occasionally

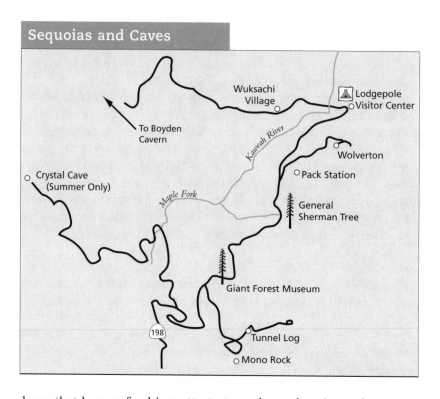

learn that human food is pretty tasty, and easy hunting to boot, thanks to careless campers. To avoid bears that are already taking after Yogi and Boo Boo, store your picnic baskets in the bear-proof boxes offered in the park's campgrounds. If you cannot find a box, or want to get into the backcountry, you can rent or buy a box at the Lodgepole visitor center. You can also leave the cooler in the trunk or hoist your pack at least 10 feet up into a nearby tree. But whatever you do, be sure NOT to store food in your tent or on the ground anywhere near your campsite. The bears want the grub, not you, but you can just happen to be in the way, especially if you are careless with your provisions. Take the proper precautions, and you'll have breakfast available when you wake up.

Take care of these minor safety issues while you're camping, and you'll have a fairly low-impact weekend adventure the whole family can enjoy. Take advantage of that fact, especially if you've got kids who do little more than lie around in front of the TV. You are not likely to forget the look of wonder on a child's face the first time he or she sees real sequoias or takes an underground hike–priceless is not too strong a word. And if you yourself have never

seen the giant trees or felt the cold damp of subterranean spaces, you'll be right there with them, wondering what it must be like to reach toward the sun for thousands of years or be without it forever.
Price: $20–$50
(Spring, Easy)

DRIVING DIRECTIONS

(Note: Gasoline is not sold anywhere inside the park, so be sure to fill up in one of the towns near the park entrance or in nearby King's Canyon or Hume Lake.) The Sequoia National Park entrance is off Highway 198; take I–5 north to Highway 99, then take Highway 198 east at Visalia. Proceed east for about one hour to the entrance. To Boyden Cavern, from points west: Take Highway 180 east toward Kings Canyon National Park. Follow Highway 180 to the bottom of the canyon where the road meets the Kings River; the parking lot is just off the road next to the bridge. From Sequoia National Park: Take Highway 198 up from the Lodgepole visitor center to the Grant Grove visitor center area, and pick up Highway 180 there. Then head east.

FOR MORE INFORMATION

Outfitters

BOYDEN CAVERN: SEQUOIA NATIONAL MONUMENT
Vallecito
(209) 736–2708
www.caverntours.com

LODGEPOLE VISITOR CENTER
(sells Crystal Cave tickets)
(559) 565–3782

SEQUOIA NATURAL HISTORY ASSOCIATION/SEQUOIA FIELD INSTITUTE
(for wild cave tours)
(559) 565–3759

Other

SEQUOIA AND KINGS CANYON NATIONAL PARKS
Three Rivers
(559) 565–3341
www.nps.gov/seki

SEQUOIA NATURAL HISTORY ASSOCIATION
Three Rivers
(559) 565–3759
www.sequoiahistory.org

GIANT FOREST MUSEUM
(559) 565–4480

Driving under a true natural bridge in Sequoia National Park. ROBERT HOLMES/CALTOUR

RECOMMENDED READING

Dilsaver, Lary, and William Tweed. *Challenge of the Big Trees: A Resource History of Sequoia and Kings Canyon National Parks*. Three Rivers, Calif.: Sequoia Natural History Association, 1990.

Tweed, William. *Sequoia and Kings Canyon: The Story Behind the Scenery*. Las Vegas: KC Publications, 1997.

SLEEP CHEAP

There are campgrounds throughout Sequoia National Park, all of which offer decent campsites for between $8.00 and $16.00. Two of these campgrounds are in the Lodgepole/Giant Forest area. Lodgepole Campground: Call (800) 365-2267 to reserve your space up to five months in advance, or visit http://reservations.nps.gov. Cost: $16/day. Information: (559) 565-3774. Dorst Campground: Open in mid-May (weather permitting), this campground is located on Generals Highway, 8 miles north of Lodgepole. Reserve up to five months in advance, via same telephone numbers and Internet address as for Lodgepole Campground. Cost: $16/day. Group sites are also available here.

Bicycling Lompoc

SoCal in Bloom

Imagine the sight: waves of blue, purple, and orange; red patches, looking as big as Caribbean islands, dotting the landscape; broad swathes of yellow extending up and over the horizon. You can't even bring yourself to believe the colors and the quantity of them— they surround you on all sides and take your breath away with every turn of your head.

We're not talking about an Arizona desert sunset or some elysian paradise across the ocean. This phantasmagorical scene is just another day of flower season in Lompoc, California's answer to the Dutch tulip fields we've all seen in postcards. Throw a couple bikes into this mix, and you have a healthful escape that will play to your love of nature's majesty, even as you stand among acres of plants put there as deliberately as conspiracy.

While you're here, you might as well enjoy the rest of what you'll see on your riding route, too: art galore, beautiful plant life (the nonflower variety), wineries, historical sites—everything you need to occupy yourself during a three-day biking excursion. And don't worry about pulling out the mega-knobby tires; most of the riding you'll do here is road work on gentle pavement, perfect for those taking their first multiday bike adventure and experienced two-wheel trekkers alike.

Sweet peas, larkspur, stock, bells of Ireland, delphinium—these are but a few of the spectacular blooms you'll see in Lompoc's

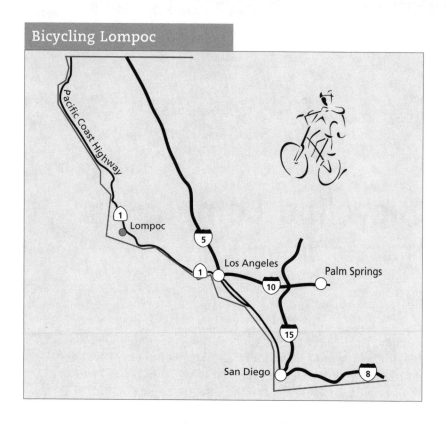

Bicycling Lompoc

world-famous flower fields. The peak season is early June through August, when approximately 1,500 acres of blooms open at once. You can drive the Lompoc Valley and see this incredible bounty, but on a bike you have the advantage of being able to stop for a picture anytime you want, along with the fresh air, the scents those blooms bring, and the rare opportunity to get close to such a unique display. After all, looking at it through the windshield of a car isn't appreciably different from looking at it on a hotel TV screen.

This does not mean you should go tiptoeing through these particular tulips. There are rules to follow here, ones that keep the flowers pretty and their growers happy enough to grow more next year. Don't go riding through the rows—the dust you kick up will damage the blooms and ruin the experience for those who follow. In addition, it goes without saying that you can't pick anything. Just as you strive for zero impact in the wilderness, you should try to eliminate traces of your presence among the blossoms. Besides, picking any flowers or vegetables here classifies as a little thing called stealing—those plants belong to the growers, not to you. Have respect, touch with your eyes, and you'll be fine.

The parade of colors and beauty doesn't end in the fields, either. Head into the city of Lompoc, and you'll find color splashing around you in the wall-sized murals scattered throughout town, courtesy of the Lompoc Murals Project. The city began this program in 1988 and based it on a Canadian model for using art as a major economic driver. Thus far, the program has succeeded admirably in both beautifying the city and drawing people from around California and the world to "The City of the Murals in the Valley of the Flowers."

Keep in mind, too, that the flowers are not the only plants you'll want to see while you're here. Between H and Locust Streets in downtown Lompoc you'll find the world-famous Italian stone pines of the valley, some of the world's most beautiful specimens of this particular plant. The trees, planted in the early 1930s, are native to Mediterranean Europe, and their cones actually produce edible pine nuts. The trees are worth at least $3 million, although their greatest value cannot be expressed in dollars and cents—they are a one-of-a-kind display and well worth checking out during your stay. In a state full of amazing plants and trees, these are truly unique.

Your ride around Lompoc will take you within sniffing distance of some other wonderful plants, namely members of the genus *Vitis*. Lompoc boasts over thirty local wineries, most of which have at least basic visitors' facilities. Many also offer tours, so get a list of local wineries from Lompoc's Chamber of Commerce, and start treating your palate in between helpings of flowers and exercise.

To sample Lompoc's human story, visit one of the area's many cultural or historical sites. Local history reaches back beyond colonization by Europeans, all the way back to the Chumash Indians, who settled what is now Lompoc Valley over 10,000 years ago. In fact, *lompoc* is a Chumash word that means "little lake" or "lagoon." (One other thing in regard to this name: It is pronounced *LOM-poke* (like "bomb smoke"), not *LOM-pock*. To avoid looking like a fool to the locals, get this right straight away.) You can get yourself caught up in this history at the Lompoc Museum, located in downtown Lompoc.

When Europeans did come, namely the Spanish, California received a valuable cultural heritage that stands strong to this day:

La Concepción Purísima Mission in Lompoc. ROBERT HOLMES/CALTOUR

the mission system. La Concepción Purisima Mission was established in 1787 and marked the earliest European settlement of the Lompoc Valley. A major earthquake struck the original mission in 1812, and a chance mix of violent aftershocks and torrential rains made the compound unlivable by the next year. The mission moved 4 miles to the northwest, where it eventually fell prey to neglect and the elements until 1934, when restoration began. Today, 1,928 acres of the original 300,000 mission acres are maintained as a state historical park, and ten restored buildings beckon visitors to experience the old days once again. You can visit the original site, too, for a look at what's left there.

For a tour full of beauty, color, history, and much more, you can't do much better than the rolling Lompoc Valley. If you haven't done much biking, this escape will reward you enough to think about bike touring again; more experienced riders will simply enjoy the offerings around them and appreciate the ability to concentrate on their surroundings rather than on switchbacks and rockslides.

Price: $50–$100

(Spring, Medium)

DRIVING DIRECTIONS

The Lompoc Valley is 9 miles from the Pacific Ocean along Pacific Coast Highway 1 and Highway 246. On the north side of the city is Central Avenue; on the east is Ocean Avenue. The best way to view the flowers is to head west on Ocean to Bailey, then turn right on Bailey to Central. Continue back and forth between Central and Ocean Avenues as you travel west. Continue westward to Artesia, and return to North H Street on Ocean or Central Avenue. There are usually flower fields on Highway 246 and Purisima Road adjacent to La Concepción Purisima Mission, too.

FOR MORE INFORMATION

Outfitters

WHEEL FUN RENTALS (RENTALS)
Santa Barbara
(805) 966–6733
www.wheelfunrentals.com

Other

LOMPOC CHAMBER OF COMMERCE
Lompoc
(805) 736–4567
www.lompoc.com

LOMPOC VALLEY BICYCLING CLUB
Lompoc
216.101.193.118/lvbc

Santa Barbara County has a free bike map available through its Traffic Solutions office. Call (805) 961–8919 to request one.

RECOMMENDED READING

Brundige, Don, and Sharron Brundige. *Bicycle Rides, Santa Barbara and Ventura Counties*. Los Angeles: BD Enterprises, 1994.

Crompe, Harry J. *Wild and Whacky Lompoc!: A Collection of Colorful Characters and Stories*. Santa Barbara, Calif.: Fithian Press, 1992.

SLEEP CHEAP

RV camping, tent camping, and showers are available at Lompoc River Park adjacent to State Highway 1 and State Highway 246 (Pacific Coast Bike Route) in the southeast part of Lompoc. River Park also features Kiwanis Lake, a small, man-made fishing pond that draws tons of wildlife. The park has thirty-five campsites with full hook-ups, as well as several park hosts and a resident city park ranger. For more information, call the Lompoc Parks and Recreation Department at (805) 875–8100.

Death Valley Ghost Towns

Disappearing into California's Badlands

Brutally hot temperatures plague the land, little more than miles upon miles of rock, salt, and sand, baked over eons into a hard crust. Barely an inch of rain falls every year, and not the smallest hint of shade provides respite from the anvil-like sun. Imagine living there, among foreboding landmarks like Starvation Canyon, the Funeral Mountains, and Hell's Gate. This is harsh, rugged country perfect for exploring.

Death Valley National Park is one of the most recent additions to our national park system (1994). Its fragile ecosystem features a diverse range of wildlife, along with amazing salt plains, clay formations stained green and pink, and winding gorges. But only a century ago, fortune hunters came to the valley by the thousands, seeking the gold and other metals that run under it. Once the mines played out, they saw no reason to continue living in such a hostile environment, so they took off for more hospitable climes and left behind what they built. These ruins still stand among Death Valley's rocks and canyons, and a weekend tour of the valley's eight major ghost towns serves as a close, spooky encounter with the West's wild and woolly past. It's as close to an American Chichén Itzá or Parthenon as you're liable to find.

Perhaps the coolest thing about these abandoned yet still sizzling settlements is their accessibility; you won't see any ticket booths or tour guides in Chloride City or Rhyolite. Travelers are

Death Valley Ghost Towns

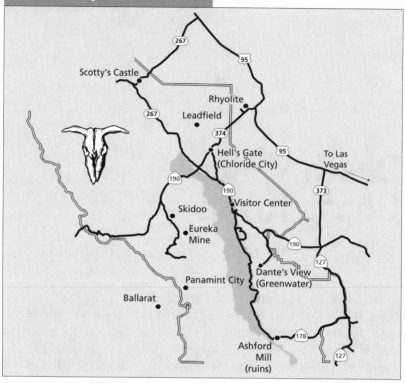

free to poke around at their leisure, exploring the ruins and taking in the silence where there was once bustling, often rowdy activity. Long ago, these towns were filled with prospectors, frontiersmen, and outlaws, all seeking their fortunes. However, as the gold ran out, so did the opportunity in Death Valley, and the fortune-seeking population moved on. Though the streets are empty today, spirits from that colorful period linger on, and it's hard not to feel at least a little spooked.

Remember one thing above all as you explore: The ghost towns' accessibility requires a certain responsibility on the part of visitors. History in such a raw state is fragile, and those of us who want to enjoy it are obligated to respect it. In other words, don't touch, burn, or take anything. Part of the reason these towns are so well preserved is that they don't see the normal volume of touchy-feely types who can't keep their hands to themselves. Bring your camera, and make your own souvenirs.

Each of the eight towns has its own story to tell, even though mining was central to all of their creations. In Harrisburg, Pete Aguereberry, one of the men who found the gold that launched the town in 1905, spent forty years working his claims in the nearby Eureka mine. Pete's home is all that remains of the town, which, at its height, was little more than a tent city. In contrast, Rhyolite, the biggest of Death Valley's towns, had a population between 5,000 and 10,000 during its heyday (along with one saloon for every one hundred people), and even boasted a stock exchange of its very own (Wall Street, eat your heart out). There are still many ruins standing here, including the train depot and a bank. Ballarat also enjoyed a brief but prosperous run, pulling 15,000 tons of gold out of the ground between 1898 and 1903.

Gold wasn't the only precious find that brought people to Death Valley, however. Panamint City was founded by outlaws hiding from the law who found silver, while Leadfield enjoyed only one year of relative prosperity before its founder, Charles Julian, went bankrupt and the town's namesake metal played out in one of its main mines. Skidoo may have hosted the spookiest bit of local history: It saw the only hanging to take place in Death Valley, a somewhat surprising distinction, given the area's general rowdiness. Hootch Simpson, an unlucky saloon owner, failed to rob the town's bank, but he did succeed in killing the owner of the store that housed it. He was actually hung twice; his executioners decided to string him up a second time for the news photographers who missed it the first time.

The towns are scattered around Death Valley, and some require four-wheel drive to access. And a few, like Skidoo, don't have much left to speak of (you'll find a sign there, but little else besides dirt). Your best bet is to set up your base at Furnace Creek, where you'll find campgrounds, hotels, and the main visitor center. From there, you can journey to the various towns, all the while taking in the desolate beauty that surrounds you. The park's southern portion, where Furnace Creek is located, contains many of Death Valley's most famous geological formations; Mesquite Flat has the largest area of sand dunes in the valley, and you should try to find your way there around sunset, when the ground changes from sand to spectacular. You can also check out Devil's Golf Course, a huge stretch of crystallized salt with a sharp, uneven surface devoid of vegetation.

If you go in the summertime, Death Valley's climate will

Be sure to visit the Stovepipe Wells Dunes in between your ghost town excursions—and bring your camera. ROBERT HOLMES/CALTOUR

demonstrate just what nature is capable of. Temperatures regularly stay above 120°F for weeks at a time, and just walking at the park's lower elevations feels like hard labor. There is an easy solution to these problems: Don't go when you can fry an egg on the ground. Avoid May through October, the hottest time of year. Late winter or early spring will also be warm but still bearable. Winter nights can get pretty cold, though, so dress and plan accordingly if you decide to camp during that period.

Death Valley is one of the planet's least friendly sites for long-term human habitation. But the valley towns and their mines sprung up anyway and made some folks very rich. Today, you can relive their experiences among the very buildings they lived in and tread on the same dust they walked on. Maybe then you'll realize just how infected with gold fever those adventurers had to be to make their homes in such a punishing, inhospitable, incredible place.

Price: $25–$100

(Spring, Medium)

DRIVING DIRECTIONS

California Highway 190 transects the park from east to west. On the east in Nevada, U.S. Route 95 parallels it from north to south, with connecting highways at Scotty's Junction (State Route 267), Beatty (State Route 374), and Lathrop Wells (State Route 373). South of the park, Interstate 15 passes through Baker on its way from Los Angeles to Las Vegas. State Route 127 travels north from Baker to Shoshone and Death Valley Junction, with connections to the park on State Route 178 from Shoshone and connection with California Highway 190 at Death Valley Junction.

FOR MORE INFORMATION

DEATH VALLEY NATIONAL PARK
Death Valley
(760) 786–3200
www.nps.gov/deva

RECOMMENDED READING

Bryan, T. Scott, and Betty Tucker-Bryan. *The Explorer's Guide to Death Valley National Park.* Boulder: University of Colorado Press, 1995.

Harder, Emmett C. *These Canyons Are Full of Ghosts: The Last of the Death Valley Prospectors.* San Bernardino, Calif.: Real Adventure Publishing, 2001.

SLEEP CHEAP

The park has a number of campgrounds, some of which are only open during the late autumn, winter, and early spring. They are located throughout Death Valley, and rates are reasonable even at the more popular campgrounds; at some, there is no charge at all. Backcountry camping is also permitted for free. For information on how to reach the campgrounds or for reservation questions, contact the park's visitor information line at (760) 786–3200.

SAMO Heritage Tour

Culture and Camping

Los Angeles—the fabled home of movie stars, beautiful beaches, palm-lined streets, and West Coast culture. Oh, and did we also mention traffic nightmares, smog, and occasionally oppressive heat?

Now, now, don't be discouraged. There's a good reason so many people make the Los Angeles area their home; it is fun, full of activity and just a bit wild, sort of like a wealthy, beautiful, devil-may-care college buddy. There's a lot to be said for that kind of town. However, there's also something to be said for slowing down the pace a little and getting to know the land and culture that was there before the glitz. You can get a lot out of learning more than where the best new club or shopping district is, and the California coast certainly has layers underneath its current gloss. Luckily, if you're in the L.A. vicinity, you have a great chance to see just these things at the Santa Monica Mountains National Recreation Area (SAMO), where the past is not gone, and the air is lighter than it is on the City of Angels' neon-bright, manicured streets.

One of the first things you'll notice about SAMO is its size— over 150,000 acres—making it the largest urban national park by a long shot. Golden Gate National Recreation Area, by comparison, is only 73,000 acres. SAMO runs 46 miles, from the Hollywood Bowl to Point Mugu in Ventura, and along the coast from Santa Monica Pier past Malibu, covering twenty-six busy zip codes (including that famous Beverly Hills 90210). SAMO is actually a chain of smaller state parks, recreation areas, and beaches that were designated one national recreation area in 1978; in fact, the park is so big that it divides the Los Angeles urban area in two, making it the only city in the world divided by both an entire mountain range and a national park. Whole cities, such as Malibu, are located entirely within park boundaries—pretty impressive, and pretty nice for folks in the area when they want to get away for a few days.

SAMO offers all the traditional activities you expect at a national park—there are over 580 miles of public trails, scattered over the smaller subdivisions within the area. Some areas are particularly suited to certain activities; Malibu Creek, for example, is an experienced mountain biker's playground (see Escape 40 for more on that spot). The park also boasts its own major, long-distance backpacking route, the Backbone Trail. When it is finished, the path will extend approximately 65 miles, linking all the major park areas and giving Los Angelenos their very own backyard backcountry. If you're not quite a backpacking fan, you can also hop in the family truck and hit the Mulholland Scenic Corridor, a 55-mile scenic drive through the Santa Monica Mountains from Griffith Park to Leo Carrillo State Park.

However you decide to go sightseeing, you'll have plenty to see. Bird-watching is a big SAMO activity, and the area boasts thirteen nesting raptor species. (This number equals that of the Snake River Birds of Prey Sanctuary, a national refuge created in Idaho.) About 450 vertebrates call SAMO home, everything from mountain lions and bobcats to deer. Steelhead trout populate Malibu Creek, representing the species' most southern habitat. In all, there are about twenty-five rare, threatened, or endangered species populating SAMO, along with another fifty candidate species.

If you're wondering why SAMO is such a hotbed for rare animals, the answer lies in the environment: The park represents one of the largest unspoiled broadleaf evergreen ecosystems in the world. The proper term is *Mediterranean*—SAMO has a Mediterranean climate, just as Death Valley has a desert climate and the Amazon has a rain forest climate. People come to California in large part because the weather is fantastic much of the time; the coast's Mediterranean climate makes these beautiful days possible. The Santa Monica Mountains have hot, dry summers (80° to 100°F) and relatively cool, wet winters (40° to 70°F), and nights can be cool any time of the year—particularly nice when the city's steamy nights start getting to

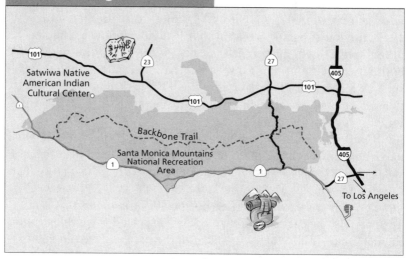

you. (The forest's proximity also provides an oxygen boost to smoggy L.A.–not a bad side benefit.)

For the critters, this means nice living conditions year-round, so before man ever showed his face, the birds and beasts congregated in Mediterranean regions to take advantage. Unfortunately, broadleaf evergreen forests are the most rare ecosystem on earth, found in only five locations and taking up far fewer acres than the deserts, rain forests, or grasslands. What's more, only 18 percent of the land classified as Mediterranean remains undisturbed, which makes SAMO that much more important from an environmental point of view.

Take advantage of this environmental heritage. See the sights any way you can, and keep your eyes open for adventure possibilities. A coastal park as big as SAMO is bound to offer something for everyone. Stargazing, surfing, whale watching, beach picnicking– all these activities are available, along with about 5,000 others. Talk to the park office staff about the many events going on in SAMO during the time you plan to spend there; they can tell you where to best engage in these activities as well as suggest others you may not have thought about.

Ask about the area's cultural heritage, and you will most certainly find yourself pointed toward the Satwiwa Native American Cultural Center, a bastion for descendants of the area's original settlers. Little known fact: Los Angeles has the largest Native American population (over 150,000) in the United States, and the area's wonderful climate attracted settlers thousands of years before Europeans ever made their way there. Two major indigenous people made their homes in the Santa Monica Mountains: the Chumash and the Gabrielleno-Tongva. These people first settled in the area about 13,000 years ago, used shells for money, and plied the California coasts in plank canoes called *tomols*. Over 1,000 archaeological sites survive in the Santa Monicas, illustrating just how populated the area was even back then.

The Satwiwa Center exists to preserve Southern California's Indian heritage, and if you are interested, you can participate in a number of activities the center puts on to promote understanding of those bygone days. You can attend talks by Native American speakers, learn native crafts and skills in workshops, or even learn dance steps and hear traditional stories at the regular evening programs at the center.

SAMO is a big deal, both literally and figuratively. You could spend a whole week just meandering through the area and taking in its many offerings, or you can find out exactly what you want to experience and go do it. Whatever your preference, just remember these nearby woodlands when L.A. gets you down. You'll be grateful that the slow lane and the fast happen to sit right next to each other.

Price: $25–$100
(Spring, Medium)

DRIVING DIRECTIONS

SAMO is located west of Griffith Park in Los Angeles County and to the east of the Oxnard Plain in Ventura County. Highway 101 (Ventura Freeway) borders the mountains on the north, while the Pacific Coast Highway and the ocean itself form the southern boundary. Access to most park areas is available via the many roads that cross the mountains between these two major highways. The Satwiwa Cultural Center is located in Newbury Park; take 101 to the Lynn Road exit in Newbury Park. Then head south for 5¼ miles on Lynn to Via Goleta; the park entrance is on the left. After parking, walk 0.3 mile up the gravel road from the parking area to the wooden building.

Hikers enjoy the Santa Monica Mountains National Recreation Area; this view is from the Malibu Creek area. CHRIS BECKER

FOR MORE INFORMATION

Providers

SANTA MONICA MOUNTAINS
NATIONAL RECREATION AREA
Thousand Oaks
(805) 370–2300 (recorded
message)
(805) 370–2301 (visitor
information)
www.nps.gov/samo

SATWIWA NATIVE AMERICAN
CULTURAL CENTER
Newbury Park
(805) 375–1930 (weekends only)
www.nps.gov/samo/fos/main
.html

Other

FRIENDS OF SATWIWA
Newbury Park
(805) 499–2837
www.nps.gov/samo/fos/main
.html

CALIFORNIA STATE PARKS
Calabasas
(800) 777–0369
www.parks.ca.gov

RECOMMENDED READING

Arnold, Jeanne E. *The Origins of a Pacific Coast Chiefdom: The Chumash of the Channel Islands*. Salt Lake City: University of Utah Press, 2001.

McAuley, Milt. *Guide to the Backbone Trail*. Canoga Park, Calif.: Canyon Publishing Co., 1990.

Schad, Jerry. *Afoot and Afield in Los Angeles*. Berkeley, Calif.: Wilderness Press, 2000.

SLEEP CHEAP

There are four California state parks within SAMO that provide camping facilities. For information, call (818) 880–0350. The least expensive alternative among these sites is the Musch Camp, located in Topanga State Park. It is a backcountry, hike-in facility consisting of eight tent spaces available on a first come, first served basis. The price is right, though—only $1.00 per slot. You will also be treated to drinking water and flush toilets. Call Topanga at (310) 455–2465 for more information.

Surf Casting at Leo Carrillo State Park

Here, Fishy, Fishy!

Southern California has an incredibly active yet very relaxed vibe.
There's always something to do, and there's always something going
on, yet it's still cool if you just want to hang out and enjoy life.
Besides scheduling ample beach time, SoCal residents are known to
always be on the lookout for a good time. As this book shows, the
opportunities for fun are incredibly vast. As a bonus, many of these
popular pastimes, after you've acquired the basic equipment, can be
enjoyed for little or no money. What's better than free fun?

Surfing has long been synonymous with Southern California
and is incredibly popular, for some simply because it is an inexpensive sport. However, while hordes of wave riders migrate to the
beaches when the surf's up, so does another breed of fun-seeker.
Instead of trying to carve a narrow plank along the curl of body-
thrashing waves, these folks prefer to set a lawn chair on the sand
next to a cooler full of food and frosty beverages, bait their fishing
hooks with nice chunks of squid, and toss lines out in the water.
The waiting game is on, but there's no hurry. The fish are out
there, and if they want to bite, they will. In the meantime, you can
just sit back and catch up on the latest bestseller, or snooze off to
the gentle lapping of the waves, or do little more than daydream,
staring out somewhere on the horizon. Before you know it, the rod
bucks in your hands, you set the hook, and, with a little luck,
you're reeling in dinner.

Fishing from the beach, known as surf casting, is a very popular California pastime. Besides the intrinsic beauty in being able to catch your own meal, fishing is about as relaxing as it gets. The scenery from shore is no less than phenomenal, and you have plenty of time to think, reflect, ponder, or just daze out. Fishing can be late afternoons merging into sunsets spent with friends—fishing buddies are often the best ones—or with a thermos of coffee in hand, you can head out before dawn to enjoy angling the ocean sunrise solo.

To get out there on the beach and start fishing, you're going to need some gear. The first essential item is a GONE FISHIN' sign to hang on the front door, and the second is your fishing license. But after that, your options are wide open. Our best advice is to head to a sporting goods shop and ask a knowledgeable salesperson to hook you up, pun intended. Your selection of rods, reels, lines, and tackle is up to your budget. The quality of the equipment, the number of lures, and a variety of other factors will affect the price, but setting up the simplest saltwater fishing gear will start out at around $75, while the best rigs may cost over $1,000. Another option is to rent gear. It's usually easy to find a bait shop on or near the beach that offers inexpensive rental packages. Sometimes, you can make a new friend and borrow their extra rod for a short time if you just want to try it out for a little while. Remember: Sharing your catch is always good etiquette whether you're borrowing gear or not.

Much of the Southern California coastline has great surf casting potential, so your options stretch several hundred miles. The fishing guidebooks or Web references mentioned below will point you in the right direction, but if you want a safe bet for a great weekend surf casting escape, head to the beach at Leo Carrillo State Park. Located just upcoast of Malibu, the park was named after the popular radio and television entertainer Leo Carrillo, a conservationist who served on the California State Park and Recreation Commission for eighteen years. Leo Carrillo State Park offers more than a mile of beautiful sandy seashore, perfect for swimming, scuba diving, kayaking, surfing, windsurfing, beachcombing, and especially surf fishing for a variety of species. Kelp bass, surf perch, sheepshead, halibut, and corbina are all common. There's hardly a day you will not see at least a few anglers standing out there, braving even the worst weather.

Spanning 3,000 acres, Leo Carrillo State Park is situated on the floor of a canyon shaded by giant sycamore trees that opens toward the ocean. The park stretches across both sides of the Pacific Coast Highway. From the canyon side and inland parking area, a paved

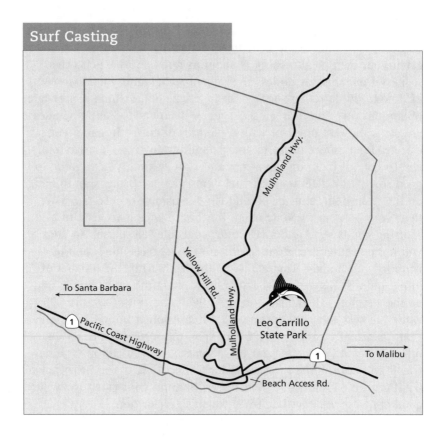

Map showing Leo Carrillo State Park with Mulholland Hwy., Yellow Hill Rd., Pacific Coast Highway (Hwy. 1), To Santa Barbara, To Malibu, and Beach Access Rd.

walkway with handrails slopes through the underpass to an observation deck with a great view of the waves crashing into the offshore sea stacks. Between November and May, you might spot migrating gray whales. More impressive scenery awaits at the wheelchair-accessible beach. Beach wheelchairs are available at the entrance, so everyone can explore this beautiful shoreline. Divided into two sections by Sequit Point, the coastal caves, tide pools, reef, and natural tunnel are other interesting highlights.

Day visitors to Leo Carrillo State Park will find a nice barbecue picnic area, along with a visitor center featuring a number of exhibits. Restrooms are located throughout the park. Two day-use parking lots, situated on each side of the Pacific Coast Highway, are easy to find and rarely full. If you plan to spend the weekend, consider bringing the old tent along—while there are numerous options for hotels and other lodging in nearby Malibu, sleeping outdoors under the night sky here is incredible. With no nearby city lights, the stars shine especially bright. A small store with basic supplies is located in the center of the campground near a small amphitheater popular for sing-alongs, campfire programs, and other group events. In addition to the watersports, hiking and wildlife watching are very popular. Before you go, be sure to call the park for a schedule of the guided nature walks, too.

If the fish just aren't biting at Leo Carrillo (which isn't the case too often), Jalama Beach is another popular surf casting spot, located 14 miles west of Lompoc. The beach sits on the farthest point from any highway on the California coastline. Healthy populations of easier-to-catch rock cod attract a strong angler following, but the real spectacle is what you can watch while waiting for the fish to bite. Late spring and summer swells from the south bring world-class windsurfers to Jalama, where afternoon breezes can kick up to over 25 miles per hour. Masterfully manipulating the colorful sails, these expert windsurfers will catch huge gusts to shoot 20 feet or higher off the water, riding the wind and giving a great show. Catching your dinner here is just a bonus.

Whether you head to Leo Carrillo State Park, Jalama Beach, or any other Southern California seashore, surf casting is a fun way to get outdoors and enjoy the bounty of the Pacific. Don't forget to purchase a fishing license. Prices range from just over $10 for a one-day permit to almost $40 for a 10-day license. It may take some time to learn how to use equipment, but once you get your bait in the water, just remember: In the end, no matter how long you wait for a strike sitting there with your toes stuck in the sand, fishing all comes down to patience. Sometimes the fish are practically throwing themselves onto shore at you, but sometimes you wait days for just a single nibble. That's the way it goes. After all, if fishing was so easy, it probably would have been called catching.

Price: $50+
(Spring, Medium)

DRIVING DIRECTIONS

Leo Carrillo State Park is located just north of Malibu, 28 miles northwest of Santa Monica on the Pacific Coast Highway. To reach Jalama Beach, drive north from Santa Barbara on Highway 101 approximately 25 miles. Exit Highway 1 (Lompoc and Vandenberg Air Force Base). Drive north for 14 miles on Jalama Road.

This fisherman seeks better position on the jettys off Leo Carrillo State Beach.
CHRIS BECKER

FOR MORE INFORMATION

LEO CARRILLO STATE PARK
Malibu
(818) 880–0350
Camping reservations: (800) 444–7275
www.parks.ca.gov/?page_id=616

WYLIE'S BAIT SHOP
Malibu
(310) 456–2321

SANTA MONICA PIER BAIT SHOP
Santa Monica
(310) 576–2014

CALIFORNIA DEPARTMENT OF FISH
AND GAME
(916) 445-0411
www.dfg.ca.gov

PIERFISHING CALIFORNIA
www.pierfishing.com

THE FISHING NETWORK ONLINE
For fishing reports, maps, tips,
message boards, and links, covering all lakes, rivers, streams,
creeks, and the Pacific Ocean,
go to www.fishingnetwork.net.

RECOMMENDED READING

Arra, Ron, and Curt Garfield. *The Ultimate Guide to Surfcasting.*
Guilford, Conn.: The Lyons Press, 2001.

Pfeiffer, C. Boyd. *The Complete Surfcaster.* Guilford, Conn.: The Lyons
Press, 1996.

Shaffer, Chris. *The Definitive Guide to Fishing in Southern California.*
Westlake Village, Calif.: Shafdog Publications, 2001.

Spira, Jeff. *Saltwater Angler's Guide to Southern California.* Belgrade,
Mont.: Wilderness Adventures Press, 2000.

SLEEP CHEAP

Leo Carrillo State Park offers excellent camping facilities. The
Canyon Campground has 135 sites, each with a picnic table and fire
pit. Restrooms and coin-operated showers are available. The state
park also features hike and bike campsites, along with a group site
that can accommodate up to fifty people. Reservations are recommended from May through October. Campsites run $13 to $16 per
night. For reservations or more information, call (800) 444-7275 or
visit www.parks.ca.gov.

Jalama Beach offers ninety-eight campsites, all beachfront or
overlooking the ocean, along with twenty-nine sites with electrical
hookups. Each site has a picnic table and barbecue pit. Hot showers,
restrooms, drinking water, and a dump station are nearby. Sites are
assigned on a first-come, first-served basis—only group sites may be
reserved in advance. Rates start at $18 per night. Call (805)
736-6316 for more information.

Coastal Bird-watching

A Cause for Adventure

You try to keep low, knowing full well that if your head slips
above the dunes you'll lose your shot and spook the target.
California least terns are endangered and quite rare, but the one
nesting just on the other side of this sandy hill doesn't seem to
know you've been looking for her for years. You take a deep
breath and steady your hand; slowly, you rise to find a gap in the
grass, coming up with painstaking quiet, until you're peeking over
the ridge and your chance presents itself. You're already loaded,
ready to fire . . .

Click. You hear your camera act as the tern sits obediently
inside the frame. Victory and another great entry for your birding
journal are yours. You didn't think we would suggest shooting such
a rare and beautiful bird in any other way, did you?

Bird-watching is not the passive activity you might think it is
at first consideration. Birders seek their quarry like hunters do,
though the outcome isn't quite the same. Both groups creep
through the wilderness silently in search of the animals they seek;
but the bird-watcher, rather than taking the trophy home for
grilling or wall hanging, simply records the sighting in a trusty
notebook, adding to a lifelong roster of birds sighted and cata-
loged. This is a competitive endeavor, with rarer specimens com-
manding the respect of fellow birders—to get the rare sightings that
make a truly interesting bird journal, they have to get out there

and beat the bushes a little, rather than sitting on a riverbank and watching the same old robins and finches fly by.

Wetlands are a paradise for birders and nature lovers of all kinds. They are some of the most biologically diverse places on earth and feature more wildlife variety than any habitat outside of the rain forest. Broadly defined, they are the places where land and water meet and create something completely different. Marshes, swamps, and bogs are the more stereotypical wetland areas, but lakes, shallow seas, deltas, tide pools, and even ocean reefs qualify as wetlands. Birds rely on these resource-rich areas even more than most species, as they often use them as stopping points on their migrations. California's wetlands, for example, lie along the Great Pacific Flyway, a migration corridor that runs from Canada to Mexico; as a result, they attract huge bird populations throughout the migratory season.

Unfortunately, California's wetlands have been shrinking for some time, and today only 5 percent of the state's coastal wetlands remain completely intact. The Bolsa Chica Ecological Reserve, located near Huntington Beach, is a 1,700-acre wetland area with a controversial recent history. The reserve originated as the result of an agreement between the Amigos de Bolsa Chica, a local citizens' group, and Signal Bolsa Corporation, which owns oil extraction facilities in this area. It is located in the middle of some very urbanized Los Angeles–area real estate and is thus under constant threat of encroaching development, despite being an avian paradise. About 10 percent of the remaining 1,200 pairs of California least tern breed at Bolsa Chica, 10 percent of the 2,200 breeding pairs of Belding's Savannah sparrow in Southern California are found there, and many of Southern California's 2,000 brown pelicans feed at Bolsa Chica and wetlands like it. It isn't hard to see that even this tiny spot of land, in the middle of Southern California's most developed landscape, is a vital natural haven for a much bigger world.

The birding here is legendary—in fact, the Huntington Beach area in general is ground zero for birding in coastal California and throughout much of the West. Almost half of the species in the entire United States have been sighted in Huntington at one time or another, and 321 of Orange County's 421 known birds have been sighted there at some point over the last ten years. Head to Bolsa Chica in the springtime, and you're likely to see great blue herons, great or snowy egrets, American kestrels, and orioles. And

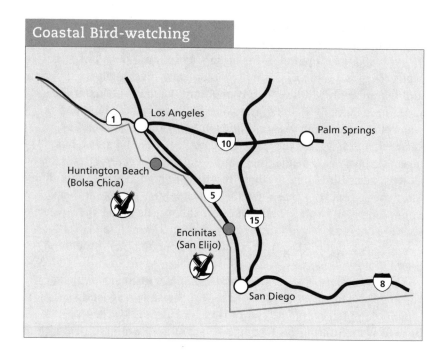

those are the ones that are *commonly* seen around the reserve; get lucky, and you may catch a glimpse of a great horned owl, an osprey, or a peregrine falcon. Even if you aren't currently a birding fan, the sheer quantity of waterfowl, raptors, and songbirds in the area will grab and hold your attention. Write down their names as you see them, and you're on your way to building a fantastic birder's journal.

If you aren't quite comfortable heading out on your own to search for birds, you can take a guided tour with the Amigos de Bolsa Chica. The group's ninety-minute tour will teach you the fundamentals of bird identification, as well as offer information about endangered species, ecology, area history, and current issues. Best of all, this tour is free, and you don't need to make reservations. If you're a true birding beginner, this is probably the way to start your odyssey into the avian kingdom.

If you're in the San Diego area, the San Elijo Lagoon Ecological Reserve near Encinitas is another wetland paradise worth checking out. San Elijo is a shallow water estuary divided into basins, courtesy of the development around and through it.

Unfortunately, this construction has reduced the area's access to the ocean, which resulted in entropy in the estuary and lack of water exchange with the open ocean. But in recent years, periodic dredging has opened an inlet and allowed this exchange to happen again, bringing a jump in the lagoon's health and viability as a migratory sanctuary. It is smaller than Bolsa Chica (900 acres), but it offers more birding opportunities along its 5 miles of trail than lakes or rivers double its size. It supports close to 700 species, about 295 of them birds—plenty enough to get your journal started.

If you're going to hit either of these areas for their bird populations, there is one thing you must absolutely bring: your camera. Binoculars are nice, as they bring your feathered friends a little closer, but a camera with good zoom capability is simply a must if you want to remember your first bird-seeking expedition. Animals, unlike majestic landscapes that tend to pale in amateur photographs (sad but true), are easily captured on film, and looking at a bevy of nice animal shots lets you relive the moment again and again. You can make California's birds yours for the taking if you snap lots of shots. Besides, how else is anyone ever going to believe you when you show them the excited chicken scratch in your brand new birding journal?

Price: $0–$2,000,000
(As much as you'd like to donate to the conservancies!)
(Spring, Medium)

DRIVING DIRECTIONS

To Bolsa Chica: From I–405 or Highway 22, take the Bolsa Chica exit south to Warner Avenue. Turn right on Warner Avenue to the Pacific Coast Highway. Turn left at the PCH.

To San Elijo: From I–5, take Lomas Santa Fe Drive west through Solana Beach to Rios Avenue (1 block before you reach the railroad tracks). Turn right; drive to the end of Rios and the trailhead. The Nature Center is located at 2710 Manchester Avenue in Encinitas on the northwest side of the reserve; there you'll find the county rangers' offices, a parking lot, restrooms, drinking water, and a 1-mile loop trail.

Low tide is feeding time for the black-necked stilt. RAY BANGS

FOR MORE INFORMATION

AMIGOS DE BOLSA CHICA
Huntington Beach
(714) 840–1575
www.amigosdebolsachica.org

THE BOLSA CHICA CONSERVANCY
Huntington Beach
(714) 846–1114
www.bolsachica.org

BOLSA CHICA LAND TRUST
Huntington Beach
www.bolsachicalandtrust.org

SAN ELIJO LAGOON CONSERVANCY
Encinitas
(760) 436–3944
www.sanelijo.org

AMERICAN BIRDING ASSOCIATION
www.americanbirding.org

RECOMMENDED READING

Clarke, Herbert. *An Introduction to Southern California Birds.* Missoula, Mont.: Mountain Press Publishing Co., 1989.

Holt, Harold R., and Brad Schram. *A Birder's Guide to Southern California.* Colorado Springs, Colo.: American Birding Association, 1998.

Rappole, John H. *Birds of the Southwest: Arizona, New Mexico, Southern California and Southern Nevada.* College Station: Texas A&M University Press, 2001.

SLEEP CHEAP

Guajome County Park, located off Highway 76 in Oceanside, is only a short drive from Encinitas and the San Elijo Lagoon. It is also very close to I–5, which will take you toward Bolsa Chica. Call (877) 565–3600 for reservations.

Biking Big Bear

Fat Tired on the Mountain

Bicycling has long been one of the most popular pastimes in Southern California. At one end of the two-wheeled spectrum are the long, leisurely tours spanning several hundred scenic miles, a saddle-sore version of heaven for some folks. On the other hand, countless people find enjoyment just from short, lazy rolls around the neighborhood. Others are stoked simply by weekends pedaling their custom beach cruisers up and down the boardwalk. There are, of course, the thousands who utilize bicycles as the perfect commuting vehicle every day of the work week—economical, environmentally friendly exercise and transportation, to say the least. And don't forget about the dedicated road riders, those likely to don snug, professional-looking digs and clip into their pedals for a Saturday "century" (a 100-mile ride often lasting five hours or longer). Finally, there are the distinct and relatively new breed of bicycle enthusiasts, easily identified by the fat, knobby tires on their bikes and their penchant for taking their pedaling off the pavement. Mountain biking is one of the most popular and fastest growing sports today. After you first throw your leg over a mountain bike, it doesn't take long for the addiction to kick in.

Southern California offers so much amazing off-road biking terrain that only the most dedicated hammerheads can hope to cover even a small chunk of it in a lifetime of weekend rides. Trails can be found nearly anywhere, from the vast expanses of desert with backdrops painted in scrub-brush brown and sea-of-sand tan, to the forested mountains full of verdant greens and granite grays. There are trails offering everyone a little bit of everything. For beginners seeking to get their wheels rolling on easier terrain, trails abound. Intermediate and expert riders will just as easily find their fix of thigh-burning single-track, lung-busting hill climbs and any kind of challenge they desire. Since fat-tired bikes can handle such a variety of terrain, the options are limited only to the rider's preference.

One of Southern California's best options for riders of all skill levels is Big Bear Valley. In mid to late spring, as the snow melts and warmer weather arrives, Big Bear becomes a mountain biking mecca. Located in the San Bernardino Mountains, yet easily accessible only 100 miles northeast of Los Angeles, mountain bikers around the world consider Big Bear one of the sport's premier hot spots. Toward the end of spring and into the summer season, the area hosts a number of mountain bike races and events, including the first stop of the NORBA (National Off Road Bicycle Association) National Championship Series. Even if you're not a professional mountain biker, however, you're sure to find plenty of terrain to suit you.

Big Bear's weather should also suit you well. Typical days are sunny with clear, blue skies. Daytime temperatures in the spring may reach 70°F, and the mercury continues to rise to highs upward of 90°F during the summer. (If you're camping, keep in mind that the night air drops to considerably cooler temperatures, especially earlier in the season. Be sure to tote along a sleeping bag and plenty of warm clothes.)

First-timers and novice riders will find a great introduction to mountain biking at Big Bear. For those who haven't jumped on a bike saddle recently or for those with kids in tow, when renting bikes be sure to inquire about any of the easy, scenic spins around the area. The ride along the lake is always spectacular. Those wishing to get off the pavement straight away should tackle either the Bristlecone Trail (located east of the base area) or the Towne Trail (to the west), as both of these rides provide great views and loads of easy two-wheel fun.

A slightly more difficult yet extremely popular mountain bike route is the Grandview Loop. This is an incredibly scenic off-pavement ride, perfect for advanced beginners and intermediates. The loop stretches 9 miles and requires roughly two hours, although the trail is mostly downhill, thanks to Snow Summit's chairlift. Years ago, when riders first seriously started taking their rigs off-road, going uphill meant thigh-burning climbs, but now, as the popularity of the sport has soared, the ski resort chairlift has developed into a popular alternative to pedaling up the mountain. The specially designed chairs feature racks to carry your bike to the top with you. Then, with gravity helping you back to the bottom, mountain biking hardly gets any easier. Keep in mind, though, the Grandview Loop isn't all downhill—yes, you will have to pedal. At the top of the Sky Chair ride, after the lift attendant unloads your bike, the trail follows signs for nearly a mile to road 2N10. From there, you'll enjoy the 3-mile roller-coaster ride to Grandview Point junction. A side trail leads to the scenic views at Grandview Point, a great place to enjoy lunch or at least take a longer rest break—the short extra ride is well worth it. After you return to the junction, you'll follow a series of roads and trails eventually leading back to the base of the Sky Chair. There are a couple of scarier, steeper sections, but most of the trail is relatively tame. Of course, if you strong intermediates and expert riders out there are looking for a bigger challenge, there's always the option to eliminate the chairlift ride and just pedal up the mountain. But be forewarned: You better have legs and lungs of steel.

Big Bear's biggest draw for more advanced riders is an incredible assortment of experts-only terrain. Mountain bikers bold enough to step up to this challenge will find miles and miles of excellent downhill tracks. Full-suspension bikes are a good idea to help tackle all the tree roots, rocks, and forearm-thrashing ruts, but don't even think about trying these trails unless you have the skills to get you down the mountain safely. Remember that mountain biking is one of the most dangerous sports out there—injuries are not uncommon. If you're confident you can hack it, head to the Summit, Log Chute, and Westridge Trails, all located at the top of the Scenic Sky Chairlift. Downhillers who don't mind a bit longer pedal to escape the crowds should search out some of Big Bear's epic downhill tracks, such as Cabin 89 and Route 1E01. (These trails are also accessed from the top of the Scenic Sky Chairlift.)

Whatever your skill level, you'll find dozens and dozens of spectacular rides in the Big Bear Valley. Peruse one of the area's mountain biking guidebooks, and when you arrive, just ask around at any of the bike shops. Everyone is very friendly and eager to help you have fun. Whether it's your first or fiftieth mountain bike trip to Big Bear, you'll soon discover it just might be impossible not to have a great time there.

Price: $50–$100

(Spring, Difficult)

DRIVING DIRECTIONS

Located in the San Bernardino Mountains, Big Bear Lake is approximately two hours from most areas of Southern California. Three main highway routes provide access: Highway 38 through Redlands, Highway 30/330 through Running Springs, and Highway 18 through Lucerne Valley. Bear Mountain is approximately 100 miles east of Los Angeles, 120 miles northeast of San Diego, and 70 miles north of Palm Springs.

Don't forget to stop and take in the view when you're biking Big Bear.
ROBERT HOLMES/CALTOUR

FOR MORE INFORMATION

SNOW SUMMIT MOUNTAIN RESORT
Big Bear Lake
(909) 866–5766
www.bigbearmountainresorts.com

BIG BEAR LAKE CHAMBER OF COMMERCE
(909) 866–4607
www.bigbearchamber.com

BIG BEAR LAKE RESORT ASSOCIATION
(800) 424–4232
www.bigbearinfo.com

BIG BEAR LAKE ADVENTURE HOSTEL
Big Bear Lake
(866) 866–5255
www.adventurehostel.com

RECOMMENDED READING

Fragnoli, Delaine, and Don Douglass. *Mountain Biking Southern California's Best 100 Trails*. Anacortes, Wash.: Fine Edge, 1998.

Pavelka, Ed, ed. *Bicycling Magazine's Mountain Biking Skills*. Emmaus, Pa.: Rodale Press, 2000.

Ross, Mark A., Paul Angiolillo, and Brad L. Fine. *Mountain Biking Southern California*. Guilford, Conn.: Globe Pequot Press, 1999.

Story, David. *Mountain Bike! Southern California*. Birmingham, Ala.: Menasha Ridge Press, 2001.

SLEEP CHEAP

One of the cheapest places to stay in the Big Bear Valley is the Big Bear Lake Adventure Hostel. These clean and safe accommodations offer a great place to sleep cheap for mountain bikers, and any other easygoing, open-minded outdoor enthusiasts who enjoy meeting others, often from all over the world, and don't mind sharing a kitchen and bathroom. Dormitory-style rooms are the cheapest way to go, starting around $20 per night. Private rooms are also available. Call (866) 866-5255 for more information and to make reservations. Contact or check the Web sites of the Big Bear Lake Chamber of Commerce and the Big Bear Lake Resort Association for more information on the area's numerous resorts, hotels, and camping options.

Rock Climbing in Joshua Tree

Papa's Got a Brand New (Chalk) Bag

Rock climbing is one of the most challenging outdoor adventures you can imagine. No other sport combines sheer strength with deftness and agility in quite the same way; it is part extreme hiking and part aerial adventure, yet suitable for just about anybody in good physical shape. In addition, both women and men are involved in rock climbing, giving the sport a universal appeal perfect for couples looking to bond, as well as singles seeking partnership.

As it does for so many other outdoor adventures, California plays host to one of rock climbing's world capitals. Joshua Tree National Park is the best-known rock-climbing destination in the United States and boasts over 4,500 established climbing routes concentrated within 100,000 acres of park area. A good percentage of the one million people who visit Joshua Tree each year are rock climbers; all skill levels are represented, from first-time scalers to the extremely talented maniacs who most would prefer to watch, rather than be.

Chances are, if you live in California and already climb, you've been to Joshua Tree. For you out-of-staters, however, or for those of you who've never given the sport a shot, the park is ripe for the picking and perfect for your next weekend escape.

Joshua Tree consists of two different deserts separated by elevation and ecological characteristics. The Colorado Desert, encompassing the eastern part of the park, sits below 3,000 feet of elevation and provides creosote bush, ocotillo, and cholla cactus with suitable habitat. If this part of the park reminds you of the Southwest, it should—the Colorado Desert is an extension of the Sonoran Desert running through Arizona. The higher, moister, and cooler Mojave Desert is home to the amazing Joshua tree, a slow-growing and beautiful plant that sports creamy white blossoms in the spring. From February to late April, if you're lucky, you might catch this fantastic display of natural finery.

As an aspiring or seasoned rock climber, you'll have your most intimate contact with Joshua Tree's geology. The park has six mountain ranges running through it: the Little San Bernardino Mountains in the southwest; the Cottonwood, Hexie, and Pinto Mountains in the center; and the Eagle and Coxcomb Mountains in the east. Between these ranges are valleys, where giant granite monoliths and rugged canyons testify to the brutal, earthly forces that shaped the park. You'll find hundreds of strange formations on your journeys through Joshua Tree, and you'll soon begin to realize that although this desert landscape looks dead and static, it is, in fact, alive with primordial geological forces that will continue to shape it long after we are gone.

Most of the climbing areas are located in the northwestern area of the park, where elevations are higher. Summers can get pretty hot in Joshua Tree no matter where you are, however; you'll be hard-pressed to find any outfitters who want to take you rock climbing under a scorching July or August sun. Your best times for hitting the routes are the fall and spring, when temperatures are more pleasant and your hands only burn from fatigue rather than from gripping sun-scorched stone. (We prefer spring because we get to see the trees bloom.)

Since Joshua Tree is such a popular climbing destination, outfitters from around the region offer trips to the area. Most head there a few times every year and require some experience to be included on their tours. After all, your guides are climbers too, and they want to enjoy what the park has to offer without having to babysit newbies who don't know a carabiner from a chalk bag. Call your local outfitter or rock gym if you're already a climber, and they can set you up with a tour you'll love.

One outfitter, however, operates in the town of Joshua Tree, and runs its adventures and classes, including the ones for beginners, within the park. The aptly named Joshua Tree Rock Climbing

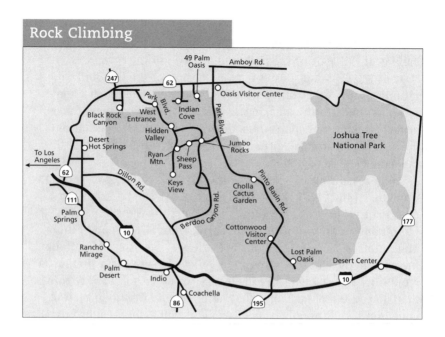

School (JTRCS) offers classes and expeditions for beginner and intermediate climbers that go from one-day seminars to four-day immersion sessions. Their most popular class is a two-day intro that combines the starter material into two one-day beginner classes. The price is certainly right—only $165 for two days of instruction—and the class provides a perfect opportunity to introduce yourself to the rocks.

If you have the time, JTRCS offers an extended class that covers both beginner sessions and brings you into more advanced territory. Already know what you're doing but want to learn more? Try the four-day intermediate class, featuring multipitch climbing and an introduction to leading skills. Or just go with a leading class, and get yourself out on the "sharp end of the rope." No matter what you decide to go with, you'll be getting your instruction inside the park. In effect, it knocks out two adventuring birds with one stone: you get to see Joshua Tree as it was meant to be seen—as you're hanging from a rock face—while you're learning a fantastic outdoor skill.

Because of its hard-core nature, rock climbing is one of the most rewarding adventures you can treat yourself to. Once you've conquered a few tough trips up the faces, you'll feel like you can do anything. Earning this confidence in a setting like Joshua

Tree, from people who are committed to giving you the best experience they can, is the kind of rush adventurous folk dream about.
Price: $50–$250+
(Spring, Difficult)

DRIVING DIRECTIONS

Joshua Tree National Park lies 140 miles east of Los Angeles. You can approach it from the west via Interstate 10 and Highway 62 (Twentynine Palms Highway). The north entrances to the park are located at Joshua Tree Village and the city of Twentynine Palms. The south entrance at Cottonwood Spring, which lies 25 miles east of Indio, can be approached from the east or west, also via Interstate 10.

FOR MORE INFORMATION

Outfitters

JOSHUA TREE ROCK CLIMBING
SCHOOL
Joshua Tree
(760) 366–4745
www.joshuatreerockclimbing
.com

VERTICAL ADVENTURES
Newport Beach
(800) 514–8785 or (949) 854–6250
www.vertical-adventures.com

Other

SOUTHERN CALIFORNIA
MOUNTAINEERS ASSOCIATION
www.rockclimbing.org

JOSHUA TREE NATIONAL PARK
www.nps.gov/jotr

JOSHUA TREE NATIONAL PARK
ASSOCIATION
www.joshuatree.org

RECOMMENDED READING

Horst, Eric J. *Flash Training (How to Rock Climb Series)*. Helena, Mont.: Chockstone Press, 1997.

Sherman, John. *Better Bouldering (How to Rock Climb Series)*. Helena, Mont.: Chockstone Press, 1997.

Vogel, Randy. *Rock Climbing: Joshua Tree*. Helena, Mont.: Falcon, 2000.

Rock climbing at Joshua Tree National Park is no picnic in the sun.
ROBERT HOLMES/CALTOUR

SLEEP CHEAP

Joshua Tree boasts a number of campgrounds, all of which are open all year and most of which do not have camping fees. Pick up a park map, and choose your area. You can make reservations (800-365-2267) at Black Rock, Indian Cove, and Sheep Pass; other sites are first come, first served. Only the Cottonwood and Black Rock sites have water and flush toilets available, so make sure you're properly equipped before setting out to your campground of choice. Joshua Tree Rock Climbing School also has a couple cabins available in the nearby town of Joshua Tree; though they are a bit pricier than camping, they are comfortable and close to some restaurants, golf, and night life. Call (800) 890-4745 for information, or write to Joshua Tree Climber Cabins, HCR Box 3034, Joshua Tree, CA 92252.

Hang Gliding and Paragliding

Sky Dancing Cloud Flirters

You feel the breezes brush your cheeks as you look down. Below, human existence is gone, swallowed by the earth and distance, and all you can see are geological features and trees swirled together into a single, rolling carpet of hues. Ahead, you have nothing but blue skies, broken occasionally by birds that, if you were close enough, you could easily look in the eye. Your wings stand rigid on either side of you, and the only sound is the constant *swish* of the air cradling you above the earth.

The high you're experiencing is one well known to hang glider and paraglider enthusiasts, a group that seeks to live the meditative life of a falcon in flight. These adventures are definitely not for everyone, but for those strong enough physically and mentally to handle them, there are few things more exhilarating. If you are ready for one of the most challenging and rewarding outdoor adventures out there, take off for the sky using nothing but the air itself, and you might just be changed forever.

California is the world capital for these sports; according to the United States Hang Gliding Association (USHGA), there are over fifty hang gliding and paragliding schools operating in the state, and three of those schools were among the top ten, by number of novice ratings issued, in 2000. One of those, Windsports, is located in Sylmar, only a short ride from Los Angeles.

Windsports specializes in hang-gliding instruction. The sport works like this: You hold the glider up and run down an incline until the wind speed reaches 15 or 20 mph. At that point, the momentum of the air moving past you creates lift under the wings, and you go up, up, and away. If there are no hills, a vehicle can tow you up like a big kite; typically, however, beginners start off learning how to perform a "foot launch," using no equipment besides their legs, their glider, the land, and the air. Paragliding operates in a similar fashion but substitutes a parachute-like canopy for the heavy-winged glider. Both pursuits are serious business and require training, a clear head, practice, and a body weight below 210 pounds or so; but for people with the right stuff, there are few things better.

The two sports are similar in some respects but differ radically in terms of equipment. The typical glider measures between 26 and 36 feet in wingspan, and weighs 65 to 100 pounds with harness and emergency parachute. Obviously, running around on the ground with one of these things can be a bit awkward, so hang gliding requires quit a bit of physical prowess; you need to be able to run with your wings balanced above you and keep the load from pitching around too much on takeoff. Once you're off the ground, however, great strength is largely unnecessary, since your body "hangs" from the glider. (Do be aware, though, that a fair degree of upper-body endurance is necessary for longer trips.) You also need to pay attention, as the hang glider moves faster than a paraglider does, requiring a constant clear head and concentration. If you don't feel comfortable with your physical abilities, you may want to hit the gym for a few months prior to your first flight. Otherwise, paragliding may be your better option—paragliding rigs are much lighter, and although the takeoff is similar to that of a hang glider, airspeeds are typically slower (12 to 25 mph vs. 20 to 50 mph).

This is not to say, however, that paragliders magically fly themselves, or that physicality isn't a factor, or that they don't require close attention during flight. Both pursuits are real aviation, and the people who fly in these ways are called pilots for a reason. Take your adventuring seriously and safely. Fly like an idiot, and you may get yourself hurt as well as answer your whole family's questions as to just how stupid you can be.

The USHGA regulates hang gliding and paragliding certifications by a set of standards all certified schools are bound to follow.

Good trainers are dedicated to ensuring that novices get the best introduction to the sport they choose. The instructors listed here each offer slightly different programs and prices; when it comes down to it, though, they all break down into essentially the same deals, depending on the time you have and how much you want to learn. Talk to each one *at length,* to get an idea of where they're coming from, teaching style, and so on, decide whether you'd rather get into hang gliding or paragliding, then make your outfitter decision.

As a beginner, your first job is to get acquainted with the whole idea—that is, going up in tandem with a professional pilot, along with taking some ground school classes and training on how to take off and land (obviously two very important things in the world of gliding). After taking part in this initial training, you can advance to the beginner's training level, which is also the first step on the standardized proficiency test. Work at it, and in a few months you can get yourself up to higher proficiency levels and start taking longer flights—hang gliders and paragliders are capable of flying at over 10,000 feet, and trips can cover dozens or even hundreds of miles. Just make sure you find a loyal driver to follow you before you get to that point.

Nonmotorized flight is one of the world's greatest outdoor adventures. Those who engage in it are a special breed and often become incredibly passionate for their chosen pursuit once they start. If you think you can handle the heights, the rigorous training, and the mental discipline required, then take your first step skyward.

Price: $50–$350, $500+ for pilot certification training
(Spring, Difficult)

DRIVING DIRECTIONS

The hang gliding/paragliding school you choose will give you directions to your flight grounds. Some flight outfitters conduct training classes at a certain flight facility (e.g., Windsports flies their tandems at Sylmar Flight Park, just east of LAX). Others will move to different locations, depending on weather, time of year, availability, and so on.

FOR MORE INFORMATION

Outfitters

WINDSPORTS SOARING CENTER
(hang gliding)
Sylmar
(818) 367–2430
www.windsports.com

UPTIMAL PARAGLIDING
(paragliding)
Ojai
(805) 646–9660
www.uptimal.com

TORREY PINES GLIDERPORT
(both hang gliding and paragliding)
La Jolla
(858) 452–9858
www.flytorrey.com

HIGH ADVENTURE
(both hang gliding and paragliding)
San Bernardino
(909) 883–8488 (call in the morning)
www.flytandem.com

FLY ABOVE ALL AIRSPORTS
(both hang gliding and paragliding)
Santa Barbara
(805) 965–3733
www.flyaboveall.com

Other

UNITED STATES HANG GLIDING ASSOCIATION
(719) 632–8300
www.ushga.org

Taking the scenic route down the Southern California coast. MAYA JEBB/TORREY PINES GLIDERPORT

RECOMMENDED READING

Fair, Erik. *Right Stuff for New Hang Glider Pilots.* Laguna Beach, Calif.: Publitec Editions, 1987.

Pagen, Dennis. *The Art of Paragliding.* Spring Mills, Pa.: Sport Aviation Publications, 2001.

————. *Hang Gliding Training Manual: Learning Hang Gliding Skills for Beginner to Intermediate Pilots.* Black Mountain, N.C.: Black Mountain Books, 1995.

Whittall, Noel. *Paragliding: The Complete Guide.* New York: The Lyons Press, 2000.

SLEEP CHEAP

Santa Monica Mountains National Recreation Area is only a short drive from Van Nuys, and it isn't terribly far from Ojai and Santa Barbara, either. There are four state parks in the area, and accommodations vary from primitive to RV-friendly. Fees are reasonable at each campground. For information and reservations, call (800) 444–7275, or visit www.nps.gov/samo.

Summer

Beach Relaxin'

Sand Combing, Cruising, and Bumming

America is one big country. In between the Atlantic and Pacific lie hundreds of thousands of square miles that don't have the benefit of an ocean shoreline, much less beaches; heck, there are tons of people in the Heartland who've never even seen the blue expanse of a truly large body of water.

California's good citizens have no such concern. The state boasts 1,264 miles of coastline, much of it covered by sandy, warm beach and cavorting, fun-loving people. Folks in the Midwest may refer to "those California folks" with a sneer, but inside you know they're just a bit envious. After all, who wouldn't want to wake up to those ocean views, that amazing natural resource, within a few miles of your front door?

It is to you, the uninitiated, that we dedicate this chapter. If you've never seen the ocean, never dipped a toe in 60,231,936 square miles of water, then go west, hearty adventurer. We also want to include those of you who, like the Arizonan who's never seen the Grand Canyon, live within a stone's throw of the sand and never seem to get on it. Welcome (or welcome back!) to California, honorary capital of beach bumming, and mecca for the sea-seeking masses.

We've all seen *Baywatch* and its less "classy" imitators. Everyone knows what the California beach culture looks like. What most of us miss out on is actually *living* that life—laying ourselves down on a blanket at sunset while the ocean swallows the sun;

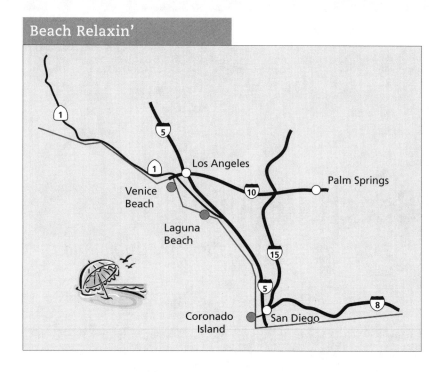

strolling down the beach at midday with the waves lapping our feet; building our own palace out of pure sand and water. These are all things you'll do on a leisurely escape to the Left Coast, where the Pacific beckons and hard-core relaxation awaits along the shoreline.

California has a ton of beaches to comb, but a few stand out from the others for pure laid-back attitude and scenic beauty. Rule number one for this adventure: Take in the atmosphere and relax. Those of you who want to attack the surf will get your chance a little later (see Escape 19). This escape is about the sand, more so than the waves. It's also about economics; it's a lot cheaper to hang out on a beach than it is to rent a bunch of equipment to use in the water. If you stick to the shore, the shallows, and the streets, you're in for a pretty low-dollar vacation (provided you can control your spending habits on the boardwalk!).

Venice Beach is probably the center of Southern California's beach culture; although it shares a name with an ancient Italian city, the two places couldn't be more opposite. While one is a center of Old World culture and charm, the other is a gathering place for all the twenty-first century people who make California such a cool and special place. The main activity here is watching the citizenry—

sit down by the beach with your eyes open, and you'll see roller skaters, street musicians, prophets, acrobats, beauties of both sexes, and the occasional entertainment personality or movie set. The movie *Speed* was filmed here, as were episodes from classic TV shows like *Get Smart, CHiPS,* and *The A-Team.* The world-famous Muscle Beach, where huge people strive to become even bigger, is another sight to see, if the muscle and iron don't intimidate you.

In all, the whole joint is a big trip and one of the few places you, as an adventurer, should check out when the population is at its densest. If you want Venice Beach's full impact—in other words, maximum cultural exposure—head there on a weekend, since that's when the most people are out and about. Go there on a weekday, and you're more likely to have a mellower, but perhaps less interesting, time.

Laguna Beach, located a little farther south, is a much more quaint, traditional beach escape spot, more suited to the old-fashioned among us. Widely known as an artists' colony, it was also a popular haunt for old Hollywood's stars. Bette Davis, Judy Garland, Charlie Chaplin, and Mickey Rooney all kept houses in Laguna once upon a time, and one look toward the shore will tell you why—the area is absolutely breathtaking and inspirational on any number of levels. Natural beauty is far more prevalent here than the surgically enhanced scenery you'll see at Venice Beach; in fact, interacting with the environment is a prime pursuit here, from wilderness park hikes to the Heisler Park Ecological Reserve, a great place for tide pool wading, snorkeling, and scuba. Art is a huge attraction too, as the town boasts quite a few galleries, museums, and rotating exhibitions. Just call or check out the Laguna Beach Visitors Bureau's Web site and see what's happening when you'll be swinging through town.

Move even farther south to San Diego and you'll hit Coronado, one of that area's best beach destinations and a place that offers something for everyone. The city of Coronado is located on the island of Coronado, and as a result you've got beach pretty much all around you. In the morning, you can take to the sand and watch the Navy SEALs from nearby North Island Naval Air Station take their 7:00 A.M. constitutional, a particularly fun activity for those interested in well-built military lads. Later in the day, you can take in the natural activity, as dolphins frolic offshore, pelicans fly overhead, and smaller birds hop and skip along the shore. Downtown Coronado offers great shopping and dining too, so you've got the best of both worlds within a few minutes' walk. Coronado is an especially good destination if you're traveling with Fido; Dog Beach is a special area where harried

If you're beach bumming in July, you might encounter the U.S. Open Sand Castle Contest. ROBERT HOLMES/CALTOUR

pets can take their owners for long, pleasurable strolls along a beach filled with other pets and their folks.

No matter which of California's beaches you decide to head to, you'll soon realize the number one reason that so many people deal with earthquakes and mudslides to live there: the ocean itself. The California coast is one of the most beautiful, vibrantly alive regions in the whole country, and just being close to it is enough to energize your depleted batteries. Come out and experience the pounding Pacific, and you will find yourself pining for it long after you return to Iowa, Arizona, or Montana and resume your oceanless everyday life.

Price: $0–$100+
(Summer, Easy)

DRIVING DIRECTIONS

Venice Beach: Take Highway 405 to Venice Boulevard. Exit west, and drive until you reach sand. Parking is available at the end of the boulevard right on the beach. Daily rates range from $3.00 to $10.00 depending on the time of year.

Laguna Beach: Laguna is about an hour away from Los Angeles proper. The easiest way to get there is to take I–5 south to Highway 133 south, which turns into the Laguna Canyon Road and ends at both the city's main beach and the Pacific Coast Highway.

Coronado: Coronado Island is located just off San Diego, across the beautiful San Diego–Coronado Bay Bridge. Take I–5 south to Highway 75, and exit toward Coronado.

FOR MORE INFORMATION

VENICE BEACH ONLINE
www.venicebeach.com

CITY OF CORONADO ONLINE
www.coronado.ca.us

LAGUNA BEACH ONLINE
www.laguna-beach.ca.us

CORONADO VISITOR'S BUREAU
(619) 437–8788
www.coronadovisitors.com

LAGUNA BEACH VISITOR'S BUREAU
(800) 877–1115
www.lagunabeachinfo.org

RECOMMENDED READING

Bisbort, Alan, and Parke Puterbaugh. *Foghorn Outdoors: California Beaches*. Emeryville, Calif.: Avalon Travel Publishing, 1999.

Caughman, Erin, and Jo Ginsberg, eds. *California Coastal Access Guide*. Berkeley: University of California Press, 1997.

Hinton, Sam. *Seashore Life of Southern California: An Introduction to the Animal Life of California Beaches South of Santa Barbara*. Berkeley: University of California Press, 1989.

SLEEP CHEAP

Crystal Cove State Park is located off the Pacific Coast Highway between Corona del Mar and Laguna Beach. The offshore area is designated an underwater park, and there are lots of shoreline, tide pools, and other features to explore—perfect for your relaxing beach weekend. Unfortunately, the campground is not located on the beach, but about 3 strenuous hiking miles inland; plus, you have to pack everything (including water) in and out. A picnic table and a pit toilet are available, but past that you're on your own. The price is certainly right, however—$7.00 per night. Call (949) 494–3539 to ask questions and make reservations.

San Diego Safari

Koalas, Komodos, and Kagus . . . Oh My!

Extinction has always been part of our natural order. There are no
dinosaurs running around anymore, no saber-toothed cats chasing
woolly mammoths, and no dodo birds flapping their flightless wings
on the island of Mauritius. The problem, however, is that the rate of
extinction seems to be rapidly accelerating—in the past few centuries,
over a hundred species of mammals have disappeared, and those are
only the ones we know about. Currently there are hundreds of
endangered birds, mammals, reptiles, and fish, along with over
25,000 endangered plant species. Human overpopulation, habitat
destruction, and increased pollution are considered the primary causes,
and although governments, zoos, and wildlife organizations are racing to save species, they cannot do it all alone—conservation only
works if everyone pitches in. So, what can the rest of us do to help?

First, recycle anything and everything you can; avoid using
products that cannot be recycled or are nonbiodegradable. Second,
conserve whenever possible—turn off lights that aren't in use, use
water more efficiently, and, maybe most importantly, walk, bike, or
use public transportation as much as possible. Third, spread the
word; kindly offer assistance to avoid needless waste and help educate
others on the importance of conservation. Finally, support indi-
viduals and organizations that are working hard to promote sustain-
able living for all species, even if this means just going to the zoo.

That's right—visit the zoo. Who says saving the planet isn't fun?

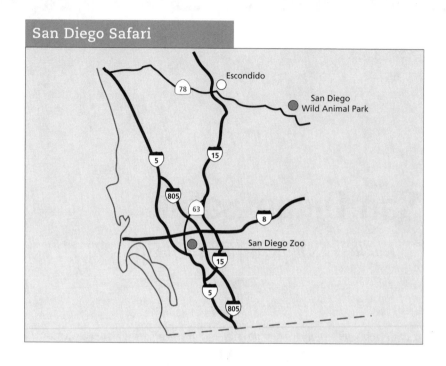

Your first trip to the world-famous San Diego Zoo will inspire awe in nature's handiwork and let you experience some of the world's rarest wildlife firsthand. Situated in beautiful Balboa Park, the Zoo was founded in 1916 by Dr. Harry Wegeforth, who started the menagerie with only fifty animals. Today, the one-hundred-acre zoo houses over 4,000. Over 800 species are represented, including the ever-popular favorites—elephants, giraffes, gorillas, giant pandas, lions, tigers, polar bears, and many, many more. Along with its 6,500 species of plants, the zoo is acknowledged as one of the planet's finest wildlife sanctuaries.

The not-for-profit Zoological Society of San Diego manages the zoo, as well as the nearby 2,200-acre San Diego Wild Animal Park. The society's mission is simply to help ensure the conservation of endangered species and their habitats around the world. Memberships of varying levels are an easy way to support the cause while taking advantage of numerous member-only benefits and discounts.

If you do become a member, you'll be optimistic about your contributions, given the zoo's recent additions. Some newer exhibits include the Ituri Forest, a complex multispecies habitat that features African rain forest natives like hippos and okapis (the only known relative of giraffes), and the Owens Rainforest Aviary, a multilevel, walk-through paradise of waterfalls and tropical plants that features more than sixty exotic and endangered bird species from Southeast Asia. Both add even more striking variety to a host of excellent exhibits, including the Gorilla Tropics, Polar Bear Plunge, Tiger River, and Sun Bear Forest. The Giant Panda Research Station is also a very popular stop.

Thanks to San Diego's ideal climate, most animals are able to live outdoors year-round in spacious enclosures that much resemble their natural habitats. Visitors will enjoy San Diego's wonderful weather as well—daily temperatures average 70°F throughout the year. As a result, lodging options abound, from beachfront mega-resorts, quaint seaside B&Bs, and high-rise hotels to campgrounds like Sweetwater Regional Park, only 10 miles from downtown.

You'll find the sweetest way to sleep, however, at the San Diego Wild Animal Park. The unique Roar & Snore experience ranks a close second to that prohibitively priced African safari—and it doesn't require painful vaccinations, either! Plan to arrive at the Wild Animal Park, located about thirty-five minutes north of downtown, around four o'clock. After checking in, camp guides arrange luggage transport and escort you on the short trek to your campsite on Kilima Point, which overlooks the stunning and wide-sweeping East Africa exhibit. Herds of antelope and giraffes span the horizon and create a stirring, almost otherworldly scene straight out of a Hemingway novel. Be prepared for a few snarls from the park's other exotic residents too, as they warmly welcome you to their domain. The Roar & Snore program costs just over $100 and with your one-day admission ticket covers both the day of and the day after your sleepover. For safety considerations, children must be at least eight years old.

Tents, camp chairs, camp pads, and lanterns are provided for your use, but sleeping bags, pillows, clothing, and personal items are your responsibility. (Don't forget the camera, of course!) After setting up your camp, the guides will lead you on walks, where you will have the opportunity to encounter some of the park's wild creatures a little closer, as well as take an after-hours peek into animal nightlife. Wear comfortable, sturdy walking shoes, as the terrain is varied and mildly strenuous at times. Restroom facilities are available at your campsite, though there are no showers, and dinner is served outdoors, as is customary on safari. Later, as the evening skies grow dark, the campfire program is sure to entertain.

After your overnight outing, a pancake breakfast fuels the day's

Giraffes are tall, but they need kisses too. This view comes from the zoo train.
ROBERT HOLMES/CALTOUR

adventures ahead. As you spend the next day moseying up and down the park's walkways (some of which are slightly steep), you'll quickly discover that the facility's layout is designed first for the animals and second for visitors. This is not a bad quality, particularly if you happen to be a resident animal; animals here wander in herds and flocks, and enclosures are measured in acres rather than square feet. This makes for some shoe-leather distance, but if your dogs get tired, hitch a ride on the Wgasa Bush Line Railway, an electric monorail that winds through and around the park's Asian and African field enclosures. The fifty-five-minute train tour is also a perfect way to relax after enjoying a hearty lunch at the Thorn Tree Terrace, located in Nairobi Village near the rail terminal.

The Wild Animal Park, like the zoo, features numerous themed exhibits. One very interactive adventure is to head down under to the Australian rain forest found at Lorikeet Landing. Hold up a cup of the specially prepared sweet nectar, a favorite food of the rainbow-colored lorikeets, otherwise known as brush-tongued parrots, and soon you'll find several birds perched on your arms and shoulders, digging in for the feast. A recent addition to the park is Condor Ridge, which presents a perfect opportunity to spot the magnificent California condor or battling bighorn sheep. Don't forget about the gorillas either, or the elephants, or the dozens of other places to see amazing animals; there is plenty of terrain to cover, and every inch offers something spectacular. Be prepared for your walkabout by bringing adequate water, a hat and sunglasses, sunscreen, and plenty of film, but don't fret over the packing list too much—you'll find anything you might have forgotten (or realize later you need) at the various concession stands around the park.

San Diego Zoo day trips present a great way to have fun, get educated, and support a good cause. (It's a year-round adventure too—both the zoo and the park are open 365 days a year.) On the other hand, if you are looking for a full weekend of safari excitement, graduate to the Roar & Snore campout. Although you are safely isolated atop Kilima Point and secure from any potential attacks, the haunting fire's flames bellydancing in the night, followed by the roars and ruckus of lions somewhere out in the darkness, will send chills down anyone's spine and remind you of exactly where you fit into the food chain.

Price: $25–$250

(Summer, Easy)

DRIVING DIRECTIONS

The world-famous San Diego Zoo is located on Zoo Drive in Balboa Park, just north of downtown San Diego. To reach the San Diego Wild Animal Park from downtown, follow I–15 north to the Via Rancho Parkway exit. Go east, and follow the signs to the park.

FOR MORE INFORMATION

SAN DIEGO ZOO
San Diego
(619) 231–1515
www.sandiegozoo.org

SAN DIEGO CONVENTION AND VISITORS BUREAU
(619) 236–1212
www.sandiego.org

SAN DIEGO WILD ANIMAL PARK
Escondido
(760) 747–8702
Roar & Snore Reservations
(619) 718–3050
www.sandiegozoo.org/wap

RECOMMENDED READING

Matthiessen, Peter. *Tigers in the Snow*. San Francisco: North Point Press, 2001.

Myers, Douglas, and Lynda Stephenson. *Mister Zoo: The Life and Legacy of Dr. Charles Schroeder*. San Diego: Zoological Society of San Diego, 1999.

Ryder, Joanne. *Little Panda: The World Welcomes Hua Mei at the San Diego Zoo*. New York: Simon & Schuster, 2001.

SLEEP CHEAP

Add up the value in the Roar & Snore program, and it works out to be quite economical, since it includes park entrance, meals, and accommodations. Check the park Web site, or call for current rates, as well as for more information or if you have any questions or special needs; children ages eight to eleven, Zoological Society members, and groups of over fifteen people receive discounts. Roar & Snore safaris take place Friday, Saturday, and some Sundays from mid-April through October. No children younger than eight are permitted, and only two youths per adult are allowed. Reservations are required.

Another interesting and inexpensive option is Sweetwater Regional Park, located only 10 miles southeast of downtown San Diego east of I–805 just off Highway 54. All fifty-three campsites have water and electricity, and some include horse corrals for equestrians. Restroom facilities include hot showers. The park features hundreds of acres of hiker and horseback habitat. Standing at the summit site, you can see San Diego Bay and the Pacific Ocean to the west, the Sweetwater Reservoir to the east, and Tijuana to the south. Campsites may be reserved up to three months in advance. Other San Diego camping parks are available. For more information, call San Diego County Parks and Recreation (858–694–3049).

Lake Havasu Houseboating

The Floating Castle

When you think of Lake Havasu, chances are you think of spring break hijinks, blazing heat, and Arizona. You do so with good reason–Lake Havasu is a spring break mecca, the mercury can hit 120°F in July, and Lake Havasu City is indeed in Arizona. What you may not know is that the lake sits directly on the Arizona–California border and that it's closer to Barstow than it is to Phoenix.

Lake Havasu (the body of water, not the city) was formed in 1938, when Parker Dam was completed. Today the lake boasts 47 miles of scenic shoreline and one of the strangest architectural landmarks in America: the actual London Bridge, removed from its home across the Atlantic and deposited in the desert sands. Robert P. McCulloch, who founded Lake Havasu City in the late 1950s, bought the bridge in 1968, then had it meticulously shipped and rebuilt between the city and a small island just off the Arizona coastline. If you take a close look at the bridge, you'll still see the numbers McCulloch's crew used to identify each piece during its journey.

Anyway, just as Arizona isn't the only state on the lake, spring break isn't the only time Lake Havasu is hopping. All summer, people looking to beat the heat in Phoenix or L.A. journey to this oasis in between and find escape on one of the greatest leisure inventions of all time: the houseboat.

Houseboating is one fantastic way to escape your daily grind and really take control of your relaxation. You can motor around the lake all day, exploring nooks and crannies while cooking burgers on your boat-supplied gas grill; rent a couple of Jet Skis and get some wind and spray in your hair; or go out to the middle of the lake, slop on some sunscreen, and soak up all the rays you can handle. Whatever you decide, you are in control the whole time—the order of the day is up to you, as is your destination. Another huge plus: instant gratification. You don't need to do much to visit the fishing hole when you're already on the lake; just drop in a line, and go to town. The same goes for just about anything you care to do in the water. Simply motor for a while and you're there, or jump off the side and you're in.

If you want to try houseboating in Southern California, this magnificent lake and its picturesque surroundings are your best bet. Lake Havasu is nestled in a valley of majestic mountain ranges, giving it beautiful scenery to match the multitude of activities you'll find there. You can enjoy not only boating around, but also swimming, fishing, golf, tennis, water-skiing, hiking, sunbathing, and about fifty other lakeside and desert diversions. You can visit the Havasu National Wildlife Refuge and take in the natural world, or head over to Havasu Landing Resort and Casino on the California shore and blow a few bucks at the slots. Luxury houseboats are available from Havasu Springs Resort practically year-round, but summer allows you the broadest range of activities. Keep in mind, however, that there are only a few houseboats to be had on Havasu; book well in advance of your trip, to ensure that you'll be floating instead of waiting. Also, remember that temperatures in the Havasu area can top 120°F; if you're going to venture away from the lake, take an ample water supply, or you won't be having fun for too long.

If you bring your rod, you won't be disappointed with Havasu's fishing. The lake's deep water, punctuated with coves and inlets, provides perfect fishing conditions for black and striped bass, crappie, bluegill, catfish, and trout. Some of the best fishing is toward the south end of the Lake in the Bill Williams Arm, near the wildlife areas. If you'd rather get your thrills on dry land, bring your ATVs and explore the two off-highway vehicle areas within Lake Havasu's Bureau of Land Management (BLM) Field Office territory. Copper Basin Dunes (1,275 acres) and Crossroads (1,500 acres) have no travel restrictions, so vehicles are free to go off the beaten path. Both locations are on the California side of the lake between Parker Dam and the Colorado River

Lake Havasu Houseboating

Indian Tribes Reservation, and there are off-highway vehicle (OHV) staging areas at each site complete with parking, restrooms, and unloading ramps. (Contact the Havasu BLM field office for more information.)

Because of all these options, a houseboating getaway is perfect for family reunions and similar events. While the adventurous types are taking to Jet Skis and OHVs, the tamer folk can enjoy their down time in a more relaxed way. Young toddlers on the boats are fine too; as long as proper precautions are taken, both you and they can have a great houseboat vacation. For one thing, make sure they have a comfortable life vest, and keep it on them at all times. Also, have things for them to do, so they stay busy during slower times and you don't end up having to entertain nonstop. If you're traveling with the tots, ask Havasu Springs about what safety equipment their boats include for a secure family adventure.

Houseboating is, more than most activities covered in these pages, a team sport. It can get a little pricey for smaller groups; Havasu Springs, for example, charges just over $1,000 for their cheapest three-day rental. It's not that you don't get a lot for your money, since even the smaller boats provide mucho amenities. But the littlest boat (a 47-footer) sleeps ten people, and the capacities go up the larger the boat is. (Keep in mind, too, that larger boats often boast more and better amenities.) Invite a crowd, and you may find yourself having a great three-day weekend for around $150 or $200 per person, including fuel, food, beverages, and additional watercraft like Jet Skis or even a water ski boat.

Enjoy feeling like you're in control? Rent a houseboat, and you're the one in charge. Feel like swimming? Jump over the side. Fishing? Open your tackle box, bait up, and drop in a line. Feel like doing nothing? Turn off the motor and float a while. No matter what you choose, you're the boss, responsible for your own instant gratification.

Price: $150–$500+
(Summer, Easy)

DRIVING DIRECTIONS

From Los Angeles, take I–10 east for about 40 miles, to I–15 north. Continue on I–15 to I–40, and go east on I–40 for about 165 miles. Leave I–40 at exit 9 and take AZ–95 south to Lake Havasu City and Parker. Turn right on AZ–95, and go south for 16 miles to the city. Call your boat rental company for precise directions to their marina.

FOR MORE INFORMATION

Outfitters

HAVASU SPRINGS RESORT
Parker, Arizona
(928) 667–3361
www.havasusprings.com

Other

LAKE HAVASU STATE PARK
(928) 855–2784

LAKE HAVASU TOURISM BUREAU
(800) 242–8278
www.golakehavasu.com

RECOMMENDED READING

Wing, Charlie. *The Liveaboard Report: A Boat Dweller's Guide to What Works and What Doesn't.* New York: McGraw-Hill, 1997.

Dropping a line on Lake Havasu. LAKE HAVASU CONVENTION AND VISITORS BUREAU

SLEEP CHEAP

You won't even have to worry about where you'll sleep or how you'll pay for it once you have your boat. Bring ten people on your houseboating adventure, and you'll all be living large for less than $200 per person. Keep in mind that the price includes overnight accommodations, food, drinks, and recreation for three days. Not too shabby, wallet-wise.

Big Sur Coastal Camping

The Scenic, Simple Life

Have you ever gone camping? If not, let us remind you there are few things more terrifying than wild animals scurrying and scampering about your campsite at night. Only the nearly transparent walls of your meager shelter, made of material akin to heavy-duty pantyhose, separate you from the wild beasts' tent-cleaving claws and flesh-ripping fangs, both probably dripping with blood from campers recently mauled at the next site over. In fact, you even thought you heard screams but weren't sure; it was impossible to tell with all the hooting owls and screeching bats and other less-than-friendly wilderness night noises going off. The full moon dances shadows all around, and you whisper to your sound-snoozing, more-experienced camping compadre, "Wake up. *I think we're under attack."*

All silliness aside, camping just does not suit some people; however, as the old saying goes, don't knock it until you try it. If you aren't whistling a different tune after a weekend trip to beautiful Big Sur, then chances are you truly aren't the camping type. Fresh ocean air, trees so tall they tickle cloud bellies, and jaw-dropping scenery await anyone courageous enough to sleep in the woods here. To seal the deal, getting attacked by a wild beast near Big Sur is about as likely as the Wicked Witch of the West showing up at your campfire.

The name Big Sur comes from the original Spanish El Pais Grande del Sur (The Big Country of the South), which is exactly

Big Sur Coastal Camping

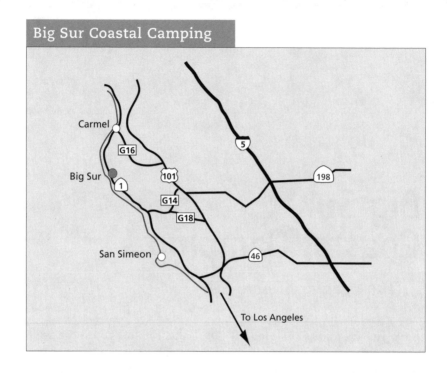

what it seemed like to early settlers. The rugged region south of Monterey was vast and relatively unexplored, bordered by almost 100 miles of treacherous Pacific coastline. The area may be more developed and significantly safer these days, but the immense grandeur remains well intact, beckoning you to discover Big Sur for yourself.

The first priority upon arrival is to set up camp. There are plenty of campgrounds in the area, but in the idyllic (and very popular) summer season, be sure to make reservations well in advance. Remember that an inflatable air mattress will make a huge difference in your sleeping arrangements, as will a warm sleeping bag or an extra blanket, just in case the temperatures dip. For maximum comfort, bring it all. For first-timers not willing to venture too far off the beaten path, one of the best campground choices is Pfeiffer Big Sur State Park. The redwoods steal the show, towering over the 218 campsites, but in this 800-acre expanse you will also find healthy populations of alders, willows, big-leaf maples, black cottonwoods, sycamores, oaks, and evergreens, to name a few. With all this lush greenery, the air is rich and fresh, perfect for soothing the soul and cleansing your city lungs.

Each campsite has a picnic table, fire ring, and plenty of space for a tent or two. Recreational vehicles less than 32 feet are welcome, though you won't find any RV hookups. Restrooms complete with running water and coin-operated showers are located within easy walking distance of every site. This is certainly not the Hilton, but in our book, Pfeiffer Big Sur is a five-star campground. For true city slickers, the Big Sur Lodge, also located in the state park, offers sixty-one clean and comfortable cottage-style guest rooms. Of course, with all the attractions and distractions available in the Big Sur area, you shouldn't be spending too much time in the room anyway, so we applaud the absence of in-room radios, alarm clocks, telephones, and televisions. The relaxing simple life is what it's all about here.

After your first night sleeping in a tent, set out and see the inspiring landscapes that have captured the hearts of countless writers, poets, and artists. If you forgot when checking in at the campground (or lodge), pick up a park map, which shows some of the local hikes, including a scenic stroll along Pfeiffer Big Sur State Creek. The Falls Trail is fairly easy and short—only 1.4 miles round-trip—however, keep in mind there are a few steps in the slightly steeper sections. Pack a picnic breakfast, maybe a bagel and orange juice, to enjoy at the end of the trail, marked by a wooden deck at the base of a 60-foot waterfall. Several optional paths verge from this main track, including the Valley View and Oak Grove Trails, but keep in mind these are a bit more difficult. However much hiking you decide on, take your time and enjoy it; these are some of the finest redwood groves in the park and in the entire Big Sur region.

The coastal redwood *(Sequoia sempervirens),* which has been around since the time of the dinosaurs, is the world's tallest tree and one of Big Sur's main attractions. Over a hundred million years ago, there were forests of coastal redwoods in Europe and China; however, major climate changes through the ages have reduced their range to a 30-mile-wide coastal strip starting in Big Sur and extending 500 miles north to just across the Oregon border. The thick, reddish-brown bark is relatively fire and insect resistant, but at the base of some older trees, you'll see black scars, known as goosepens, from wildfires of ages ago. Located near the group picnic area, the Colonial Tree is the largest in the park, with a circumference of 27 feet. In the Proboscis Grove, some of the redwoods are over 1,200 years old.

Plenty of other hiking paths wind throughout Big Sur; your best bet is to pick up a book from the "Recommended Reading" list below and peruse your options. The variety of terrain is truly spectacular, no matter which trail you choose. If you come from the city, be sure to spend a lot of time in the area's dense redwood groves; interestingly (but not surprisingly), many people report experiencing a peaceful, calming effect when walking among the giants.

Wherever you decide to explore, you'll be driving along Highway 1 to get there, so you are sure to see some incredible coastal views, another main attraction in the Big Sur region. Don't be shy about stopping at any of the pull-off areas to soak in the scenery and snap a photo or two—even meditate, if you want. One of the most beautiful spots for such contemplation is just 11 miles south of the campground at Julia Pfeiffer Burns State Park. The wheelchair-accessible Waterfall Trail leads through a pedestrian underpass beneath Highway 1 and is less than a mile round-trip from the parking lot. The breathtaking view of McWay Falls may even convince you to book one of the environmental campsites for the next trip. (These two walk-in sites can be reserved up to seven months in advance: because of their popularity, be sure to plan ahead.) At the end of the Waterfall Trail, an observation deck offers more Pacific panoramas and, in the winter months, a chance to see migrating whales.

Your weekend in Big Sur is sure to offer relaxation, fun, and most importantly, quality sleep in the comfort of your tent. And don't worry—as you drift off under the moonlit shadows of soaring redwoods, keep in mind that scurrying is probably just raccoons raiding the stash of s'mores you forgot to put back in the car. *Probably . . .*

Price: $25–$250

(Summer, Easy)

DRIVING DIRECTIONS

Pfeiffer Big Sur State Park, located 26 miles south of Carmel on Highway 1, is surrounded by the Ventana Wilderness Area and the Los Padres National Forest. Julia Pfeiffer Burns State Park is 11 miles farther south.

FOR MORE INFORMATION

PFEIFFER BIG SUR STATE PARK
Information: (831) 667–2315
Reservations: (800) 444–7275

BIG SUR CHAMBER OF COMMERCE
(831) 667–2100
www.bigsurcalifornia.org

BIG SUR LODGE
(800) 424–4787
www.bigsurlodge.com

RECOMMENDED READING

Henson, Paul. *Natural History of Big Sur.* Berkeley: University of California Press, 1996.

Schaffer, Jeffrey. *Hiking the Big Sur Country: The Ventana Wilderness.* Berkeley, Calif.: Wilderness Press, 1998.

Steakley, Douglas, et al. *Big Sur and Beyond: The Legacy of the Big Sur Land Trust.* Portland, Ore.: Graphic Arts Center Publishing Co., 2001.

Weekend Sailing

Blue Water Daydreams

If there's one thing we may have overlooked in all the talk about exciting hiking, flight adventures, perfect beach days, speeding roller coasters, and off-roading Hummers, it's the ocean beyond the California coast. Not the fish in that ocean, or its beaches, or even the islands that dot it; we mean the ocean itself, as a destination all its own, to be savored and appreciated as the amazing natural wonder it is. The Pacific does, after all, cover more than 28 percent of the earth's total surface, more than all its landmasses combined. Journeying to, or living in, California should require homage to this great natural resource, some communion to acknowledge its presence. Few activities fit this bill better than sailing.

To sail on the ocean is to enter a partnership with it. While there are times that sailors are at the mercy of the seas, they more frequently work in tandem with its forces to move forward or outward, away from the shore and farther into blue water. Taking a few days' sail with one of Southern California's many charter boat companies is a perfect way to introduce yourself to this world, and to the Pacific itself. Afterwards, you will find yourself, at odd, high-stress times, remembering your time on that ship and wishing you had that kind of peace again.

The two most important features of your sailing adventure will be the sea itself and the boat you find yourself on. The Pacific, obviously, you have no control over; that doesn't mean you can't be prepared. No matter what the forecast, you should bring rain gear of some kind, as the weather can change out there fairly quickly, and if the temperature is a little low, you might want to protect yourself from sea spray. Also, know what weather you're getting into before you set out. If you haven't been boating in the past, you'll want to look for peaceful seas and clear skies. That way, you have less chance of having to deal with heavy chop and possible seasickness.

Now we know what you're thinking: "Seasickness? Nuts to that! Nothing fun about it." This is true, but seasickness is by no means unavoidable or even inevitable. Before you head out, try reading a newspaper in a moving car; if you feel okay doing that, you should not have much trouble on your voyage. If you feel nauseous, prepare yourself before and during the trip, and you should be just fine. While you're sailing, get plenty of fresh air (that's sort of the point anyway!); stay to the stern (the rear of the boat, which moves less); and keep away from alcohol, cigarettes, and greasy foods. In addition, pick up some medication before your trip. Bonine, Dramamine, or scopolamine patches (need a prescription for this one—ask your doctor) will all make your trip infinitely more fun if you tend to get seasick and help most any landlubber forget his or her lack of sea legs. Finally, keep in mind that motion sickness is mostly mental. Getting caught in ridiculously rough seas will make just about anyone heave, but don't think about the balance-defying boat movement, or at least distract yourself from any such seasick thoughts. With the proper mental conditioning, you should be fine.

Once you've got your seasickness licked, you're ready to get to sailing. Although the ocean will do what it will, your charter and the area in which your charter sails are up to you. There are as many chartered boats in Southern California as there are marinas, so you need to do your homework and choose the company and boat that best suit your needs. Do you want to go for a few hours or a few days? Sail through the Channel Islands or down Mexico way? Is sailing the most important thing to you, or are you using the boat to get into prime snorkeling, fishing, or kayaking grounds? Do you want to see wildlife?

Santa Barbara Sailing Center (SBSC) offers most of these options, plus a few more. This is an especially good outfitter to start with if you want to sample the sailing life before charging headlong into it. SBSC's *Double Dolphin,* a 50-foot catamaran, offers whale-watching cruises, wildlife cruises to Santa Cruz Island, champagne sunset cruises, dinner cruises (which include the food), even cigar cruises for the tobacco aficionados among us. It's a perfect atmosphere for getting acquainted with the feeling of sailing over a few hours, and the prices are very reasonable ($20 to $40 for any of these activities, not including bar drinks when available). If you want a charter sail with a captain, SBSC can set up a custom voyage for you—just call and tell them what you want, and they can make it happen.

The other charter companies listed also offer a variety of voyages to destinations up and down the coast. Their vessels are different, as are what they include as far as nonsailing activities. If you want to head for the Channel Islands, for example, and explore mysterious saltwater caves, then call Sunset Kidd Sailing Charters. Want to see the Sea of Cortez and Baja California? Contact Jim Elfers at Restless Spirit Enterprises, and book a two-day excursion into some of North America's most beautiful waters. You have all the say in what your sailing adventure is to be, and your options are nearly endless.

Most charters also present a range of options as far as what the guest crew is required to do. Chances are that, at some point, someone will ask you to do something, whether it's just moving out of the way or pulling on a particular line. Just do what you're asked unless you don't feel comfortable doing so, and everyone should get along famously. Of course, we do encourage you to become involved with the goings-on, taking orders from your captain and performing necessary tasks. Longer trips will generally require more participation, so if you set out for a long weekend, expect a little more action. Above all, be respectful of your captain and crew, as they are the ones who know what they're doing; even if you've been sailing before, let them run the show without your input.

The Pacific is one of California's greatest natural resources, as well as a source of mystery and adventure. Taking a sail on her waves, you can't help but feel part of something else, a tiny cog inside something much bigger. Give yourself a chance to get lost inside it, and you'll come out the other end more peacefully relaxed than you've ever been before—not a bad goal when it comes to weekend escaping.

Price: $20–$500+

(Summer, Easy)

DRIVING DIRECTIONS

Your outfitters will obviously keep their craft in marinas on the coast. Once you decide which charter company to go with, they will give you exact directions to their vessels' resting places.

FOR MORE INFORMATION

Outfitters

RESTLESS SPIRIT ENTERPRISES
Oxnard
www.bajaadventure.com

BLUE DOLPHIN OCEAN ADVENTURES
(310) 540–9575
www.bluedolfin.com

CLASSIC SAILING ADVENTURES
San Diego
(800) 659–0141 or (619) 224–0800
www.classicsailingadventures
.com

SANTA BARBARA SAILING CENTER
Santa Barbara
(800) 350–9090 or (805) 962–2826
www.sbsail.com

SUNSET KIDD SAILING CHARTERS
Santa Barbara
(805) 962–8222
www.sunsetkidd.com

TOUR BAJA
Calistoga
(800) 398–6200 or (707) 942–4550
www.tourbaja.com

Unfurling the sails with the Santa Barbara Sailing Center. SANTA BARBARA SAILING CENTER

RECOMMENDED READING

Jobson, Gary. *Sailing Fundamentals: The Official Learn-to-Sail Manual of the American Sailing Association and the U.S. Coast Guard Auxiliary.* New York: Simon & Schuster, 1998.

Patterson, Kevin. *The Water in Between: A Journey at Sea.* New York: Alfred A. Knopf, 2001.

Seidman, David. *The Complete Sailor: Learning the Art of Sailing.* New York: McGraw-Hill Professional, 1995.

SLEEP CHEAP

Jalama Beach County Park is located in Santa Barbara County and provides inexpensive camping for those of us who aren't yet sleeping on boats. The park is right on the beach, so you'll be able to keep an eye out for passing ships. Call (805) 736-6316 (recorded info) or (805) 736-3504 (park office) for more information and reservations.

Beach Action

*Parasailing, Jet Skiing,
and Boogie Boarding*

A few chapters ago, you heard the rundown on where to relax on
Southern California's most laid-back beaches, the places to go
when you want to slow your life down to the pace of spent waves
licking your toes. Now, however, it's time to see how the other half
of California's beach people live—a little farther from the shore.

If you're not interested in waiting for the waves to hit the beach
before you experience them, you need to go on the offensive. Attack
them with all the tools at an adventurer's disposal: true grit, a fun-
loving spirit, and the right equipment for the job. Don't be apprehensive;
all the mini-adventures here are quite safe and don't require much
physical prowess past general fitness. But they are first steps, both into
the water and towards more difficult (and often more rewarding) pursuits. Try them out, and you may find yourself ready for much more.

Tool #1: Big Parachute, Little Boat

Parasailing involves flying above the ocean on a parachute,
attached to a long (and we mean long) tether pulled by a boat. If
this sounds a little crazy, it used to be; early parasailers took off
from behind trucks or, when boats were involved, from the shoreline. Of course, either way, you were likely to get busted up or
drowned once you came back to earth.

Special winch boats solve these problems by letting you out
slowly and towing you back to the deck without any broken bones.

Blue Edge Parasailing, based in Santa Barbara, is happy to introduce you to the wonders of flight, and will even throw in some pictures of you soaring for a small fee (perfect for those of us who are better at forgetting our cameras in hotel rooms than using them!). You don't even have to hit the ocean to parasail; if you're vacationing inland and still want the thrill, visit Big Bear Parasail and Watersports at Big Bear Lake, and you can get your flight on.

After experimenting with this controlled, simple form of flight, maybe you're feeling frisky. Do some introductory paragliding or hang gliding (Escape 13), and see if you're ready for your own wings.

Tool #2: Waterlogged Motorcycles

Jet Skis are pretty much standard equipment on most lakes, but riding them on the ocean is a completely different, much more exciting experience. You've got the waves to contend with, for one thing; and then there's the feeling of flying along, looking at the horizon beyond you, and seeing nothing but more water and sky. Drive straight out there, and the first thing you hit is likely to be Japan, a few thousand miles to the west. It's just you, the ski, the promise of far-off lands—and those waves, of course.

If you decide to go wave jumping, hit them before they break, or you'll jump straight up and possibly flip onto your back. (Painful and not much fun, to say the least—Jet Skis and other personal watercraft weigh over 450 pounds, generally, more if they're big and beastly.) Although there are some areas of the California coast where personal watercraft have been banned for their noise and sometimes negative effect on the local ecology, there are still plenty of beaches you can visit that will welcome you and your multicolored seaborne steed. Off Shore Watersports out of Long Beach is one outfit that can hook you up with the craft you need; just give them a call and see what they have available.

Once you've got your fill of wave running, take the next step up the speed ladder: Strap in to a real stock car (Escape 32), and see what *real* speed feels like. Or, if you're more the "Freebird," Hell's Angel type, try a Harley tour of the Pacific Coast Highway (Escape 47).

Tool #3: A Board for Your Belly

This is a universal activity available at just about any California beach you go to, and cheap to boot. Meet the longboard's rowdy little cousin: the boogie board.

Beach Action

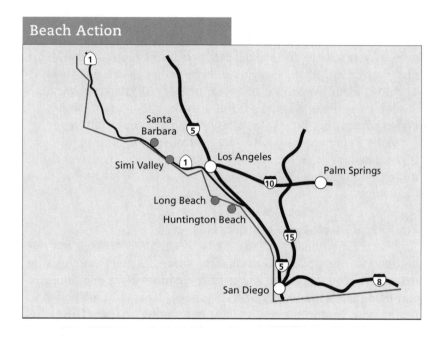

Boogie boards (or body boards) are lay-down surfboards, an accessible way to ride waves for anybody willing to swim out to meet them. Boogie boarding is, in truth, a lot more popular than surfing in terms of pure numbers; tons of people do it, while only a few move on to conquer the waves standing up. Boogie boarding is a great way to introduce yourself to the ocean, and eventually prime yourself for bigger and better things—namely, surfing, which you can learn on your own (sometimes a bit painfully) or at one of Southern California's surfing schools (Escape 25).

Boogie boards are available more or less everywhere, from surf shops to discount stores to drugstores, so you shouldn't have any trouble finding one. Most beaches have rental stores or stands, if you just want to try one out; Huntington Beach, for example, offers boogie board rentals from a number of sources. If you happen to be at another beach, just check with the local bike/surfboard rental shop, and they should be able to hook you up or at least tell you where to go. Keep your eyes open too, because it's usually easy to spot boogie board rental shops from the beach.

Just ask anyone at Home Depot: Pick the right tools for the job, and you can do anything. The equipment mentioned above is exactly what you need to slice up the waves before the land eats them up; they present your opportunity to attack the ocean on its terms, rather than the beaches'. In addition, you may find yourself wanting more once you've got the flight/speed/surf bug—keep pursuing your chosen sensation, and you may find yourself involved in a lifelong love affair with hang gliding or surfing. And, looking back, you'll always know that it was the Pacific that brought you together. Ain't love grand?

Price: $10–$250
(Summer, Medium)

DRIVING DIRECTIONS

To Huntington Beach: The city is located 35 miles southeast of Los Angeles and 90 miles northwest of San Diego, in Orange County. From San Diego, take I–5 north to State Route 73 north, then get off on I–405 north and follow the signs. You can take I–5 from Los Angeles, too; take it south to I–605 south, then to I–405 south.

To Santa Barbara: The city is almost two hours north of L.A. Just take the Pacific Coast Highway (or U.S. Route 101) north, and you'll hit it.

FOR MORE INFORMATION

Outfitters

BIG BEAR PARASAIL AND
WATERSPORTS
Big Bear Lake
(909) 866–4359
www.pineknotlanding.com/
sports.html#para

BLUE EDGE PARASAILING
Santa Barbara
(805) 966–5206
www.spiderside.com/blueedge

Other

OFFSHORE WATERSPORTS
Long Beach
(562) 436–1996
www.owsrentals.com

MOTORSPORTS RENTALS
Simi Valley
(805) 527–9802
www.motorsportsrentals.com

Kitesurfing and other adventures await in the surf zone. CHRIS BECKER

RECOMMENDED READING

Epting, Chris. *Huntington Beach, CA (Images of America Series)*. Charleston, S.C.: Arcadia Press, 2001.

Hastings, Karen. *Insider's Guide to Santa Barbara: Including the Channel Islands National Park*. Guilford, Conn.: Globe Pequot Press, 2004.

Stone, Robert B. *Day Hikes around Santa Barbara, CA: 46 of the Best*. Guilford, Conn.: Globe Pequot Press, 1999.

SLEEP CHEAP

The Cachuma Lake Recreation Area is located close to Santa Barbara and provides extensive facilities—including tent, yurt, and RV camping—along with naturalist-guided lake cruises, some of the best fishing in the region, boating, hiking, and picnicking. From Santa Barbara, take Highway 101 to the San Marcos Pass exit, Highway 154; the park entrance is about 20 miles from this point. Rates are $16 (less for seniors and disabled persons), although yurt camping is more expensive. For more information, call (805) 686–5054 or (805) 686–5055.

Backpacking Kings Canyon

Sequoia Roughin' It

Ever say to yourself, "Man, I wish I had some *real* wilderness space to kick around in," only to come to the rapid realization that you don't have the funds to buy your own tropical island, or Montana ranch? Funny to think that in a state as populous as California, you can make that wish come true with nothing but a map, a backpack full of supplies, and your own two feet. Stuff your pack and roll up your bag, because you're headed for an amazing overnight experience in Kings Canyon National Park, one of the largest untouched wilderness areas in the West.

Those of us who enjoy our solitude with nature as solitary as possible are out of luck most of the time. Hiking and biking areas are pretty sparsely populated as far as most people are concerned, sure, but most of our public nature areas are still *developed* in some way and bear some scars of human presence. You're liable to pass big groups of hikers even if you're 10 miles from the nearest parking lot; drive ten minutes or so from most trailheads, and you're bound to find a 7-11, gift shop, or tourist trap. This isn't to say that spending time with folks who share your outdoor interests is always a drag, or that gift shops are somehow evil—only that sometimes, as Garbo did, you just "vant to be alone."

Kings Canyon is similar to Yosemite and Zion National Parks, in that a deep valley (or canyon, if you will), accessible from only one end and surrounded by huge areas of back country, is the main

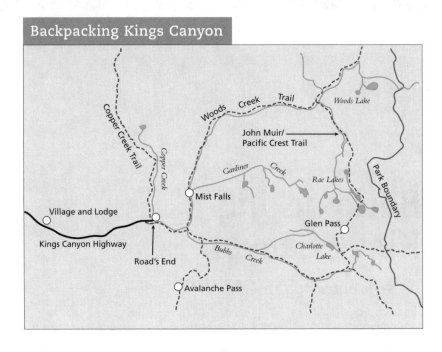

attraction. Kings Canyon is probably not quite as spectacular as the other parks, in terms of raw grandeur; it is, however, much less affected by development, and thus perfect for those of us interested in more than driving along a road and stopping at viewpoints. In fact, vehicular access is much more limited than at Yosemite—the dead-end canyon approach is the only major road within the largest section of the park. Kings Canyon is perfect, then, for those of us who want to get off the well-beaten trails a little and experience the wild on our own.

A few words of advice, however, before you set out for the bush. There is a good reason why this area remains so pristine: The people who hike here follow zero-impact camping guidelines religiously. Those of you already familiar with the outdoors should know what these rules are, but we'll remind you anyway: Pack out your trash, don't camp near water or paths, don't alter sites that you find, and only light campfires when regulations allow it (and only in established firepits). Check with Kings Canyon personnel for a complete list of these regulations, and *follow them*. The park's future as an untouched sanctuary for hikers and wild things alike depends on all of us taking these rules and guidelines seriously.

There are actually two separate sections to Kings Canyon, one of which includes Grant Grove and Redwood Canyon, the two most famous attractions in the park. If you're new to overnight hiking, this smaller, less challenging area is probably where you should go. Redwood Canyon is home to the world's largest sequoia grove, and it's easy to get around in; in addition, people are allowed to sleep most anywhere inside the area. It makes for one of the easier Sequoia/Kings Canyon hikes and is thus a great place to start your backcountry experience if your tent is brand-new and your pack is still stiff from its cardboard inserts. There are two easy 6-mile loop trails through the grove, but backcountry permits are also available, and it is fairly easy to get around off the beaten path. You'll pick up the trail at the Redwood Saddle trailhead, and from there the world's largest collection of the world's largest living things will inspire you and draw you into its depths. You're only allowed to camp in Redwood Canyon for two nights, but you should be able to see a lot of the area in that time. Bring your camera, and don't forget to hike the main paths as well as the ones you tenderly beat yourself.

If, however, you are in the mood for something a little more wild, head north on the Kings Canyon Scenic Byway into the largely untouched main section of the park. Overnight hiking is the only way to visit most of this area, and you can potentially lose yourself for a few weeks in the park's roughly 460,000 acres. The most popular trail group is the Rae Lakes Loop, a 46-mile trek that climbs from 5,035 feet at the trailhead to 11,978 feet at its highest point, Glen Pass. You can set off on one of two trails, either Bubbs Creek or Woods Creek, and stopping points are fairly frequent, even though you're out in some pretty untouched territory. From the loop, you'll find a number of branching trails that lead farther into untouched Kings Canyon wilderness; you can even pick up the famous Pacific Crest Trail, a mega-hike that stretches from Canada 2,650 miles down into Mexico. (Obviously, if you go that route, you'll need to pick up *52 Great Eight-Month Escapes in North America*—as soon as we publish it, we'll let you know!)

High water at stream crossings along the loop can be a problem in early summer, and Glen Pass may be dangerous to hikers until mid- or late July, so be careful. Make sure to follow bear safety rules too; keep your food in portable bear-proof containers (available for rent or purchase at visitor centers throughout Sequoia/Kings Canyon). Some campsites do have permanent bear-proof storage,

Hike deep into Kings Canyon for amazing views like this. NATIONAL PARK SERVICE

but don't take the chance. Bring your own container and you can camp wherever you want, instead of if and where you can find storage space.

Kings Canyon is an escape from your everyday world and a return to a much simpler one. Once your feet hit the trail, time seems to take on a different meaning; after all, when was the last time you spent the day doing little more than traveling 6 or 7 miles? As your frame of time reference changes, you'll find your mind speeding up, taking in the sights around you and the pleasant warmth in your limbs—you may even start to think about things you haven't covered in a while, things that hectic everyday life tends to push into the background. Strap on your backpack, and use the opportunity to catch up with yourself, as well as see the sights. You will emerge from the bush with a clearer head and greater appreciation for the earth's gifts to us.

Price: $10–$50
(Summer, Medium)

DRIVING DIRECTIONS

Gasoline is not sold within the park's boundaries. Be sure to fill up in one of the towns near the park entrance or at two locations in nearby national forest areas—Hume Lake (year-round) and Kings Canyon Lodge (closed in winter).

You can reach the Kings Canyon Park entrance from Highway 99. At Fresno, take Highway 180 east about seventy-five to ninety minutes. To get into the large, untamed section of Kings Canyon, you need to take Highway 180 (the Kings Canyon Scenic Byway) into the Cedar Grove Visitor Center area.

FOR MORE INFORMATION

SEQUOIA AND KINGS CANYON
NATIONAL PARKS
Three Rivers
(559) 565–3341
www.nps.gov/seki

SEQUOIA NATURAL HISTORY
ASSOCIATION
Three Rivers
(559) 565–3759
www.sequoiahistory.org

RECOMMENDED READING

Curtis, Rick. *The Backpacker's Field Manual: A Comprehensive Guide to Mastering Backcountry Skills.* New York: Three Rivers Press, 1998.

Department of Defense. *U.S. Army Survival Manual.* Gainesville, Fla.: Apple Pie Publishers, 1992.

Harvey, Mark. *The National Outdoor Leadership School's Wilderness Guide: The Classic Handbook.* New York: Fireside Press, 1999.

SLEEP CHEAP

If you are planning to hike the Rae Lakes Loop in the summertime, you should make reservations, as trailhead quotas often fill up. Backcountry permits for the loop are issued at the Road's End station, 5.5 miles beyond Cedar Grove. Even if you have a reservation, you must still check in and pick up your permit prior to starting your trip.

The maximum stay in Redwood Canyon is two nights, and the maximum group size is ten people. All overnight users must obtain a permit from the Grant Grove Visitor Center prior to starting their trip. Reservations for permits may be made no less than three weeks before the start of the trip. Unreserved permits will be issued on a first come, first served basis, beginning the afternoon before the trip is scheduled to begin. Again, even if you have a reservation, you must still check in and pick up your permit before going out. Call (559) 565–3341 for more information on getting your backcountry permits.

Sea Kayaking Catalina

Paddling on Island Time

The scorching sun pounds down on your group. After dilly-dallying
most of the morning and snorkeling around in that secluded cove,
everyone agreed over an early lunch picnic that getting to the
campground would be the next priority. Although making good
time for the past hour or so, your arms and shoulders are getting a
little tired. The summer weather is quite agreeable, as it usually is in
Southern California, but all this paddling is causing a serious sweat.
"Man overboard!" you yell with devilish delight, as everyone turns
just in time to see you capsize your kayak . . . .

Sea kayaking Santa Catalina Island is truly one of California's
top-notch adventures. This great weekend presents the perfect
chance to flee humdrum, work-a-day life on the mainland, and
throw yourself (sometimes headfirst) into a new and exciting world.
After an hour-long ferry ride (about $40 round trip), the island's
outline greets visitors with dramatic landscapes rising over 2,000
feet above the sea and stretching over 20 miles in length. Santa
Catalina is one of the largest of California's Channel Islands and
one of the two located in Los Angeles County; unlike the other
islands, however, Catalina has developed into a tourist mecca that
attracts thousands of visitors every day.

Lodging, dining, and entertainment options abound in Avalon,
Catalina's largest town, and the moment you step off the ferry,
you'll immediately realize the place has its own special feel. The

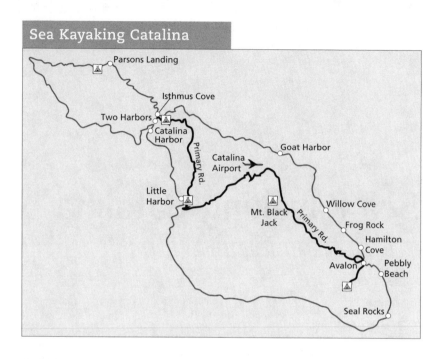

Sea Kayaking Catalina

Parsons Landing

Isthmus Cove

Two Harbors
Catalina
Harbor

Goat Harbor

Primary Rd.

Catalina
Airport

Little
Harbor

Mt. Black
Jack

Primary Rd.

Willow Cove

Frog Rock

Hamilton
Cove

Avalon

Pebbly
Beach

Seal Rocks

bubbling anticipation of adventure and the ocean breeze lifting your spirits with each passing mile culminate in a wonderful feeling of exquisite escapism; you'll practically float on air as you make your way to the kayak rental spot.

You'll find that sea kayaking off Catalina offers adventure regardless of your time constraints, skill level, and budget—the details of your adventure are all up to you. Rental boats are available by the hour if you just want a taste of something new before spending the rest of your time exploring the island. Guided trips are perfect for those less experienced or for those who want all the little details taken care of for them. Either way, your most important decision is how long you want to paddle.

Guided tours start with shorter specialty trips that last only a few hours, such as the Meet the Morning trip or a two-hour excursion to Frog Rock, both offered by Descanso Beach Ocean Sports (DBOS); seasonal evening trips, full moon, and astronomy tours are also available. Catalina Kayak Adventures leads half-day trips to Seal Rocks, while both outfitters take guests on half-day paddles to Willow Cove. Both companies offer full-day tours and custom itineraries as well. Longer trips include picnics on secluded beaches and allow adequate time to strap on a mask and snorkel to get a closer look at the marine life underwater; sunbathing and relaxing are encouraged too. Whatever tour you decide on, rest assured that most outfitters employ well-informed and safety-conscious experts as their guides, people who know how to maximize your enjoyment.

While shorter tours are certainly a lot of fun, the best way to explore Catalina by kayak is to take a couple of days or more to ensure total relaxation and serious fun. Eleven primitive boat-in beach campsites located between Avalon and Two Harbors combine with the gentle, warm waters on the protected leeward side of the island to provide the perfect setting for longer trips. The natural beauty and abundant wildlife keep you in awe the entire time. Before you start saying that this is way too much adventure for your urban-outfitted self, keep in mind that even for overnight trips, you do not need much as far as paddling skills. (You should, however, be a decent swimmer in reasonably good shape to take on a longer trip.)

Self-planned trips are not difficult to organize if you have some backpacking or kayak touring experience, and you will save some money; however, the better and much easier idea is to get a group together and hire DBOS to lead the trip. Just show up with a small duffle containing a few personal items, clothes, and a sleeping bag, and they will take care of everything else for you. Keep in mind that most kayak tours require advance registration, no matter how you decide to go—if you still want to go solo, without guides, you need to reserve your campsites well in advance. Goat Harbor is the halfway point to Two Harbors, just over 6 miles of paddling from Avalon, making for a good campsite choice to start with. Even beginners will find that a full day allows plenty of time for exploring and having fun in addition to the paddling you'll do. The snorkeling and scuba diving are excellent, and some hiking is accessible, but don't forget to pack your boots, as trails on the more remote parts of the island are usually rugged and steep.

Going it on your own also puts meals and drinking water into your realm of responsibility. The coastal ranger who patrols the campsites sells jugs of potable water, but they usually need to be ordered in advance (your campsite confirmation will have information). Campfires are not allowed, though boating enthusiasts are working to get this changed—be sure to ask your outfitter for any updates. For now, if you want hot food you will need to bring a (charcoal-only) barbecue grill or propane stove. Boaters are also required to pack out all trash, and since there are no latrines, that

Taking in some rays off Catalina Island. RAY BANGS

includes human waste. (The ranger and kayak rental shops sell specially designed latrine bags.) Finally, sleeping on the beach under the stars is great, but bring a tent, or at least a tarp; on especially sunny days, you will want the shade. Store your gear and provisions in heavy-duty waterproof bags, which can also be rented. And, of course, don't forget your camera.

Once you have the rental gear or are set up to depart with an organized tour, your itinerary is as simple as paddling for a while, stopping to have fun, paddling a little more, having more fun, then sleeping on a pristine beach where the chief entertainment is stargazing to the tune of the waves. Spend the next day snorkeling, hiking, or doing nothing. If you choose, on the day of departure paddle back to Avalon and arrive a few hours before the return ride to the mainland, so you have a little time to enjoy the relaxed lifestyle the island is famous for. Take two or three days kayaking on Catalina, and you should be totally revived and refreshed upon your return to civilization; but for the sake of your soul, don't wait too long until your next paddle. Escape to sweet Santa Catalina, and let the stars be your blankets.

Price: $100–$500

(Summer, Medium)

DRIVING DIRECTIONS

Santa Catalina Island is located 21 miles off the California coast near Los Angeles. Catalina Express has the fastest ferry service to Avalon with up to 25 daily departures from San Pedro and Long Beach. The Catalina Flyer departs Newport Beach while Catalina Explorer departs Dana Point; both are slightly slower with limited trips. The fastest way to Catalina Island is via the Island Express helicopter service, with flights departing Long Beach and San Pedro. Contact each company for reservations and more information.

FOR MORE INFORMATION

Outfitters

CATALINA KAYAK ADVENTURES
(310) 510–2229
www.catalinakayaks.com

DESCANSO BEACH OCEAN SPORTS
(310) 510–1226
www.kayakcatalinaisland.com

Ferry and Helicopter Services

CATALINA EXPLORER
(877) 432–6276
www.catalinaexplorerco.com

CATALINA EXPRESS
(800) 481–3470
www.catalinaexpress.com

CATALINA FLYER
(949) 673–5245
www.catalinainfo.com

ISLAND EXPRESS HELICOPTERS
(800) 228–2566

Other

CAMPING CATALINA
(boat-in campsite registration form)
www.campingcatalinaisland .com

CATALINA ISLAND CHAMBER OF COMMERCE
www.visitcatalina.org

CATALINA ISLAND CONSERVANCY
www.catalinaconservancy.org

SANTA CATALINA ISLAND COMPANY
(other campsites registration form)
www.scico.com

RECOMMENDED READING

Automobile Club of Southern California. *Catalina Island*. Los Angeles: Author, 2000.

Martin, Terrence, and Peter Howorth. *Santa Catalina Island: The Story behind the Scenery*. Las Vegas: KC Publications, 1984.

Seidman, David. *The Essential Sea Kayaker: A Complete Guide for the Open Water Paddler*. Columbus, Ohio: McGraw-Hill, 2000.

Wicklund, Bruce. *Boating and Diving Catalina Island*. Avalon, Calif.: Black Dolphin Diving, 2000.

SLEEP CHEAP

In addition to the eleven boat-in campsites, Catalina Island has five established campgrounds to provide an inexpensive lodging alternative. Located near Wrigley Memorial, the Botanical Garden, and numerous Catalina hiking trails, the closest to Avalon is Hermit Gulch campground, only 1.5 miles from the landing. Many campers enjoy the short hike, but taxi service is also available (310–510–0025); for larger groups, call for shuttle service (310–510–2500, x223). Lighted restroom facilities include flush toilets and coin-operated hot showers. Sites have picnic tables, fire rings, and charcoal barbecue grills. Camping equipment rental is available. Campsites can be reserved by calling (310) 510–8368; reservations are recommended in July and August.

Yahoo for Yoga

It's So California

Just when you think you can't hold the asana another half-second,
suddenly it seems like your spine snaps into alignment, your other
joints tweak crazy but true, your muscles tensing yet surprisingly
relaxed. It's your first hatha yoga class, and even on day one, you
realize it's like no health or fitness regimen you've ever tried before.
You know that if you can just twist and turn your body at least
somewhat close to this next posture, you'll be hooked for life.
Already you feel that powerful surge that comes from practicing
yoga. Already, you have started down the path of the yogi.

Hatha yoga is the science of yoga postures, called asanas. The
asanas differ considerably from ordinary calisthenics because
instead of trying to get the body all worked up toward exhaustion,
the goal here is to assume the correct posture and then relax while
holding the pose. Since the asanas can be difficult, especially when
you're just starting out, don't try to force or strain yourself to get
into the prescribed position. Remember that practicing yoga is about
relaxing to calm your body and your mind. There should be no
pain, but there will be pressure. The different postures are designed
to exert a beneficial tension on various internal organs and glands.
Each asana allows energy to flow freely through the nervous system, flushing toxins and poisons from the organs, the joints, and
the rest of the body. The various asanas are intended to help the
practitioner learn a stimulating system of movements in efforts to

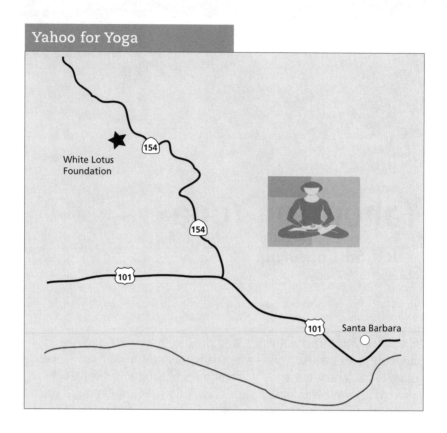

promote longevity and to ensure healthy, radiant living.

Well known for its physical health benefits, yoga increases flexibility, but muscle tone and strength are also improved. Body weight rapidly normalizes, and the immune system gets a real boost. Lesser known are yoga's incredible mental fitness benefits. Yoga is a spectacular stress buster, promoting peace of mind, improved concentration, and a greater sense of overall well-being. Even after only minimal training, you'll soon see the benefits. As a result, yoga is growing more popular than ever in California. After all, what better place to live the best life you can?

After you've taken a few classes at your local studio, an excellent way to indulge in a long weekend of yoga is to treat yourself to a trip to the White Lotus Foundation, a nonsectarian spiritual foundation dedicated to the development of the total human being. Overlooking Santa Barbara and the Pacific Ocean, tucked away in the Santa Ynez Mountains, the foundation features acres and acres of old growth oaks, bay trees, and manzanita forests, perfectly secluded for recharging your spirit. Throughout the year, the White Lotus Foundation offers various weekend retreats. The Memorial Day and Labor Day programs are very popular. Your weekend itinerary will include hatha yoga classes and pranayama breathing techniques practiced twice daily. Hikes and walking meditations along wooded paths under towering canyon walls are also popular. In the evenings, discussions and workshops about yoga philosophy, diet, and other information are offered in addition to musical presentations and art workshops. The gourmet vegetarian meals are the perfect complement to your yoga training.

The easiest way to escape and give yourself time to relax and recharge, especially if your weekend doesn't happen to fall on Friday, Saturday, and Sunday, is to try out another foundation offering, the Personal Retreat. Slip away from busy city living for a few days, and enjoy the kind of peace and tranquility only to be experienced at the White Lotus Foundation. Guests will find the traditional canvas tent yurts quite comfortable, although there's plenty of space to pitch your own tent in the bay laurel forest or along the spring-fed creek. Time is yours to hike, meditate, swim, soak in the hot tub, read, or just enjoy relaxing outdoors in the beautiful surroundings. Weekly hatha yoga classes are offered, although guests may also arrange for private instruction and body work. Personal Retreats are usually limited to Monday through Thursday and can be reserved on a space-available basis. Rates run $75 per person per day, which includes lodging and use of the facilities.

The White Lotus Foundation also offers a number of extended programs for those who would like to designate more time to relaxing, doing yoga, and finding their balance. One popular option is an eight-day program that teaches traditional Thai massage, a unique method of yoga therapy combining stretching, acupressure, massage, and meditation. This program's fees, like several of the other courses, are more expensive than a day or weekend, but they are considered a tax-deductible donation. Another extended duration program if you already have several years of yoga experience is the complete yoga training course offered three times a year. This sixteen-day residential program provides comprehensive instruction in how yoga works, the origins of yoga, and an exploration into the classical and contemporary techniques of the most respected yoga systems. Students of this course will learn how to set up and teach classes, along with the theory of, purpose behind, and hands-on correction techniques for each asana. The course includes teacher certification.

Whether you are a beginner or a yogi with years of experience, the White Lotus Foundation will certainly help improve your yoga techniques and knowledge. The instructors are extremely capable of sharing their decades' worth of experience and expertise with you. Besides just teaching yoga students, the foundation has certified thousands of teachers. Since yoga is noncompetitive, you don't have to worry about trying to keep up with everyone else. The instructors not only help you improve what you can do, at your own learning pace, but eventually they'll have you winding up your body in ways you never imagined you could.

Don't think that yoga is just some effort to be a circus contortionist, even if some of the advanced asanas seem to bend bones. To better introduce yourself to yoga—also the perfect training for your trip to Santa Barbara—pick up a copy of one of the videos created by White Lotus Foundation founder Ganga White and codirector Tracey Rich. *Total Yoga I* is the best-selling yoga video of all time, and the learning continues with *Total Yoga: The Flow Series,* three programs of progressive difficulty. You can also head to any bookstore to find a number of great books and more videos to give you an idea of what yoga is all about. You can at least try out a few of the easier asanas, so you won't be completely lost when heading to your first class. Soon enough, as you see the incredible results and feel the rewards of truly taking care of yourself, yoga will become your lifestyle. Eventually, retreats to the White Lotus Foundation or one of the other yoga institutes to be found all around the world may become an annual or even more frequent routine. And, even though it might have seemed different, even strange at the time, that first yoga class when you were living a different life will seem so long ago. Everybody starts there, so in the words of diva yoga advocate Madonna, "Just strike a pose."

Price: $75–$500+

(Summer, Medium)

DRIVING DIRECTIONS

Go north on U.S. 101 from Santa Barbara. Exit on State Street/Cachuma Lake (Highway 154), then turn right onto San Marcos Pass (which is also 154). Go about 5.5 miles and you're there.

FOR MORE INFORMATION

WHITE LOTUS FOUNDATION
Santa Barbara
(805) 964–1944
www.whitelotus.org

RECOMMENDED READING

Coulter, H. David, and Timothy McCall. *Anatomy of Hatha Yoga: A Manual for Students, Teachers, and Practitioners.* Honesdale, Pa.: Body and Breath, 2002.

Schiffmann, Erich. *Yoga: The Spirit and Practice of Moving into Stillness.* New York: Pocket Books, 1996.

White, Ganga. *Double Yoga: A New System for Total Body Health.* Santa Barbara, Calif.: White Lotus Foundation, 1998.

SLEEP CHEAP

The best way to experience a program with the White Lotus Foundation is to stay right on the grounds, sleeping in one of the yurts if available or in your tent. If the foundation is full, you'll find a number of excellent campgrounds in the Santa Barbara area. In Goleta, check out El Capitan Canyon, a unique resort-style campground that offers your choice of cabins, safari tents, or traditional campsites. Other amenities include a general store and children's day camp, as well as kayaking, hiking, and mountain bike excursions. Visitors to El Capitan Canyon enjoy the no-car policy. For more information and reservations, call (805) 685–3887, or visit www.elcapitancanyon.com. Another nearby option is Carpinteria State Park, one of the most popular parks in California's state park system. Reservations are required, especially if you want to be one of the lucky campers pitching a tent just inches from the sand. The park rents a variety of bicycles as well as in-line skates (safety padding too). Call (805) 968–1033, or browse www.parks.ca.gov.

Whitewater Rafting the Lower Kern

Permagrin Free of Charge

"Splish, splash, we're taking a bath!" a fellow paddler chants somewhat nervously as he spots the impending eruption of roaring whitewater straight ahead. The once-mild rapids have escalated into especially ferocious foam-filled stampedes, and that frantic moment of hitting the swells head on now rockets through you—an adrenaline surge so powerful that your newfound vigor would send the Incredible Hulk running for cover. Your guide shouts instructions, which are sure to get everyone through safely as you've had no spills yet, but you barely hear the row commands over the locomotive churning of the river and the rush of your own excitement. As the mighty Kern tries to swallow your raft whole, you paddle furiously just to survive, and you do, emerging from the hootin' and hollerin' roller-coaster ride sloppy as a drenched dog and having the time of your life.

Drive only three hours north of Los Angeles to Sequoia National Forest, and you'll find your own whitewater adventure, complete with screams and squeals, a sure symptom of the good life. The farthest south of the Sierra rivers, the Lower Kern offers more Class III–IV rapids than some California rivers twice its length. This makes it an ideal place for a formal introduction to river running—no prior skills are needed; however, any training or experience certainly will help. The two-day overnight trip is one of the best and most popular excursions available and perfect for first-timers and families, though more experienced folk will also love it.

River rapids are rated on a scale from Class I to Class VI. The safest and easiest are Class I, which consist of fast-moving water with easy to negotiate hazards and only a low chance of injury if you are forced to exit the boat. The highest level is the extreme Class VI, considered unrunnable by most sane people. Groups of expert paddlers might occasionally attempt Class VI runs when water levels are favorable, but only after serious scouting and taking all safety precautions. The risks grow more significant as the ratings get higher, but remember that increasing your paddling skills helps decrease the danger.

The Lower Kern's Class III–IV rapids can get a little scary, but for most people, especially beginners, the trip's biggest appeal is that for the first few miles the pace is gentle and perfect for practicing techniques needed to navigate the rowdier stuff later. After your lunch stop, the rapids start to grow as you become more comfortable and confident working your paddle, while others in the crew steer the boat. With everyone contributing toward the one goal of successfully navigating the raft down this river, the down times around meals and breaks start to provide a little opportunity for instant realization of how much fun you are actually having. Two days on the Lower Kern pack enough punch to make up for even the worst two weeks of work—exactly what weekend escaping is meant to do.

Your outfitters strive to create a truly spectacular experience for you and usually surpass expectations. Adventure appetite aside, the meals are definitely worth mentioning; backcountry fare is often hit-or-miss, but with any of these two-day trips you can expect a wide variety of fresh foods that are healthy, wholesome, and distinctly delicious. Many raft guides and cooks spend the equivalent of months on the river each year, so you will soon forget any preconceived notions you may have about outdoorsy types subsisting on tins of beans cooked over campfires. Your scene will more likely be chomping hors d'oeuvres before dinner and mingling with the other boaters over an unbreakable plastic cup of boxed wine, while the experts whip up the main course. Feel free to help out with preparing the meals or any other camp work as much or as little as you want. Also, be sure to mention any special dietary considerations, as your chefs can accommodate just about anything with enough advance notice.

Make a couple calls, or check the outfitter Web sites, as they can provide you with more information and specifics as far as trip planning, packing lists, and prices. One of the best aspects of this weekend

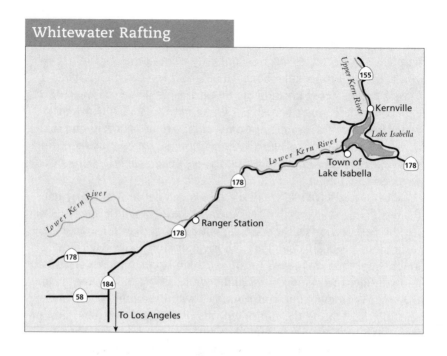

escape is that everything is taken care of for you, and no special gear is required. You may need to rent a wetsuit if you run the river early in the season, but summer weather on the Lower Kern is warm and dry—perfect for getting wet. No matter when you go, keep in mind that these trips are somewhat strenuous at times; for example, one cumbersome section of the river is choked with monstrous boulders, meaning everyone must portage the rafts and gear around, a significant shock to most people's lifestyles. Just the paddling part alone can be demanding as well, but anybody who is reasonably healthy should be able to participate. If you have any questions, check with your outfitter and your doctor.

As the first day of adventure draws to a close, you may find yourself a little sore, probably a little tired, but quite content with a full stomach and literally boatloads of river pals—camaraderie and new friends is what river running is all about. Your body, mind, and soul feel pretty darn good sitting around that campfire, reminiscing about the close encounters and other breathtaking moments from the day's paddle. Soon your guides will tell of bigger and badder rapids waiting tomorrow, and you'll get to watch a giddy enthusiasm work its way through your small crowd. Luckily, with the day's experience, a somewhat Zen-like anticipation of the fun to come should eventually settle on you. Soon, after yawns are exchanged and goodnights bid, everyone will excitedly slink into their sleeping bags for a night of wilderness slumber under southern Sierra skies.

After a hearty breakfast, the rafts are launched, and your second day on the river begins. Now is when many people realize they are a little bit sorer than they thought, so make sure you are warmed up and ready to go. Fortunately, the rapids are going to be doing most of the work today. Galloping along with strong currents from the start, you will surprise yourself with a reborn swagger, despite the day's heftier torrents. The snaking cauldron of whitewater bubbles viciously, but your crew will start to feel the rhythm of the river, leaning into the plunges instead of away; soon paddling becomes more efficient and easier, and it's normal to realize the rapids are all too quickly catapulting you to the end of your 21-mile escape.

"Pinball rapids dead ahead!" the guide announces. With a flex of your forearms, you pound out a couple hard paddles and make a determined promise to return every summer for the rest of your life to run this and other sections of the Kern, or at least some river. You fantasize about becoming a river guide, and even find out what it takes from your captain. You imagine that tales of your out-landish adventures running the raging waters across the world filter their way back to the place you once called home, and soon enough, all of your flabbergasted, former couch-potato friends are now diehard converts, dedicated river buddies to the end. All of a sudden, like a thousand buckets of chilly water crashing onto your head, you startle from your lucid daydream, soaked alive from the latest foaming blitz. Riding the surge through it, water dripping from your nose, ears, even your eyeballs, it could well be at that exact moment the characteristically silly river-runner grin grips your mug for the first time and never lets go. See you on the river!

Price: $250–$500

(Summer, Medium)

DRIVING DIRECTIONS

From the Los Angeles Basin, take I–5 North. Descend the Grapevine Grade, and follow Highway 99 North to Bakersfield. Take the Lake Isabella exit, and continue along Highway 178 East. Kernville is located north on Highway 155. Check with your outfitter for exact meeting locations.

Keep in mind that rafting isn't a spectator sport. You're going to do some paddling.
ROBERT HOLMES/CALTOUR

FOR MORE INFORMATION

Outfitters

CHUCK RICHARDS WHITEWATER
(760) 376–2242
www.chuckrichards.com

KERN RIVER OUTFITTERS
(800) 323–4234
www.kernrafting.com

KERN RIVER TOURS
(800) 844–7238
www.kernrivertours.com

SIERRA SOUTH
(800) 457–2082
www.sierrasouth.com

WHITEWATER VOYAGES
(800) 400–7238
www.whitewatervoyages.com

Other

KERN RIVER VALLEY CHAMBER OF COMMERCE
(866) 578–4386
www.kernrivervalley.com

KERNVILLE CHAMBER OF COMMERCE
(760) 376–2629
www.kernvillechamber.org

RECOMMENDED READING

Bennett, Jeff. *The Complete Whitewater Rafter.* Columbus, Ohio: McGraw-Hill, 1996.

Boyd, William. *Lower Kern River Country, 1850–1950: Wilderness to Empire.* Bakersfield, Calif.: Kern County Historical Society, 1997.

Kuhne, Cecil. *Whitewater Rafting: An Introductory Guide.* Guilford, Conn.: The Lyons Press, 1995.

SLEEP CHEAP

If you need a place to stay before or after your whitewater trip, two campgrounds stand out. Hobo Campground is located 42 miles east of Bakersfield off State Highway 178 on Old Kern Canyon Road; 2 more miles and you'll find the Sandy Flat Campground. Both campgrounds are situated along the Lower Kern, and both are very scenic. Toilets and drinking water are available, and sites have fire pits and tables. Sites are limited to six people per. Reservations are recommended and can be made by calling the National Recreation Reservation Service (877–444–6777).

Learning to Waterski

The Big Bear Lake Barefoot Boogie

Your friends and family members just finished whipping around the lake, the last skier going two full loops with hardly a wobble. The performance earned huge applause from the others. Everyone is waterskiing surprisingly well. You were feeling excited, but now it's finally your turn, and so the excited feeling has shifted to nervous butterflies. You're wearing a life vest, and you've slid your feet into the ski bindings, cinching them tight. Soon you're floating in the water, flailing awkwardly thanks to the skis, and you're thinking it's impossible to be even half as graceful as the last skier.

"Keep your knees bent, arms straight, sit back, and let the boat pull you up!" the instructor hollers over the rumble of the boat's motor. He repeats it, and you try to follow the instructions exactly, step by step. You flop around for a moment more as the skis try to have their way with you, but then as the towrope tightens, you come into position. You're strong and you're ready, so you scream, "Hit it!"

The instructor guns the motor, and in a roaring second, the handle of the towrope nearly yanks your arms out. You've kept a strong grip, though, and somehow manage to hold on. The boat pulls faster. You try to stand up, and all of a sudden, you get yanked forward, straight out of the ski bindings, and do an acrobatic faceplant right into the lake's surface. "Oh!" the folks in the boat yell. Yes, it stung a little, but it probably shocked you more than it actually hurt. After all, water is rather soft, especially going at that slow start-up speed. The boat circles around, and you get set up again. It takes a couple more tries, but finally, you do everything you're supposed to do and spring right up on the skis. In seconds, you're cruising. You're flying. The feeling is extraordinary. You skim across the water's surface, quickly gain confidence, crank your body into a lean, and then you're out of the boat's wake. The lake is like glass. Smooth skiing ahead. You're doing it!

One of Southern California's best places to learn to waterski or wakeboard is located in the San Bernardino Mountains, only 100 miles northeast of Los Angeles. Big Bear Lake is phenomenal in the summer time. Stretching roughly 8 miles long and almost one mile across at its widest point, located at an elevation of nearly 6,800 feet, Big Bear Lake has over 20 miles of spectacular shoreline. A number of private homes, several marinas, public parks, hotels, and lodges surround the south side of the lake. Day temperatures during the summer months comfortably range around 70° to 88°F. Typical summer days are clear with blue skies. In fact, Big Bear is one of the sunniest places in the world, although the occasional afternoon thundershower is part of the mountain magic. You're all set for great sleeping too, with the night air dropping to a cool 45° to 60°F. While temperatures are scorching in other parts of the state, country, or world, fun lovers will find paradise at Big Bear Lake.

Waterskiing is only one of the countless activities to be enjoyed in the region, but being out on a boat on this beautiful lake is one of the most fun and exciting times you can ask for. Various types of boat rentals are available at several locations, and most marinas can set you up with waterski or wakeboard equipment and instruction. Holloway's Marina & RV Park is one of the more popular rental providers, thanks to their fleet of Ski Sanger competition waterski boats and expert staff of certified drivers and instructors. The crew will have you up and skimming the water's surface in no time.

We'll let you in on a little secret: Getting up on waterskis is really as easy as following those four easy instructions—keep your knees bent, keep your arms straight, sit back, and let the boat pull you up. Sometimes friends aren't the best people to learn to ski with because even though they may have been skiing, wakeboarding, and kneeboarding for years, it takes a very experienced person at the boat's controls to pull a novice. Sometimes, if you just can't get the hang of it or your grip is too weak, the experience can be frustrating for everyone. With a professional at the helm, however, you

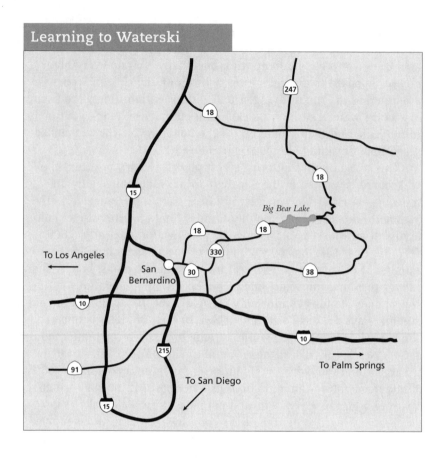

maximize your chances of learning how to waterski in just a weekend, probably in just a few hours. Likewise, if you're an advanced skier, these professionals can help you learn to slalom or, if you think you're ready, even try to ski barefoot.

If you have your own boat, ski and wakeboard gear is also available for rent or purchase at several sports shops in the village. While you're in town, also be sure to pick up a private boat lake permit if needed, as well as a National Forest Adventure Pass. This inexpensive recreational pass is required for visitors using the San Bernardino National Forest. Fishing boats and equipment, pontoon boats, Jet Skis, windsurfers, canoes and kayaks, sailboats, and paddleboats are also available to rent. Be sure to call ahead to make reservations for everything you plan to rent, as you can be sure this cozy little enclave sitting on the edge of such an immense playground sees a busy tourist crowd.

Since Big Bear Lake is such a popular destination, basic regulations have been established for waterskiing (which include and cover similar sports such as tubing, kneeboarding, and wakeboarding). First, waterski hours are limited from 7:00 A.M. until sunset, and an observer on the boat in addition to the driver is required to watch the skier's progress. Waterskiing boats must maintain a counterclockwise course, and a red flag must be flown whenever a skier or equipment is in the water. Of course, all skiers must wear a personal flotation device, or life jacket.

When the skiing is done, anchor the boat. Even if you didn't get up on the wakeboard or going barefoot still baffles you, there's always next time. Your surroundings are so incredibly beautiful, it's easy to enjoy just being out on the water. Swimming to and jumping off the nearby boulders is always a local favorite, and there are plenty of picnic and barbecue sites to be found. Ask around at the village sports shops to learn about fishing hotspots. Big Bear Lake is well known for healthy populations of largemouth and smallmouth bass, rainbow trout, catfish, black crappie, and a variety of other panfish. (Don't forget to purchase a fishing license.) With your choice of fun accessories galore, head out, explore, and have a great weekend. Find solace in just lazing about and relaxing. Forget the hustle and bustle. Escape. Ski a while.

Price: $250–$500+
(Summer, Difficult)

DRIVING DIRECTIONS

Big Bear Lake is located 100 miles northeast of Los Angeles and only 30 miles from San Bernardino. From Los Angeles, take I–10 East to the Running Springs Highway 30 exit in Redlands. Follow Highway 30 to Highway 330 to Highway 18.

FOR MORE INFORMATION

Outfitters

BIG BEAR MARINA
Big Bear Village
(909) 866–3218
www.bigbearmarina.com

HOLLOWAY'S MARINA & RV PARK
Big Bear Lake
(909) 866–5706
www.bigbearboating.com

Slicing up Big Bear Lake. ROBERT HOLMES/CALTOUR

Other

BIG BEAR DISCOVERY CENTER
(909) 866–3437
www.bigbeardiscoverycenter
.com

BIG BEAR LAKE CHAMBER OF
COMMERCE
(909) 866–4607
www.bigbearchamber.com

BIG BEAR LAKE RESORT ASSOCIATION
(800) 424–4232
www.bigbearinfo.com

RECOMMENDED READING

Desmond, Kevin. *The Golden Age of Waterskiing*. Osceola, Wisc.: Motorbooks International, 2001.

Firestone, Mary, and Scott N. Atkinson. *Extreme Waterskiing Moves (Behind the Moves)*. Mankato, Minn.: Capstone Press, 2003.

Olesky, Walter. *Barefoot Waterskiing (Extreme Sports)*. Mankato, Minn.: Capstone Press, 2000.

SLEEP CHEAP

All around Big Bear Lake you'll find excellent camping. There are a number of campgrounds in different areas of the valley that provide camping anywhere from right next to the lake to remote spots in the mountains. The remote campsites offer a great opportunity to "rough it" in amazing solitude. One to consider is Yellow Post site #25, which is located in a very lush area, next to a mountain stream and beautiful meadow of wildflowers and ferns. From the Village, drive west on Big Bear Boulevard to Mill Creek Road to the 2N10. Yellow Post site #30 is even more remote and can be reached by continuing along the 2N10 to the 2N86. A paid Adventure Pass and a permit (free) are required to camp at these sites. Campers must apply in person at the Big Bear Discovery Center for the permit. Since this type of campsite is first come, first served, be sure to arrive early, especially on busy or holiday weekends. Check out the Big Bear Discovery Center's Web site (www.bigbeardiscoverycenter.com) or call (909) 866–3437 for more camping information.

California Surf School

Hang Ten 101

The alarm sounds off, but no worries, you're already up. You were so excited that you awoke almost an hour early, and now you're ready to go. You turn off the coffeepot, grab your beach bag, and cruise out the door. Not long later, you're standing ankle deep in saltwater as the waves soak the sand gritting between your toes. As the sun pokes up over the mountains behind you to the east, you bend and twist your torso, flex and stretch your legs, rotate your shoulders, and swing your arms about to work out all the kinks. Your wetsuit is snug and warm, and there's nothing in front of you but the deep blue sea. It's another beautiful day at the beach. *Surf's up, brah.*

Southern California boasts one of surfing's most famous shore-lines. Hundreds and hundreds of breaks all along the coast offer plenty of options to those who want to catch a wave. And once you learn the basics, this huge watery playground is just waiting to provide a lifetime's worth of weekend adventures for you. Surfing is, however, one of the tougher sports to get the hang of, so your best bet, instead of trying to figure it out yourself, is to find some-one to teach you.

Before you get started, you should be in good physical condi-tion, and, of course, knowing how to swim certainly helps. Your first attempts to stand up on the board will be in shallow water, but as you progress, you'll find that the big waves are usually found deeper than where you can still stand with your head above the water. If you're not comfortable with this depth out at the surf zone, surfing could be very dangerous. After working on your swimming skills, the quickest way to catching your first wave is to go to surf school. Although schools are located all along California's coast, the San Diego area offers numerous options, and thanks to the spectacular weather, most schools can operate all year long.

An excellent choice located just north of San Diego at San Elijo State Beach is the Groundswell Surf Camp hosted by professional board shaper Terry Senate. Beginners will enjoy starting out with the softboard, but with a little practice, students can try out new Terry Senate longboards and shortboards. Groundswell offers single-day and weeklong lessons for novices and more experienced waveriders, but the fastest track to surf god status is to start with the weekend two-day, two-night trip. Camping accommodations at San Elijo State Beach are semi-deluxe, as you'll be sleeping in tents with cots, and the hot shower feels great after a long day of surfing. A big-screen TV with VCR and DVD allows students to see video footage of each other catching waves while the teachers comment on technique, making for an excellent instructional tool. Field trips to local points of interest are included, as well as an educational tour to see how surfboards are designed and manufactured.

San Diego Surfing Academy is another school that operates at San Elijo State Beach, offering lessons year-round for all ages as well as trips to Baja and summer surf camps for adults and families. Another good choice in the San Diego area is Kahuna Bob's Surf School, where fundamentals are stressed to get students up and surfing as quickly as possible. A two-hour program is often all it takes to start beginners riding smaller waves, and after just a few lessons, most students are surfing at the next level. Another school well worth mentioning is the Rusty K. Farrel Surfing School, which operates in Pacific Beach at the Tourmaline Surfing Park. This school is unique in that it is run by pro surfer Rusty Farrel, who plans his teaching schedule to accommodate his competition schedule.

While all surf schools generally teach anyone who wants to learn, some can be quite specialized. If business brings you to the San Diego County area, the Executive Surfing Club, operating out of La Jolla, offers an excellent corporate and team-building program,

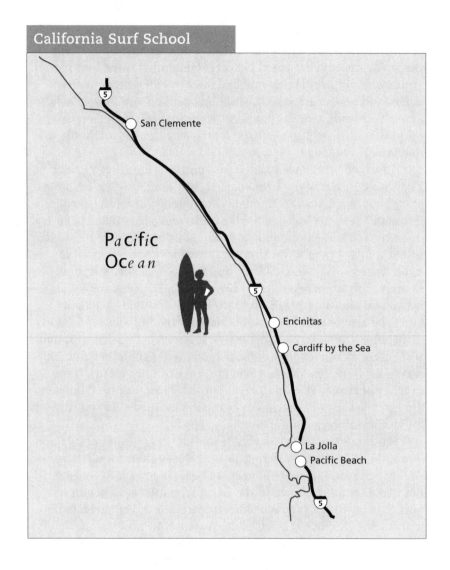

California Surf School

Pacific
Ocean

San Clemente

Encinitas

Cardiff by the Sea

La Jolla
Pacific Beach

but caters to any group, large or small. Also operating out of La Jolla, Surf Diva specializes in teaching women of all ages how to catch a wave in the span of a great weekend escape. Over ten hours of instruction is included with the standard weekend package at La Jolla Shores. Additionally, Surf Diva hosts specialized weekend trips, such as the Family Weekend, where the whole family can have a blast while starting to learn to surf together. On the other hand, another option is to leave the kids behind and head out to enjoy Surf Diva's Adults Only Weekend. Both of these excursions feature gourmet campfire meals, incredible ocean views at the beautiful South Carlsbad State Beach campground, and, of course, plenty of time playing in the water.

Finally, for those who can spare more than just a weekend, many of the aforementioned schools offer longer instructional sessions and trips. Check their Web sites to see what is offered. Some of these schools actually specialize in longer surf camps, most lasting five days or a week. Many of the longer sessions, especially in the summer, are camp programs for children, but most schools teach all ages. One notable camp that has a variety of extended programs is the Endless Summer Surf Camp, which features a beautiful campsite overlooking the Pacific Ocean in the San Onofre State Park campground, located just south of San Clemente. Roughly halfway between Los Angeles and San Diego, San Clemente is a surf mecca, an uncrowded area that offers a variety of waves, from the easy rollers for beginners to the world-class point surf of Lower Trestles for more experienced waveriders.

Besides just teaching students how to paddle and stand up on the board, surf schools also discuss safety, wave selection, ocean conditions, and, as more people discover this life-changing sport and breaks get more crowded, the importance of surfing etiquette and priority rules. Of course, most schools also make it a big priority to stress ocean awareness and conservation. Surfers are proud stewards of the sea.

Although you are welcome to bring your own equipment, all the surf schools will provide surfboards and wetsuits. If you are extra big or tall, mighty short or small, you might want to mention it when making your reservation so they put aside the proper sized wetsuit and board for you. When you show up to the lesson, you'll be fitted to the right equipment. Besides surfing gear, outfitters will let you know what other equipment is required. Don't forget drinking water, a towel, a sweatshirt, and waterproof sunscreen. A hat and sunglasses are also mandatory beach gear. Be sure to inquire whether meals are included.

So sign up for surf camp today, and in just a few lessons, you could find yourself graduated from the foam softie and toting a well-waxed fiberglass board. In just a few months, you may realize you're setting your sleep schedule to the surf and unavoidably talking in surfer lingo. As your skills improve, you'll find it's all about that moment, popping up and gliding along big open-faced

Surfing is for everybody; some schools cater to women, while others will teach the whole family. DANIELLE BECKER

ground swells, riding because you can. It's all about the stoke. Surfing becomes life. And it all started in a weekend.

Price: $50+

(Summer, Difficult)

DRIVING DIRECTIONS

Contact individual outfitters for specific directions to where instruction will take place. Otherwise, just go west. You'll get to the ocean eventually.

FOR MORE INFORMATION

Outfitters

ENDLESS SUMMER SURF CAMP
San Clemente
(949) 498–7862
www.endlesssummersurf
camp.com

EXECUTIVE SURFING CLUB
La Jolla
(858) 344–5336
www.executivesurfingclub.com

GROUNDSWELL SURF CAMP
Cardiff by the Sea
(949) 361–4906
www.surfcamp.com

KAHUNA BOB'S SURF SCHOOL
Oceanside (lessons/camps usually in Leucadia or Encinitas)
(760) 721–7700
www.kahunabob.com

RUSTY K. FARREL SURFING SCHOOL
Pacific Beach
(858) 274–1843
www.rustysurfschool.com

SAN DIEGO SURFING ACADEMY
Cardiff by the Sea
(760) 230–1474
www.surfSDSA.com

SURF DIVA
La Jolla, CA
(858) 454–8273
www.surfdiva.com

RECOMMENDED READING

Guisado, Raul. *The Art of Surfing: A Training Manual for the Developing and Competitive Surfer.* Guilford, Conn.: Globe Pequot Press, 2003.

Kampion, Drew, and Bruce Brown. *Stoked: A History of Surf Culture.* Los Angeles: General Pub Group, 1997.

Warshaw, Matt. *The Encyclopedia of Surfing.* San Diego: Harcourt, 2003.

SLEEP CHEAP

Surf culture has long been about keeping it cheap. There are still plenty of waveriders living in that fringe category, with no permanent address except a Volkswagen van parked down by the beach. Unless you want to quit your job, move into the car, and ride waves all day, the next best way to live the Southern California surf bum life is to rent an RV. Rentals are large enough to accommodate an entire family or a group of friends. Amenities vary with rental model. When the cost is split between several people, an RV rental is comparable to an average hotel room. Additionally, meal costs decrease because RVs have built-in kitchens. Check your local yellow pages, or contact Cruise America RV Rentals (800-327-7799; www.cruiseamerica.com). The ultimate ride for a surfing safari!

Mountaineering Whitney

The Crown of the Lower 48

Step, step, rest, slide backwards a foot. Step, step, rest, slide backwards a foot. You breathe hard for a minute, but the air is so thin it feels like you're breathing through a straw. As you try your best to catch your breath, you look up and around; it hardly seems you're making any progress. Your lungs are burning, and the muscles of your legs have been reduced to little more than jelly. For the past hour, you haven't felt anything except pain. But the summit can't be too long off, because you can see it right there, almost close enough to touch, yet with all this loose scree causing you to slide backwards half the distance of each step, it's hard to say how much longer the last push will take. It doesn't matter, though—you can't think about that. Breathe, breathe. You can only think about taking two more steps and then resting again. Looking forward any further doubles the pain. Luckily, for the moment, emotion has faded away. By this point, you're running solely on will power. With every ounce of your being, you lift your foot to take one more step.

Perhaps the most incredible aspect of mountain climbing is that one experiences every type of human emotion during a climb. Excitement, anger, disappointment, greed, confidence, betrayal, fear, loneliness, lust, despair, love, and hate are just a few feelings that mountaineers face. While all of these emotions may be experienced hoofing up any respectable hill, the way it generally works out is that the greater the climb, the greater the glow of the human condition. Of

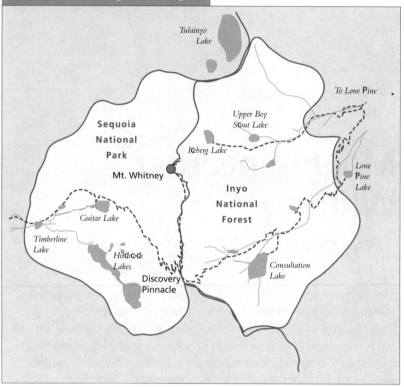

Mountaineering Whitney

Tulainyo Lake

To Lone Pine

Upper Boy Scout Lake

Sequoia National Park

Iceberg Lake

Mt. Whitney

Lone Pine Lake

Inyo National Forest

Guitar Lake

Timberline Lake

Hitchcock Lakes

Discovery Pinnacle

Consultation Lake

course, keep in mind that the climb does not necessarily refer only to what one's hands and feet are doing—there are often obstacles and challenges greater than rock or ice. Nonetheless, the intensity of emotion is often consistent with elevation gain: The higher the climb, the more intense the exhilaration on succeeding. But no matter mountain or molehill, climbers will see at least a glimpse of the entire gamut of emotions during the climb. It might hurt; it might even hurt a lot. But when you reach the top, it's worth it. At the top, you can feel only joy.

Mount Saint Elias, Mount Foraker, Denali/McKinley . . . When people talk about climbing big mountains in the United States, Alaska usually dominates the conversation, with nineteen of the twenty tallest peaks in the country. California's 14,495-foot Mount Whitney is the sole exception. For those experienced hikers seeking a serious adventure, those possessing enough desire to stand atop the highest peak in the Lower 48 states, the summit of Mount Whitney is only a weekend away.

First, however, unless you maintain a phenomenal level of physical fitness, making an earnest summit attempt on Whitney means at least several months of training. If you're out of shape, plan on training for at least six months to a year. The hike to the top may only be 11 miles, but the tough part is that you also face an elevation gain of over 6,100 feet. And, of course, you have to make it back down too.

One of the most reasonable ways to see the summit (as far as safety and physical exertion are concerned) is to allocate three days in late summer for the trek. In July and August an ice ax and crampons are probably not required, though they should both be carried in your pack just in case. The first day of the journey offers a good warm-up hike getting to Trail Camp, which covers a little more than 6 miles and takes you to just over 12,000 feet. Be sure to get some good sleep, then get up early on day two because it's ninety-seven grueling switchbacks to the summit. After reaching the top and taking plenty of photos, some hard-core mountaineers, full of energy and feeling healthy, hike all the way back to the trailhead. A likely better idea is to stop again at Trail Camp, limiting the mileage on the second day and saving the last 6 miles back to the trailhead for day 3.

There is one other way to scale Mount Whitney. If 22 miles round trip and more than a vertical mile both up and down doesn't intimidate you, you just may be of that peculiar breed of nutcase mountaineer who, by possessing extraordinary fitness and diehard determination, will actually attempt to reach the summit in a single day. The only advice we can offer to dayhikers is start early (you should be on the trail no later than 3:00 A.M.), and best of luck. That is an ultimate challenge. However, no matter what way you split up the hike (or don't), getting to the summit of Mount Whitney and back will likely be the toughest 22 miles of your life.

Located in Sequoia National Park, Mount Whitney is only a five-hour drive from Los Angeles and San Francisco. The trail is one of the most popular paths in the California Sierras, and therefore, to limit impact, a permit is required from the start of May through the first day of November to enter the Mount Whitney zone. It is especially difficult to acquire the backcountry permit for a two- or three-day hike in the prime season of July and August. Climbers may apply for permits in the February lottery. Permit applications for other trails can be submitted up to six months in advance. Keep in mind that permit procedure and regulations are subject to change, so ask about this when you call the permit office. Another requirement to ask about is the bear canister, a metal case used to conceal the delicious smell of your foodstuffs from any curious bears. Although bears are generally not a problem, the canisters are required and are available for rent or purchase at the permit office.

Besides the permit, the bear canister, and healthy doses of commitment and fortitude, other essentials you'll need to remember on your Mount Whitney hike include sturdy boots, plenty of warm clothing, sufficient water storage, a filter or iodine tablets to purify and replenish your water reserves along the hike, toilet paper for the solar toilets, and plenty of food. Don't forget to apply sunblock and lip balm regularly, because the sun is much stronger at altitude. Although July and August are generally free of ice and snow, finding yourself in a sudden storm without an ice ax or crampons may mean trouble, so, again, it's a good idea to pack them along anyway. Your trip also requires additional research, starting with our recommended reading list, continuing with a thorough perusal of online journals and trip reports, and finally, as much additional advice from Whitney veterans as you can find. Be sure to read up to know the signs and effects of acute mountain sickness (AMS). To top Mount Whitney, you need to be as prepared as possible.

Finally, once you've got your permit squared away, after you've done plenty of training, and at last as you've packed everything on your list, it's time to head out to the mountains and start climbing. Go for it, but no matter whether you make it to the top or not, just stepping foot on the Mount Whitney trail is an incredibly beautiful and rewarding experience. With alpine lakes occupying grand cirques, steep breathtaking drop-offs, and views that stretch on forever, the interior of the High Sierra is only to be seen from within. Wildflowers are found scattered through high scenic meadows, while marmots and other mountain creatures scurry all over this monstrous mound of granite. Majestic waterfalls splash down from mountain streams. Along the way, you're guaranteed to meet some interesting folks. You're also guaranteed a workout no matter how great the shape you're in. And you're guaranteed some of the purest, most powerful emotions you have ever felt.

Price: $25+

(Summer, Difficult)

DRIVING DIRECTIONS

Lone Pine is the gateway to Mount Whitney, and is located on U.S. 395 on the eastern side of the Sierra Nevada Mountains. From the

Los Angeles area, follow State Highway 14 north until it becomes
U.S. 395. Lone Pine is roughly 210 miles from Los Angeles, and 260
miles south of Reno. Whitney Portal Road intersects Highway 395
at the traffic signal in downtown Lone Pine. Drive 13 miles west of
Lone Pine on the Whitney Portal Road. The road is usually open
from May through November. The last 6 miles of the road are not
plowed in the winter.

FOR MORE INFORMATION

INYO NATIONAL FOREST
Lone Pine
(760) 873–2400
www.fs.fed.us/r5/inyo

WILDERNESS PERMIT OFFICE
Bishop
(760) 873–2485

RECOMMENDED READING

Richins, Paul. *Mount Whitney: The Complete Trailhead-to-Summit
Hiking Guide.* Seattle: Mountaineer Books, 2001.

Salony, Sharon. *How to Climb Mount Whitney in One Day.*
Gardnerville, Nev.: Dublin-Shore Publications, 1997.

Winnett, Thomas. *Mt. Whitney: The Peak and Surrounding Highlands
(Hiker's Guide to the High Sierra).* Berkeley, Calif.: Wilderness Press,
2003.

SLEEP CHEAP

The Whitney Portal Campground at the trailhead is some of the best
camping to be found in Southern California. It is also at over 8,000
feet in elevation, so arriving a day or two in advance of your hike
will give your body extra time to acclimate to the altitude and
hopefully avoid any problems with AMS. Reservations are recommended. Call (800) 280–2267 for more information. Another option
is the Tuttle Creek campground located just a couple miles west of
Lone Pine on Whitney Portal Road (760–872–4881). Stay on
Whitney Portal Road to reach Horseshoe Meadows Campground,
just another mile and a half west (760–876–6200).

Fall

Ballooning in Temecula

Hot Air over Grape Country

On September 19, 1783, a sheep, a duck, and a chicken became the first passengers to see the world from a working hot air balloon. Since then, millions of people have followed them upwards, jumping into wicker baskets and soaring miles above the ground in these brightly colored, sometimes peculiarly shaped craft. In general, hot air ballooning has not changed much since then, despite new technology and materials such as nylon and stainless steel; the object is to heat the massive pocket of air in the balloon (or envelope) to over 100°F, at which point it becomes lighter than the outside air and begins to rise. Good old air, heated by propane burners, is the only force of locomotion the pilot controls. Otherwise, the balloon floats on the atmospheric currents surrounding it, moving as they move.

The Temecula Valley is Southern California's ballooning capital, and with good reason. The valley is filled with vineyards and wineries, and the atmosphere both above and on the ground is perfect for ballooning. This adventure is a mellow yet exhilarating way to see some of California's most beautiful country from a spectacular vantage point, and also gives wine connoisseurs the chance to sample some of the world's best wines.

Recreational ballooning is one of the safest airborne adventures you can take, suitable for the whole family. Very young children may be a little scared by the noise the flames make as they shoot into the envelope, but past that, it's fun for everyone. However,

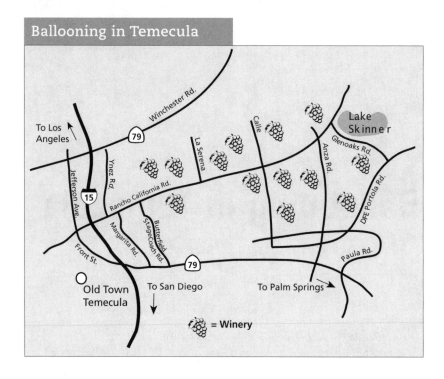

To Los Angeles

79

Winchester Rd.

La Serena

Calle

Lake Skinner

Glenoaks Rd.

Anza Rd.

Jefferson Ave.

Ynez Rd.

15

Rancho California Rd.

DFE Portola Rd.

Margarita Rd.

StageCoach Rd.

Butterfield

Front St.

79

Paula Rd.

Old Town Temecula

To San Diego

To Palm Springs

= Winery

floating through the Temecula Valley is especially suited to a certain tyke-less set: couples looking to get away for the weekend, without little ones in tow.

Yes indeed, grown-up-style celebration is the name of the game for this escape. If you have a special occasion coming up, or if you're just in the mood to treat your significant other right, this is the way to do it. The Temecula Valley is a great little playground for fun-loving adults; five championship golf courses occupy the valley, as does picturesque Lake Skinner, home of the annual Temecula Balloon and Wine Festival. Dining and shopping in Old Town Temecula provide diversion after your day of flight and exploration. And, of course, there's the wine; kids don't get quite the same satisfaction from touring vineyards and receiving numerous (and delicious) samples.

But back to the ballooning. Most of us have only seen hot air balloons from a great distance and have no idea how impressive they really are, towering a few stories above the ground. Once you're in the air, take the time (between burner blasts) to look up into the balloon's mouth. That's almost 100,000 cubic feet of hot air you see, all of it required to keep the basket buoyant in the sky. Watching the envelope fill up is an amazing sight, as the long stretch of nylon lying on the ground becomes the rigid, round carriage for your flight. Not often will you see such a blossoming of power with little more than air and heat driving it.

Once you are aloft, your balloon will float along silently, and you'll have a great chance to take in the sunrise or sunset. (Balloon flights almost always take place near dawn or in the evening, as midday sun heats the earth's surface and causes strong, variable winds.) The altitude you'll be flying at depends on weather and your wishes; you may coast along the treetops or find yourself nearly a mile up. If you opt for the wuthering heights, you'll soon notice that a mile up in a balloon feels a lot farther than a mile flying down Highway 5; enjoy the view, and do your best to lean over and look down. It's a rush—just remember to bring your camera! (You may even want to bring two—one for you and one for the ground crew following your balloon, to chronicle your trip from the ground.)

That said, don't let the height scare you or dissuade you from taking your first ride. Balloon gondolas are very safe and much bigger than they look from the ground. They are built to hold up in wind and weather, and you won't feel like you're hanging on by a thread in a little Easter basket once you're up and away. If there is anything objectionable about ballooning, it's the propane burners; they create a whole lot of radiant heat, and anyone with a bald or shaved pate should take care to protect it. Wear a loose-fitting hat, and you should be just fine. The burner is most active when the balloon is rising, though, so once you're up, don't be afraid to take off the hat and lean out for a look-see.

Temecula's ballooning outfitters cater to just about everyone, and each one offers different packages. The less expensive flights are shorter (fifteen to twenty minutes) and don't include many bells or whistles. Pricier flights are, well, pricier, but they also include breakfast, lunch, and bottles of wine or champagne after the flight, as well as much longer durations. Most of Temecula's ballooning companies also fly from other locations and provide more experiences than the lazy floats over wine country. The Great American Balloon Company, for example, offers balloon skydiving from its Perris Valley launch spot. The balloon lifts off at dawn and takes divers up to about 3,500 feet, at which point the pilot starts pushing passengers out (with parachutes strapped to the pushees, of course). Call around to find out which one suits you best, and be sure to ask what comes with each flight to maximize your adventure dollars.

Ballooning will stoke your sense of wonder and show you just

Ballooning is a relaxing, early-morning activity. ROBERT HOLMES/CALTOUR

how huge this planet of ours is. Just think: What you're seeing from a few thousand feet over the Temecula Valley is one little wine region in one small corner of the earth. Look at it in these terms, and you'll start to realize just how much adventuring there is left to do. When you feel that realization, just wrap your arms around the significant other who's sharing all that beauty with you, say something nice and sweet, point to the horizon, and ask, "Where next?"

Price: $60–$350

(Fall, Easy)

DRIVING DIRECTIONS

Temecula Valley wine country is located off I–15, 90 miles from L.A. and 60 miles from San Diego.

FOR MORE INFORMATION

Outfitters

ADVENTURE FLIGHTS
(800) 404–6359
www.advflights.com

A GRAPE ESCAPE
Temecula
(800) 965–2122
www.agrapeescape.com

GREAT AMERICAN BALLOON COMPANY
Hemet
(15 miles outside the Temecula area)
(909) 927–2593
www.greatamericanballoon.com

Other

CITY OF TEMECULA
(888) 836–3285
www.ci.temecula.ca.us

TEMECULA ONLINE
www.temecula.com

TEMECULA VALLEY WINEGROWERS ASSOCIATION
www.temeculawines.org

RECOMMENDED READING

Brigandi, Phil. *Temecula: At the Crossroads of History.* Carlsbad, Calif.: Heritage Media, 1999.

Elwood, Ann. *Wineries: San Diego County and the Temecula Valley.* Cardiff by the Sea, Calif.: Chalk Press, 1999.

Kalakuka, Christine, and Brent Stockwell. *Hot Air Balloons.* New York: Metro Books, 1998.

SLEEP CHEAP

Loma Vista Bed & Breakfast is located 5 miles east of downtown Temecula. It has eight wineries within a mile, and fantastic restaurants are also close by. In addition, Loma Vista provides complimentary wine and cheese in the evenings, along with a full champagne breakfast in the morning. Rates run between $115 and $195, which usually wouldn't be considered cheap, but for the location, amenities, and all the extras included, along with the romantic Temecula atmosphere, it's a small price to pay. Call (909) 676–7047 for reservations, and treat your sweetie right.

Sportfishing San Diego

Bass, Bonitos, and Barracudas

The water lapping against the hull practically puts you to sleep where you stand, helping the setting sun and the huge albacore dinner you had that afternoon put your already mellow disposition into a state of near-perfect relaxation. Your hands are barely wrapped around your rod and only grasp tight enough to prevent it from slipping out and into the drink. Your mind is just starting to go under, you feel your head nod just a touch, your eyes drift closed, when . . .

BAM! Your rod tip shudders, and instantly you're back on the alert. Your hands come alive suddenly, tightening their grip, and you ease back to set the hook. You know that you're going to bring up another one if you're lucky and don't do anything stupid. Just got to set a good hook first . . . BAM! Fish on! Fish on!

After landing your third contender for biggest fish of the day, you become conscious again of the people around you, the shouts and hollers of anglers hauling in, and you wonder how you could have felt so drowsy in the first place. You settle in again, thinking, *just this one more, and I'm done for the day,* knowing you couldn't possibly stop while there are still albacore and yellowtails swimming underneath you.

Sportfishing has a long, hallowed history in California, particularly in San Diego. Anglers have been pulling marlin, shark, tuna, sea bass, and mackerel out of the ocean between Los Angeles and

Baja for the past eighty years. But they haven't done it alone; San Diego's charter fishing fleet has provided the opportunities for these fisherfolk, and today the various outfitters operating throughout San Diego are glad to take you wherever you need to go to catch the big one that swims in and out of your dreams.

For the most part, tuna fishing is the name of the game on longer cruises, as the majority of your action will be from albacore, yellowfin tuna, and bigeye tuna. Beyond these staples, what kind of fish you'll be catching depends largely on what your destination is and how long you're cruising. Shorter trips obviously don't move as far into the ocean, so you'll catch more barracuda, bonito, bass, and other coastal water fish. Longer trips (two or more days) put you out where the albacore, yellowtail, and dorado concentrate most heavily. Go out longer still, say, on a three- or four-day cruise down to the waters off Baja California, and you may find yourself hooking some grouper or wahoo, along with everything mentioned above. For those of you with really big dreams, there are still healthy populations of sharks and sailfish lurking out in the blue depths off Baja and the Coronado Islands.

There are tons of charter choices, and each offers different strokes. Most break out their available trips by the half, three-quarter, and full day first, then have multiple-day excursions on top of that. H&M Landing, for example, offers half-day trips that leave first thing in the morning and mid-afternoon, as well as less expensive twilight trips that don't head out until 6:30 P.M. H&M's full-day trips are excellent too, as they leave at 11:00 P.M. the night before, to ensure you're at the fishing grounds by sunup. The company's long-range trips down to Baja can last from two to twenty-one days, include bait and food for you, and are pretty much the pinnacle of fishing in style. Ask about these longer trips if you have the time—they are more expensive but worth every penny when you're pulling up more pounds of fish than you can add without a calculator. If you have a limited budget or just want to spend more shore time in San Diego, the twilight trips, costing roughly $40, are an amazingly inexpensive way to have a blast, not to mention fill up the freezer.

Some companies and individual boats offer expeditions especially for the high-profile marlin and shark. The *Aristokat,* for example, runs trips for Islandia Sportfishing, but her crew also will take you out especially for the big fish if you so desire. Keep in mind that on a trip such as this one, you may catch fewer fish. What you will get

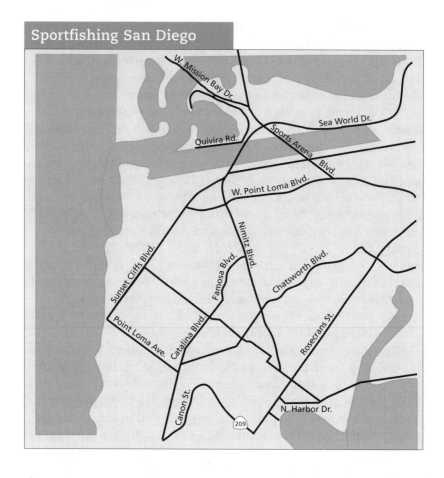

is the chance at the proverbial "Big One," and perhaps a Hemingway-style fishing story to tell your grandkids. If you're interested, ask the charters you call whether they run trips like this, and when was the last time they had any success. That information should help you make up your mind between a higher-volume cruise and the possible glory of a wall-mountable, trophy catch.

Seasickness is something you may have to deal with out there; check out Escape 18 (Sailing) for tips on what to do about your deck queasiness. Just make sure you deal with the problem before setting out on your trip. Also, don't worry too much about the cutting and gutting—part of the reason you're taking a charter is to avoid that whole mess. Your boat's crew will generally handle cleaning duties, but make sure you know beforehand to avoid getting stuck. And remember: If you were gutting hundreds of fish every day, you'd want to get tipped for it. Gratuity is not an option, so pony up to the folks who are making your catch fit for the dinner table.

Sportfishing is a classic California adventure, one you'll want to repeat regularly if you're into action. Fishing under these conditions is far from the solitude and quiet that is fly-fishing; deep-sea angling is a busy, social, activity-packed escape that involves pulling fish that can weigh over 100 pounds up into your boat over and over again. There's time to relax, sure, but why would you want to with all those fish waiting to be caught? Go out ready for the hard core, and if you're lucky, that's just what you'll get.

Price: $70–$500+

(Fall, Easy)

DRIVING DIRECTIONS

San Diego's fishing charters are located up and down the city's coast. Ask the outfitter you choose how to get to their dock area.

FOR MORE INFORMATION

Outfitters

H&M LANDING
San Diego
(619) 222–1144
www.hmlanding.com

ISLANDIA SPORTFISHING
San Diego
(619) 222–1164
www.islandiasportfishing.com

POINT LOMA SPORTFISHING
San Diego
(619) 223–1627
www.pointlomasportfishing.com

SEAFORTH SPORTFISHING
San Diego
(619) 224–3383
www.seaforthlanding.com

There are many individual boats available for specialty charters too. Most of the good ones run tours for these larger companies as well as their own charters. Each company's Web site lists the boats in their fleet; if you want to, check out the individual boats to see which one provides the kind of trip you want, and go with it.

RECOMMENDED READING

Greenlaw, Linda. *The Hungry Ocean: A Swordboat Captain's Journey.* New York: Hyperion, 2000.

Hemingway, Ernest. *Hemingway on Fishing.* New York: The Lyons Press, 2000.

Ries, Ed. *Tales of the Golden Years of California Ocean Fishing 1900–1950.* Laguna Hills, Calif.: Monterey Publications, 1998.

SLEEP CHEAP

Sleeping on the boat is just about as economical as you can get; sure, the trip will cost more, but you're saving on food costs, campground fees or motels, and gas money. Plus, you'll be up bright and early to start hooking that night's dinner. If you need a place in San Diego, try Sweetwater Regional Park, located only 10 miles southeast of downtown east of I-805 just off Highway 54. All fifty-three campsites have water and electricity, while restroom facilities include hot showers. Standing at the Summit Site, you can see San Diego Bay and the Pacific Ocean to the west, the Sweetwater Reservoir to the east, and Tijuana to the south. Campsites may be reserved up to three months in advance. Other San Diego camping parks are available. For more information, call San Diego County Parks & Recreation (858–694–3049).

Gold Rush Revisited

The Mother Lode of Adventures

They have a football team named after them and enjoy a hallowed
place in this country's gallery of frontier heroes. There are songs,
stories, movies, and books dedicated to their adventures in pursuit
of golden, metallic wealth. They may be the most American adventurers of all—people who set out for a strange land in pursuit of
their fortunes, put their hands into the earth, and pulled out their
dreams. Everyone raise a pan and shovel, please, to California's
illustrious 49ers (the ones from the mines, not the gridiron). And
when you're done, set out on your own gold-digging adventure
among California's metal-rich deserts and rivers.

News flash: There's a reason it's called the Golden State. Gold
rush history is the history of California itself; in January 1848,
James Marshall discovered the first gold along the American River,
kicking off the following year's mad migration and the explosive
immigration that continues today. They came pouring in by the
thousands, and with good reason—imagine finding 10 pounds of
metal worth a small bank (in those days), and it's easy to figure out
the allure. Prospecting was a common pursuit across the entire
West, and a dedicated little community of miners practices it to this
day from New Mexico to northern California. They ply the rivers
and deserts searching for deposits, using a combination of tried and
true methods, like panning and dredging, and powerful metal detectors that seem to part the earth's crust.

Gold Rush Revisited

Some of the more enterprising and successful of these prospectors are happy to take the uninitiated on gold-hunting expeditions, allowing the rest of us to experience the fever without giving up our families and jobs in search of the mother lode. In fact, prospecting is a much surer bet than Vegas; weekend diggers often, thanks to experienced guides, go out on two- or three-day excursions and actually find gold, sometimes enough to pay for their trips. If there's anything to keep in mind while you're panning or scanning, it's to be patient, because the gold is definitely there; in 1992, for example, miners found a 45-pound nugget in California's Jamestown Mine. You may not be quite that lucky, but with the right guidance and a steady hand, you may find yourself yelling "Eureka!" just like those old-school grizzled guys.

River and desert prospecting are very different activities, involving different tools. Simply speaking, river prospecting involves moving silt through sluices either by hand or machine and separating the gold from everything else. Desert prospecting, on the other hand, involves more use of high-tech metal detectors, which are capable of finding treasures 18 inches down in the ground. In California, both activities resulted in huge claims, and the same holds true today. You stand a good chance of finding treasure using either means; factors like location, price, amenities, and the landscape you prefer will end up being the basis of your decision, rather than success rate. Talk to each outfitter, get your questions answered, and make your decision based on what you hear.

Granted, if you're a beginner, you won't have a detector of your own to hunt with, nor will you really know what you're looking for or where to look for it. That's why on your first prospecting trip, you should tag along with people who can provide you with both the knowledge you lack and the equipment you need. The Lifestyle Store, a California-based operation that runs desert prospecting adventures near Barstow, provides equipment, including deep-seeking metal detectors. The workshops last three days and allow participants to hone their searching skills and socialize with other people who share the gold bug. The Lifestyle Store also runs metal detector workshops at its store and in the gold fields; these one-day activities are meant to get you acquainted with the equipment and serve as a nice introduction if you're not sure about a longer trip.

If you want to get your feet wet, Get Gold Adventures & Outfitters specializes in stream prospecting, and though they are in northern California, they are definitely worth checking out if you want to get into prospecting big time. They offer overnight tours around the California River that boast mucho gold, as well as the best sourdough in the mother lode. Get Gold even offers claims-for-rent; for a small fee, you can buy the right to prospect on the company's claims as much as you want for a whole year. It's well worth it if you plan on prospecting as a hobby, and at the very least you'll have exclusive access to some beautiful California camping land for a whole year.

In fact, camping is an important feature for both of these outfitters; prospecting is a complete outdoor experience, with the added bonus of income potential. Its lack of domesticity also makes it an inexpensive escape for those of us without a lot of gold in our bank accounts. The Lifestyle Store's adventure is about forty minutes from Barstow, so you could bed down there if you wanted to; the best way to go, however, is to bring your own tent or camper and rough it, spending your nights under the stars and above the gold you'll surely find the next morning. Count on camping, and you'll feel

Sifting through water and silt produces sweet, sweet gold—if you're lucky.
GEORGE L. ELDRIDGE

immersion in your adventure, rather than a worklike "gotta be there by eight" obligation.

After all, total involvement is really what prospecting is all about. The more dirt you move or ground you cover, the better your chances for striking. That being said, don't forget about immersing yourself in the countryside too, whether it be desert dunes or lush greenery. You'll have time to sit back and enjoy the scenery in between loads of silt, so don't pass up the opportunity. There is also a lot of time to get to know your comrades and guides. Look forward to sharing good company, acquiring a new skill, and spending a weekend learning about one of the most American pursuits there is. Prospecting is adventure for fun *and* profit, the kind of activity that pays for itself if you're lucky, but is relaxing and enjoyable even if you find nothing but more mud.

Price: $100–$500+

(Fall, Easy)

DRIVING DIRECTIONS

The mining outfitter you choose will tell you how to get to your mining destination. Because claims "dry up," your site could be different every trip.

FOR MORE INFORMATION

Outfitters

GET GOLD ADVENTURES & OUTFITTERS
Sonora
(209) 588–1523
www.getgold.com

THE LIFESTYLE STORE
Hesperia
(800) 900–6463
www.lifestylestore.com

Other

OAKLAND MUSEUM OF CALIFORNIA
(510) 238–2200
www.museumca.org

MUSEUM OF THE CITY OF SAN FRANCISCO
(online gold rush exhibits)
www.sfmuseum.org

RECOMMENDED READING

Alt, David, and Donald W. Hyndman. *Roadside Geology of Northern and Central California.* Missoula, Mont.: Mountain Press Publishing Co., 1999.

Angier, Bradford. *Looking for Gold: The Modern Prospector's Handbook.* Mechanicsburg, Pa.: Stackpole Books, 1982.

SLEEP CHEAP

Your best bet on a Lifestyle Store jaunt is to sleep on your claim. Your outfitter provides a shaded common meeting area and portable outhouses. You will, however, have to bring your own tent or camper.

South of the Border in Tijuana

Shopping, Bullfighting . . . and Tequila

Tijuana evokes a lot of images, many of them less than wholesome:
Sailors fresh from Pacific voyages tearing up the town; spring
break tales involving booze, sex, and more booze; broken down
horse tracks filled with drugged nags and down-luck gamblers.
Rumors of legendary deviance seem to swirl around the Gateway to
Mexico's reputation, as does a certain fear on the part of many
Americans. They believe the stories and see this arid, almost
Saharan city as some kind of sin mecca, where crazy Americans
and their Mexican counterparts can engage in the kind of behavior
that makes decent folks run for Branson.

   Times have changed. Although it was a pretty lawless place not
very long ago, the Tijuana of today is not only much safer, but
makes a great weekend getaway for anyone visiting the San Diego
area. The entry point to Baja's Gold Coast sits less than thirty minutes from downtown and is even accessible via the city's trolley
system. It offers a little taste of Mexican history and culture without
requiring a passport or visa (visitors to northern Baja California do
not need either document if staying in the country for seventy-two
hours or less), along with more universal pleasures like shopping
and bar hopping. (Just because the place has mellowed doesn't
mean it's dead!) Thanks to its location and many attractions,
Tijuana sees more international traffic than any other city in the
world; in 1995, its border was crossed more than fifty million times.

The city was founded in 1889 and may be named for the Indian word *Tiguan,* which in the Cochimis dialect means "close to the water." However, another story maintains the name comes from a ranch near the region owned by *Juana Tia,* or aunt Jane *en español.* And once upon a time, the big reason Americans came to Tijuana *was* to engage in things that weren't quite legal on this side of the border. In the 1920s, folks who didn't approve of America's Prohibition laws simply moseyed south to enjoy their favorite cocktails and the casinos that opened there in the decades following.

As time passed, though, Tijuana developed a powerful (and legitimate) local economy based on technology and a cleaner brand of tourism. "Sin tourism" plays a fairly insignificant part in modern Tijuana's economic life; a visit to the city's beautiful, tree-lined Zona Río, where shopping has largely taken the place of debauchery, is all any visitor will need to realize that today's Tijuana is no more dangerous than a typical American city. Of course, this is no reason to be foolish. Just exercise a measure of common sense when kicking around in Tijuana. Don't be ignorant, and you'll have a great, safe time.

The Zona Río is one of the best examples of Tijuana's growth and modernization. Its shopping centers are filled with posh department stores and specialty shops that carry both European finery and traditional Mexican crafts. More good news for shopaholics: Purchases in Mexico are duty free, and there is no state sales tax. Each shopper can bring $400 worth of merchandise back across the border free of charge, including 1 liter of alcohol (if over age twenty-one), 100 cigars (except for Cubans—bummer), and 200 cigarettes. If you drop major change in Tijuana, the U.S. duty fee is 10 percent for the first $1,000 of merchandise above $400. And don't worry much about currency problems—dollars, pesos, and major credit cards are accepted all over the city.

But don't come to Tijuana just to max out your credit card. There is local culture galore here; contact the Tijuana Cultural Center for detailed information about the cultural landmarks that dot the city, or take in some of its many interesting sporting events. Tijuana boasts two bullrings (one of which is the only oceanside ring in the world) and a dog track. Or, if you're feeling more adventurous, take in a game of jai alai while you're in town. Jai alai, a Basque phrase meaning "merry festival," was first introduced in the United States in 1904, and Tijuana opened its first court, or fronton, in 1947. The game is the unruly offspring of racquetball and lacrosse; players throw a small, rock-hard ball against the court's

To San Diego · 5 · 805 · 905
Boundary Monument
International Border
San Diego Trolley Station
San Ysidro – Tijuana Port of Entry
Otay Mesa Port of Entry
MEX 1
Bullring by the Sea
Tijuana Int'l Airport
MEX 2
Ave. Revolucion
Peseo de los Heros
Blvd. Cuauhtemoc
To Ensenada
Cuauhtemoc Monument
Toreo de Tijuana Bullring
Tijuana River
Bus Station
Blvd. Agua Caliente
1 Abelardo Rodrigues
Agua Caliente Racetrack
La Mesa
MEX 2
To Tecate
Libramiento Oriente

walls with a scooplike basket, and the ball often exceeds 100 mph as it flies around the fronton. It is a dangerous pastime, but incredible fun to watch. Tijuana is one of the few places that boasts jai alai as a spectator sport, so don't miss it.

So there's a lot to do here, even if you're not into tequila and tattoos. But let's not forget that nightlife, either—it is, after all, one of Tijuana's claims to fame. Even if the town has mellowed a bit since the rough-and-tumble old days, it still knows how to throw a party. You'll find some of the West Coast's wildest times here, where both Mexican and American adventurers unwind in smoky bars with cold cervezas, white-hot tequila, and just about any kind of scene you can think of. If you want to mix and mingle with the dance club crowd, head over to Baby Rock; or go to the TJ Brewery Co., where they brew Tijuana-brand beer. If you're feeling adventurous, check out some of the smaller, seedier places to get tequila slammed down your throat. And where but Tijuana could you see a live, indoor rodeo at midnight? Rodeo Santa Fe's got a mechanical bull too, so give it a ride after you check out this three-level, nocturnal version of the wild, wild West.

Whatever your preferences might be, Tijuana really does offer something for everyone. Hotel accommodations range from five-star to cut-rate, and you can reach the city via trolley, car (though you do need to buy Mexican auto insurance if you choose this route), or on foot. You can go home with bags of clothes, or get half in the bag before returning to the USA. It's easy to spend a week in and around Tijuana, but a weekend escape is the perfect recipe for sampling what this one-of-a-kind town has to offer.

Price: $10–$500+

(Fall, Easy)

DIRECTIONS

Tijuana is 15 miles south of San Diego on I–5, although traffic is frenetic, parking is difficult, and there may be long waits to get back into the United States. It's better to drive to San Ysidro, drop your car off in a parking lot, and walk across the border. You can also take the bus or trolley into Tijuana and avoid traffic headaches. Make sure you buy Mexican auto insurance if you drive!

FOR MORE INFORMATION

BABY ROCK
(011) 52–66–34–2404

COMPLETE GUIDE TO TIJUANA
www.tijuana.com

BORDER INSURANCE SERVICES
(800) 332–2118

TIJUANA CULTURAL CENTER
(011) 52–664–687–9600

RODEO SANTA FE
(011) 52–664–682–4967 (or
682–4968)

TIJUANA TOURISM BOARD
www.seetijuana.com

Keep in mind that many of the phone numbers on these and other Web sites may be incorrect. Mexico changed its conventions for international calls in November 2001; dial (011) 52–664, then the seven-digit number, if there is one. Many numbers at tijuana.com are still listed in the previous six-digit form.

RECOMMENDED READING

Harris, Richard. *Hidden Baja*. New York: Ulysses Travel Guides, 2000.

Kershul, Kris. *Spanish in 10 Minutes a Day*. Seattle: Bilingual Books, 1997.

Profitt, T. D. *Tijuana: The History of a Mexican Metropolis*. Lanham, Md.: University Publishing Association, 1994.

SLEEP CHEAP

The Tecate KOA, about thirty minutes from Tijuana and minutes from the town of Tecate, is a perfect place to spend the night if you want to camp south of the border. Proprietors Hernan and Zella Ibanez Bracamontes are more than happy to share their knowledge of the area with you, so be sure to ask them about attractions outside of Tijuana if you're staying in the region for a while. Call (011) 52–665–655–3014 for more information, or visit either www.koa.com and look for the Tecate site or go directly to the campground's own site, www.tecatekoa.com. Accommodations range from cabins, to RV spots, to tent areas, and there is a pool on site, golf nearby, and a ton of other fun stuff.

Golfing Torrey Pines and Barona Creek

Thirty-six Holes of Natural Wonder

Golf isn't very high on the list of nature-centric outdoor activities. Sure, you're outside; there's lots of green all around; you might even see a rabbit or two while you're whipping around asphalt pathways on your speedy cart. But you're often not *connected* to the land, to what lies underneath the manicured greens and fairways. Golf courses have more to do with the people who play on them than the natural world that was there before the tee boxes.

The game doesn't have to play that way, though. Just because a course is built doesn't mean its foundation should be plowed flat first. What you have here is a golf adventure for those of us who want *more* out of our golf than eighteen holes, a refreshment cart, and those wonderful putting/driving/short iron frustrations. If you're into run-of-the-mill, fine—there are plenty of courses up and down the California coast that will satisfy you. But if you want to escape the ordinary (without necessarily mortgaging your house for the greens fees), check into Torrey Pines and Barona Creek, two San Diego–area courses that are sure to provide you a weekend's worth of natural beauty, nineteenth hole entertainment, and spectacular golf.

Torrey Pines is the more famous of the two courses, the lifetime all-star to match Rookie of the Year Barona (more on that later). Torrey has been a San Diego golf landmark almost since golf came to the city; the San Diego Open (now known as the Buick Invitational) came to the course in 1968 and has remained there

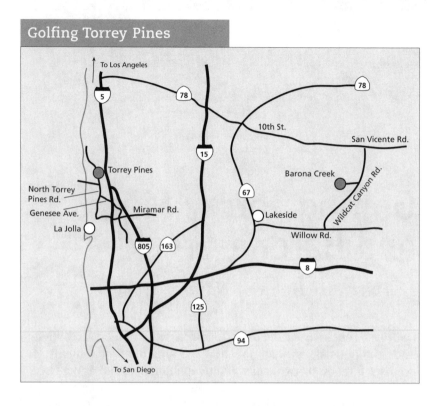

To Los Angeles

5

78

78

10th St.

San Vicente Rd.

15

Torrey Pines

Barona Creek

North Torrey Pines Rd.

Genesee Ave.

Miramar Rd.

67

Wildcat Canyon Rd.

La Jolla

Lakeside

Willow Rd.

805

163

8

125

94

To San Diego

until this day. (If you happen to be in town during February, head over and see some real golfers swing.) Arnold Palmer, Jack Nicklaus, and homegrown champ Billy Casper have all seen victory at Torrey Pines. It boasts two eighteen-hole masterpieces, the north and south courses, and the more difficult south links host the Buick Invitational's final every year. Both courses feature incredible ocean views, as well as the feeling that you're treading where the great ones once did. You egalitarian, anti-country-club types should not pack up your clubs in protest: You will be happy to know that despite this storied pedigree, the course is a municipal facility, open to the golf-playing public.

What makes the courses even more special, for our purposes, is their proximity to the Torrey Pines State Reserve, home to the rarest native pine tree in the United States: the indomitable Torrey. This tree probably has one of the smallest native distributions in the natural world, as it has never set root outside California. Today, it is found only around the course and reserve grounds, and in a small stand on Santa Rosa Island.

Torrey pines are not the most beautiful trees around; in fact, they are a bit beaten-looking—twisted, gnarled, and weakened by constant inbreeding. They cling to the beautiful sandstone cliffs that shoot up over the Pacific shore and are subjected to the hard winds, brutal sun, and pounding rain that periodically assault the coast. Despite all that and their proximity to such a metropolitan area, they live, symbolizing toughness, character, and fortitude—three things you can surely use when you're hitting the links.

After playing your round, go take a closer look at the pines and their natural, unspoiled home. You'll see the last of the Torrey pines, as well as miles of untouched beaches and a lagoon that serves as a popular stopover for feathered migrators. The area boasts 8 miles of trail too, enough to check out the landscape and give yourself a taste of the natural beauty of the area after you view it in the course's context.

Another San Diego–area course, Barona Creek in Lakeside, boasts an even stronger commitment to the land, and demonstrates that human leisure and the natural world can exist side by side without sacrificing either. Completed in 2001, Barona Creek is the centerpiece for the $260 million Barona Valley Ranch Resort and Casino, completed in 2003. The course took three years to build and is a golfer's dream; for one thing, it is only the second course in San Diego to proceed from all sod, thus giving it an instantly mature look and feel. For another, it lives with its surroundings, rather than on top of them. More than 170 full-size oak trees, native to the Barona Indian Reservation, were incorporated into the design, as was a low-usage irrigation system designed to use recycled moisture from the casino's wastewater treatment plant. The layout of the course is meant to take advantage of the land's natural contours, complementing what nature has already laid down. Throw in around one hundred bunkers and plentiful water play, and you're both amazed by the beauty of the place and cursing at the top of your lungs.

The Barona Band of Mission Indians, who owns the land, the casino, and the course, has gone to great lengths to ensure Barona offers challenging, exciting golf and an environmentally gentle recreation experience. And though the course is a newbie, in that it was the first built on a California Indian reservation, it hasn't acted like one. Barona has won a number of awards since its opening; *Golf Week* magazine named it the fourth-best course in California (Torrey Pines, incidentally, came in ninth), and in 2002, *Golf* magazine

The view from Barona Creek Golf Club's 11th green. BARONA CREEK GOLF CLUB

named it one of the top ten new courses in the country. All this, and the price is better than nice: only $80 weekdays, including cart and range balls or—get this—$50 at twilight (after 2:00 P.M.) Monday through Friday. Playing such a great course at those prices is a steal, and it's well worth taking a San Diego excursion just to sample the bunkers and creek beds.

Plus, there's the casino. The tribe claims its slots are loose, and any place with table gambling offers something worth checking out if you've got a little Vegas in your blood. Now that the hotel's completed, you have even more resort-style options to choose from. It might not be the natural world you'll see on the course, but you may get pretty wild anyway.

Playing the links is the big priority here, of course. But when you're out on these two beautiful courses, look around and remember you are here for more than the golf. They offer something more, both in terms of leisure and communion with nature. Each one presents you with a different way to get closer to California's natural world, even while you feel like beating your five-iron repeatedly into the pretty ground.

Price: $225–$250

(for two weekday greens fees without specials)

(Fall, Easy)

DRIVING DIRECTIONS

Barona Creek: Take I–8 to Highway 67 north in El Cajon. Proceed through Lakeside, then turn right on Willow Road and left on Wildcat Canyon Road.

Torrey Pines: From I–5 heading north, exit at Genesee Avenue, and turn left. Stay on Genesee as it curves to the right and becomes North Torrey Pines Road. Look for large, green course signs on the right after Science Park Way. From I–5 heading south, exit at Carmel Valley Road and turn right; then turn left on Camino Del Mar. Stay on this road as it passes the Torrey Pines State Beach, the State Preserve, and the golf course driving range. You'll see the course lot on your right.

FOR MORE INFORMATION

BARONA CREEK GOLF CLUB
Lakeside
(888) 722–7662 or (619) 443–2300
www.barona.com/golf

BARONA CASINO
Lakeside
(888) 722–7662 or (619) 443–2300
www.barona.com/casino

TORREY PINES GOLF COURSE
La Jolla
(800) 985–4653
www.torreypinesgolfcourse.com

TORREY PINES ASSOCIATION
www.torreypines.org

TORREY PINES GOLD CLUB
(organization for club specials and reservations)
(858) 452–3296 or (760) 944–3707
www.torreypinesgc.com

TORREY PINES STATE RESERVE
San Diego
(858) 755–2063
www.torreypine.org

RECOMMENDED READING

The Torrey Pines Association has published *Torrey Pines, Landscape and Legacy*, with text and photographs by Bill Evarts. It is available in a second printing at the reserve itself or from local bookstores. Warwick's, a store in La Jolla (619–454–0347), will send copies by UPS upon request. Paperbacks are $17.95, and the hardcover edition is $29.95.

Margolin, Malcolm, ed. *The Way We Lived: California Indian Stories, Songs and Reminiscences.* Berkeley, Calif.: Heyday Books, 1993.

Rotella, Bob. *Golf Is Not a Game of Perfect.* New York: Simon & Schuster, 1995.

SLEEP CHEAP

This space is normally reserved for camping options available nearby (and you will get one here), but you may want to consider splurging on a few nights at the Lodge at Torrey Pines, a beautiful resort overlooking the course and the ocean beyond. Sure, the prices are a little steeper, but the lodge offers specials that will include your round of golf, parking, and basic club amenities. Call (858) 453–4420 for more information, or visit www.lodgetorreypines.com. For truly cheap sleeping, head to Lake Jennings County Park, located just outside Lakeside and only a short jaunt from La Jolla, where Torrey Pines is located. Call (877) 565–3600 for reservations.

Auto Racing School

Your Own Days of Thunder

So you're into speed—very into speed. Cars are your passion, particularly the ones capable of obscenely quick lap times. You are a Sunday morning driver, glued to whatever race happens to be on, and you appreciate the skill, strength, and daring it takes to maneuver a 400-horsepower machine around a track filled with similar vehicles. You've tried to re-create the experience for yourself, with go-karts, super-karts, electronic simulations—you even sneak down in the middle of the night to see if the new extreme driving game you just bought "for the kids" really gives the same thrill as being behind the wheel does. At each turn, though, you're disappointed, knowing in the back of your mind that the track, the real track, is still calling. "It's obviously better than this," you think as you guide your electronic machine through yet another virtual hairpin. "But how much better?"

Well, quit asking, and find out for yourself behind the wheel of an actual NASCAR-ready stock car. Not a simulator, not a souped-up civilian model or a go-kart—the real thing. Call California's Drivetech Racing School, and make your inner speed demon's dreams come true.

Although there are a whole lot of stock car driving schools in the southern United States, there are far fewer in Southern California. Luckily, the state does make up in quality what it lacks in quantity. Drivetech offers its drivers-in-training things that

Auto Racing School

many other driving schools do not. First off, the whole experience is meant to teach you something about stock car driving, not just give you a glorified amusement park ride. Instead of being led around the track by bored instructors riding in the car with you and pacing you out front, Drivetech students get to be in their cars by themselves, without having to play "follow the leader" with another driver. You can pass as you catch your rivals, another activity some driving schools strictly prohibit. You're in touch via radio with your instructors, but you're doing the driving, making the decisions, and living the dream.

Then there's the cars themselves. These ain't no glorified sports cars, partner—these are 350-cubic-inch V-8s with around 400 horses under the hood. You'll get racing tires and suspension to boot, allowing you to stick to the track like glue. Don't fear for your safety or that of your loved ones, either; the cars all feature steel roll cages and a fire suppression system, just in case. (As with all great adventuring in whatever capacity, prepare for the worst and you'll usually enjoy the best.) In addition, every driver gets helmeted, belted, and driving-suited, to ensure maximum safety. It's a real race car with real precautions taken—you can't help but take the whole thing a little more seriously than the Indy 500 go-kart ride down at the county fair.

If you want to spend an entire two days living the racing life, sign up for Drivetech's longest class. The Championship Adventure lets you take on three driving sessions, adding up to two hours behind the wheel, and teaches one-on-one pursuit, side-by-side racing, starting, and just plain straightaway driving and cornering. Between your drives, you'll work with instructors and watch other students, learning while preparing for your next run. The two-day deal gives you more bang for your buck than shorter classes; the two-day class at the California Speedway, for example, gives you ninety laps (plus all your training, food, and drinks) at around $27.50/lap. The Racing Adventure, a twenty-lap sampler, gives you—well, twenty laps—at a much higher per-lap price. Splurge just a little, and you'll be very glad you did.

Part and parcel to this fantastic driving experience is some work on your part. Drivers are required to sign a waiver, and spectators are occasionally asked to do the same (ask Drivetech what the requirements will be when you make your reservations). Because this is not simply a prepackaged simulation you'll be doing, you need to take a little more responsibility than you would on the bumper cars down on the boardwalk. These are 2,600-pound machines with more power than most people know what to do with. Control yourself, and don't be a moron behind the wheel. Unlike hanging your arms out of the flume, screwing around on the track with Drivetech could get somebody besides you seriously hurt; listen to your instructions, and follow them.

Also keep in mind that Drivetech classes are somewhat nomadic; the school sets up at different tracks throughout the year. Visit Drivetech's Web site for a list of classes, along with when and where each of them is taking place; ask for your vacation time according to where you want to race, and choose your class on how much you want to spend. Racing on the super speedways (ovals longer than 1 mile) is a bit pricier than doing so on shorter ovals or road courses, but they also most approximate the professional racing experience. The school spends most of its time at the California Speedway in Fontana (a bigger track), although it also conducts

Suiting up and strapping in for a few laps at Drivetech. DRIVETECH RACING SCHOOL

classes at the Willow Springs road track in Rosamond and the ⅜-mile Cajon Speedway just outside San Diego.

Drivetech does offer go-kart classes in addition to its stock car program. Although this won't give you the whole NASCAR experience, many current drivers on the various professional circuits got their start driving the smaller, but still burningly fast, karts. These are especially good for younger drivers; Drivetech offers classes in ages eight and up and sixteen and up categories, as well as for thrill-seeking adults. It's a great way to introduce your kids to your speed fixation in a safe, supervised, yet killer fun environment. The karts are also quite a bit cheaper than the stock cars, and they're perfect if you want some speed without the larger financial commitment.

Drivetech is absolutely your best bet if you want to learn what it takes to be a stock car driver. Sign up for their two-day class, and you've got stories to tell for the rest of your life. Not many of us get to experience the thrill of flying through our thirtieth lap about to overtake the lead car; doing so is an experience you won't soon forget. Even if you're not necessarily into this sort of thing, chances are you know someone who is—Drivetech sells gift certificates, perfect if your favorite speed freak's birthday is coming up. Whether you're driving or watching, Drivetech has the velocity thing down, and they are happy to share the rush with you or anyone you know. Buckle up, put on your helmet, and drop the hammer.

Price: $500+

(Fall, Medium)

DRIVING DIRECTIONS

To California Speedway: Take I–10 East from Los Angeles to Fontana. Exit left at Cherry Avenue. Travel 1 mile, and the track is located on the left.

FOR MORE INFORMATION

DRIVETECH RACING SCHOOL
(800) 678–8864
www.drivetech.com

NATIONAL AUTO SPORT ASSOCIATION
www.nasaproracing.com

RECOMMENDED READING

Assael, Shaun. *Wide Open.* New York: Ballantine Books, 1999.

McCullough, Bob. *My Greatest Day in NASCAR: The Legends of Auto Racing Recount Their Greatest Moments.* New York: Griffin, 2001.

SLEEP CHEAP

Glen Helen Regional Park is located at the northern junction of Interstates 15 and 215. Call (909) 887-7540 for more information.

Horseback in the Santa Ynez Valley

Dude Ranching, California Style

The tough thing about cool history is that, usually, it's gone. Whether from time's passage or safety concerns, many adventures we read about that make us say "I wish I could try that!" are unavailable to us. After all, chances are you'll never stand on the deck of a wooden man-o-war with a hundred cannon as the sails whip around you. Ditto the old-time jousting match; sure, you might *see* two guys in plastic armor lance it out at Ye Olde Buffet in Vegas, but most likely you won't be up on that horse bearing down on your opponent at full gallop, steadying your shield for the inevitable blow.

If you decide to visit a California dude ranch, though, you'll get about as close to reliving history as you can. And what a history it is—the Old West reborn, cowboys and cattle drives, complete with a whole host of villains and heroes for make-believe. Want to be a good guy with a bad attitude? You're Wild Bill Hickok, who once killed a bear single-handedly with a 6-inch knife. Bad girl with some style? How about Pearl Hart, a pretty Canadian lass who used to rob stagecoaches on the Arizona frontier? Whatever your preference, taking to horseback and roaming the rugged California landscape is just the way to pay tribute to the spirit of your favorite cowpoke, outlaw, or gunslinger.

Dude ranches specialize in leisure, of course, and the ones mentioned here are far more than a stable with some cabins nearby. But they are also interested in taking their guests to another time and place, one where you might have to work a little harder than you do sitting by the pool. Ranches require that their patrons be in at least decent physical shape and weigh less than a small Volkswagen. Keep these factors in mind before you go, and if you're not in acceptable physical condition, hit the pavement running and reward yourself with a weekend spent roping dogies.

Of course, this *is* Southern California, where the air of celebrity and its corresponding luxury seem to pervade everything. Celebrities love adventure vacations, and in this part of the world you might find yourself riding next to someone you've seen riding on the big screen before. No ranch boasts more star power than the Alisal Guest Ranch and Resort, nestled in the gentle hills of the Santa Ynez Valley. Located 150 miles north of L.A., Alisal stands close enough to provide quick escape to city-bred mortals and screen legends alike; in 1949, for example, Clark Gable married Lady Ashley in the resort's library. Modern screen idols, including Jeff and Beau Bridges, Kevin Costner, John Travolta, Kurt Russell, and even Barbra Streisand, have also called Alisal their home on the range.

The facilities and amenities mirror the high-end clientele; golf and tennis compete with horseback riding, as do fishing, kayaking, and sailing on the ranch's one-hundred-acre spring-fed lake. Other amenities, such as fine dining (California fresh cuisine, complete with wonderful wine dinners throughout the year) and in-room massages, might make you forget where you are once the range rides are over. But Alisal doesn't skimp on the good stuff— twice-daily jaunts set out to challenge all riders, from greenhorns to leathery folks who spent their infancy on horseback. In the summertime, you can get in on Alisal's weekly rodeos, where guests can compete in various events, brand steers, or check out quick draw demonstrations and professional wranglers' skills. Alisal combines the special activities dude ranches have to offer with amazing extras, adding up to a trophy getaway you'll remember for many moons.

The price of a weekend escape at Alisal is more expensive, but well worth the splurge. Rates range upwards of $400 per night for a couple, with breakfast and dinner included. By the time you pay for riding (no, the horses do not eat old shoes and dirt) and the other per-use amenities, you're into the green pretty far. If your wallet isn't quite Hollywood material yet, the less expensive Circle

Bar B Guest Ranch, near Goleta, is another ranch just a quick trip from Los Angeles that delivers rip-roarin' cowpokin' for a bit less cash. The ranch, owned and operated by the Brown family for three generations, is just down the way from the late Ronald Reagan's Rancho del Cielo, again reminding would-be cowboys both of the area's rich history and the fact that Tinseltown's only a short jaunt toward the coast.

The Circle Bar B is small and cozy, with accommodations for only thirty-five people or so, but it still offers its share of first-class extras; the pool and spa give you a place to cool off after a hard ride, and a nighttime dinner theater, complete with family-style barbecue, runs through most of the year. The Circle Bar B also offers western riding instruction, so if you're up to it, ask your neighborhood rustler to show you how to throw a lasso. You'll pay for your riding here too, but the rates start out lower—about $225 per night.

Both of these ranches provide a number of chances to chow for free, often including food in the various riding activities they offer. Take half-day rides to take advantage both of the food and the extra time on horseback. Keep in mind, too, that both Alisal and the Circle Bar B are kid-friendly establishments and offer a ton of stuff to keep little hands and heads busy.

These ranches aren't places to visit if you're looking to save a few pennies, but they do present an amazing chance to both physically relive the past and enjoy the luxuries of the present. There's nothing quite like working out trail-beaten muscles in a beautiful Jacuzzi, or coming back from a long, dusty ride to enjoy an in-room massage and a glass of local merlot. Life's certainly rough on the range!

Price: $500+

(Fall, Medium)

DRIVING DIRECTIONS

To Alisal, from L.A.: Take Highway 405 north to Highway 101, going north through Oxnard, Ventura, and on through Santa Barbara toward Buellton. At Buellton, exit 101 (on the right) to Highway 246/Solvang-Lompoc. Turn right onto Highway 246, and follow the signs to Solvang. Once you have entered Solvang, proceed to the third stoplight, Alisal Road. Make a right turn onto Alisal Road, and proceed south for approximately 3 miles past the Alisal's golf courses and tennis courts to the main entrance. Make a left turn, and proceed to the building at the end of the lane.

To the Circle Bar B: Take Highway 101 to the Refugio State Beach exit. Drive 3.5 miles up the canyon on Refugio Road. Circle Bar B is adjacent to the late president Ronald Reagan's ranch, overlooking the Pacific.

FOR MORE INFORMATION

Outfitters

ALISAL GUEST RANCH AND RESORT
Solvang
(800) 425–4725 (4–ALISAL)
www.alisal.com

CIRCLE BAR B GUEST RANCH
Goleta
(805) 968–1113
www.circlebarb.com

Other

GUEST RANCHES OF NORTH AMERICA
www.guestranches.com

Riding the range with Alisal's talented equine "staff." ALISAL GUEST RANCH

RECOMMENDED READING

Erickson, John R., and Fay E. Ward. *The Cowboy at Work: All about His Job and How He Does It.* Norman: University of Oklahoma Press, 1987.

Morris, Michele. *The Cowboy Life: A Saddlebag Guide for Dudes, Tenderfeet, and Cow Punchers Everywhere.* New York: Fireside, 1993.

Starrs, Paul F. *Let the Cowboy Ride: Cattle Ranching in the American West (Creating the North American Landscape).* Baltimore: Johns Hopkins University Press, 2000.

California Skydiving

The Pacific, Bird's-eye Style

Ask most people, and they will tell you something's wrong with
anyone who would open an airplane door and jump out. They
could be right, if they consider adrenaline addiction a serious
medical condition.

If it is, the tens of thousands who have already tried the
adventure that is skydiving must suffer terribly from it. More than
a sport, skydiving is a lifestyle, a communal activity like scuba
diving or surfing—one that attracts people of all walks of life with
one thing: the kind of freedom you just can't find in cubicles or
workstations. To the skydiver, "flying" in a plane is akin to "swimming" in a boat; they live for the wind whipping past as they
plummet toward the earth during freefall, and the thrill of floating
on the air currents once their 'chutes are safely open. They live on
the edge, though not in danger—amid the elements, but not at
their mercy. If this world sounds like one in which you'd like to
live, give California skydiving a try, and join one of the world's
most exclusive, yet accommodating, clubs.

Among all the aerial sports you can try, skydiving seems on its
face to be the craziest. There's nearly a minute of freefall, for one
thing, along with the 120 mph you'll rack up during that period.
Then there's the off chance that the nylon foil packed tightly on
your back won't respond to frantic tugs on the rip cord.

California Skydiving

These factors are enough to scare away even the most serious extreme sports fanatics, even though their fears are mostly groundless. Today's parachutes are head and shoulders above their old school, round-'chute, G.I. Joe–style predecessors—they are lighter, stronger, more durable, and better maintained, thanks to strict repacking regulations that govern the skydiving community. (Reserve parachutes, for example—the backup to the main found on all modern 'chutes—have to be repacked by certified parachute riggers every 120 days, whether they've been used or not.) What's more, safety is concern numero uno at any reputable jump school you'll find; your instructors will make sure you are well taken care of in terms of instruction and equipment, and if you do what they tell you to do, you should be just fine.

Skydiving is not just for thrill junkies of the extreme sort, either. People upwards of eighty have enjoyed it, and tandem diving with experienced instructors makes the experience accessible to just about anyone with the will to take the plunge. There are some health and fitness considerations to keep in mind, though: Ideally, you should weigh less than 200 pounds, give or take, as many drop zones won't take you up if you tip much higher on the scales. You also want to be in very good physical shape if you're a heavier jumper, as a nimble 220 pounder is far safer and more able to land comfortably than a 220-pound couch potato. Age is also a factor—few if any drop zones will let you jump if you're under eighteen, so this is one activity for the grown-ups to try out solo.

Southern California presents a perfect set of conditions for skydivers, both inland and out on the coast. Perfect weather and sunny skies will keep your jump simple most days of the year, and the state's multitude of great drop zones and skydiving outfitters will give you the ability to choose just the right experience for you. The Santa Barbara–Los Angeles corridor is particularly thick with skydiving; you can find experienced, professional operations all over the place, though some certainly stand out for the quality of their facilities and instruction.

One of these major facilities is Perris Valley Skydiving School, which lays claim to the title "Largest Skydiving Center in North America." Founded in 1965, Perris has safety on the mind 24/7, and its tandem jumping record is flawless. (For those not in the know, tandem jumping is leaping with an instructor sharing your parachute, in order to keep track of your jump and make sure all goes well.) This site offers tons of extra perks as well—there's a full restaurant on-site, along with lodging facilities (bunk houses for visiting experienced jumpers, tent space for everyone else) and a wind tunnel for practicing your skydiving technique.

Another great choice is Skydive Santa Barbara, located in Lompoc. Jumping from here gives you the chance to check out one of the best views of coastal California you can possibly ask for—the one from 10,000 feet. The facility is at the Lompoc Airport, only ten minutes from the Pacific and forty-five minutes from Santa Barbara, where a host of nonaerial diversions await.

If your first tandem dive whets your appetite for more freefall, both Perris and Skydive Santa Barbara can help you get certified to jump all by yourself. The cost is higher and the time required stretches across a couple weekends, but the end result is well worth it—your ability to feel the rush alone and take responsibility for your own jumps. Ask the jump school you attend what their procedure is for advancing students to the "A" license—skydiving's first tier of expertise. With this rating, you'll be able to pack your own main 'chute, do basic group/formation jumps, and otherwise take care of yourself up there. Beyond that, other ratings await, each with a new set of requirements

Skydivers exiting plane. BRENT FINLEY

for you to fulfill as you live the dream. If you're so inclined, explore the options and make jumping a regular part of your exercise routine.

Don't shy away from challenging yourself up in the wild blue yonder. If you want to soar, to feel what the most modest birds feel on a daily basis, take that first step and let the wind hit you full in the face. Do so knowing that, as the people in planes buzz through the sky miles away, they have no idea what the meaning of *fly* really is.

Price: $200–$300

(depending on site and perks, e.g., photo or video of your jump)
(Fall, Medium)

DRIVING DIRECTIONS

Perris Valley Skydiving: From Los Angeles, take Highway 60 east to Highway 215 South, toward San Diego. Exit on D Street in Perris, then go 1 mile. Turn left on Eleventh Street, drive 2 blocks, and turn right on Goetz Road. The facility is on the left side 1 mile down; look for the large airplane wing at the entrance.

Skydive Santa Barbara: From Santa Barbara, head north on Highway 101. Just past the Gaviota tunnel, take the Highway 1 North exit. Take Highway 1 until it ends in Lompoc at the traffic light, and you will see a sign for Lompoc across the road on the left-hand side. Turn left. This road becomes Ocean; take this until you reach H Street, then make a right. Take H Street through town until you pass Central Avenue—the Lompoc Airport will appear on the left shortly after Central. Turn left into the airport on George Miller Drive, and park in the second parking area on your left.

FOR MORE INFORMATION

Outfitters

PERRIS VALLEY SKYDIVING SCHOOL
Perris
(800) 832–8818
www.skydiveperris.com

SKYDIVE SANTA BARBARA
Lompoc
(877) 652–5867
www.skydivesantabarbara.com

Other

UNITED STATES PARACHUTE ASSOCIATION
(703) 836–3495
www.uspa.org

RECOMMENDED READING

Poynter, Dan, and Mike Turoff. *Parachuting: The Skydiver's Handbook.* Santa Barbara, Calif.: Para Publishing, 1999.

SLEEP CHEAP

Perris Valley Skydiving School has accommodations about as cheap as they come: free. You can pitch a tent at the facility's Tent City as long as you don't bring any animals or let your kids run around unattended. There are showers and washing machines available, as well as the aforementioned on-site restaurant. Just think—if you take a few jumps over a couple days, you can put the amount you save in lodging toward jump fees. Not a bad deal at all! Call (800) 832–8818 for more information.

4WD Mojave

Silver Mines and Dusty Miles

Southern California is covered by a lot of backcountry desert, most of which you wouldn't want to be stuck in on foot. Every year, there are stories about poor lost hikers, desperate immigrants from Mexico, and unlucky drivers who get stuck in the desert and end up dehydrated and sick (or worse) when they are finally found. These folks tell stories of boiling daytime temperatures, freezing cold nights, and thirst unlike anything they've ever felt before, coupled with the sinking feeling that, on foot, the desert certainly has the upper hand in the struggle for survival.

Put yourself in a four-wheel-drive vehicle, however, and the odds change substantially. You've got a mobile shelter, a place to put your food and water, fast movement over large stretches of territory, and the means to cruise up and down the desert floor on your own terms, rather than nature's. Four wheeling is man's way of evening the score with the California desert, and no place lets you do so with such reckless abandon as the Mojave National Preserve, located between I–15 and I–40 in Southern California's desert badlands.

The preserve is named for the Mojave people, who lived on the land long before white people came looking for quick cash through trapping and mining. They were renowned as desert traders and traveled extensively throughout the Southwest. Relations between the Mojave and the white trappers and miners who settled nearby were strained, at best, and took a big turn for the worse when the

United States won the Mexican-American War and took possession of the Mojave's territory. Sadly, the Mojave suffered the typical Native American humiliations at the hands of the U.S. government—relocation, destruction of native culture, and economic exploitation. Today the remnants of the tribe live on the Fort Mojave Reservation, 33,000 acres in California, Arizona, and Nevada, and operate two casinos—an interesting place to end up, after such a long and difficult road.

Speaking of roads, the Mojave Preserve has a bunch of them, most made of nothing more than dirt and rocks. It is an offroader's paradise, where you can turn into the dirt and lose yourself for days. Here you'll find about 1,200 miles of desert roadway, with quality ranging from paved two-laners to rough, clearance-challenging four-wheel-drive routes. Contact one of the park's information centers for questions on specific roads, or pick up a map before you set out (the Baker and Needles information centers have detailed maps, as does the Hole-in-the-Wall Ranger Station on weekends). Keep in mind, too, that although storms don't hit the desert often, they cause a ruckus when they do. Good dirt roads can melt away after a hard rain, so be careful if you're out in the backcountry and get caught in one. Drive carefully, and you won't end up telling those terrible lost-in-the-desert stories mentioned above. Also keep in mind that you will be trekking through the desert—bring enough water for the trip and some extra for your radiator just in case.

The byway you'll want to seek out most bears the indigenous peoples' tribal name. The historic Mojave Road once connected military barracks in Wilmington, California, with Prescott, Arizona, the brand-new state capital at the time. It has seen Native American travelers, Spanish missionaries, fur-trapping adventurers, military excursions, and one camel expedition. Yes, only one—a guy named Edward Fitzgerald Beale came up with the bright idea and sent a ship to the Middle East to pick up some of the humped, spitting creatures. Being desert dwellers, they did work out quite nicely, but they scared the bejeezus out of every horse they passed. Needless to say, any animal that frightened horses in the mid-nineteenth century wasn't going to be very useful, given equestrian popularity; the experiment went nowhere, and Mojave travelers made do with less exotic locomotion.

Today, the road crosses the Mojave Preserve between Piute Springs in the east and Soda Dry Lake at the west, and presents a perfect route for enterprising offroaders. History is as big a part of this trip as driving; military outposts once stood at Soda Dry Lake, Marl Springs, Rock Springs, and Piute Springs, all prominent landmarks

Map showing 4WD Mojave area with locations including Baker, Kelbaker Rd., Lava Beds, Grotto Hills, Piute Range, Searchlight, Ivanpah Valley, Soda Dry Lake, Mid Hills, Woods Mountains, Mojave River Wash, Devil's Playground, Kelso Mountains, Kelso, Providence Mountains State Recreation Area, Devil's Playground Wash, Kelso Dunes, Blind Hills, Fenner, Granite Mountains, Clipper Valley, Essex, To Calico Ghost Town, To Barstow, To Needles. Highway markers 127, 15, 95, 40.

along the road today. In addition, you'll see plenty of the desert landscapes and wildlife that make this area so special from the naturalist's point of view. The fabled tarantula graces Mojave, complete with its legendary, and mostly phony, reputation—they are not poisonous to humans (unless you consider bees poisonous), nor are they aggressive in the least. Desert tortoises also populate the park, slowly inching around and requiring careful attention on your part as a driver. Watch the road for them, check under your vehicle before leaving any location (tortoises enjoy the shade), and never, ever touch one; the trauma causes them to empty their bladders, thus expelling fluids that, in this punishing environment, are necessary for survival.

If you're truly lucky and happen to find yourself in the preserve during the spring or fall, you may experience one of the area's rare (about once every ten years or so) big wildflower blooms. Although some Mojave plants bloom every year, it takes a special convergence to get a heavy, consistent bloom through all the area's plant life. The last big bloom was in fall 1997 and continued through to the spectacular spring of 1998; El Niño gave the area more rainfall than usual, and the temperatures stayed warmer longer in the fall and stayed cooler as spring rolled around. It was truly an impressive performance, and one to keep in mind next time you hear the desert's in for a lot of rain and mild temperatures.

Once you've cruised the Mojave and checked out the natural history it has to offer, you may want to get into more of the area's human heritage. Head down the highway to the Calico Ghost Town, and you'll get a close approximation of what an Old West boomtown might have looked like in its heyday. Calico started as a small silver mining camp in 1881, and it eventually became one of the West's most prosperous silver towns. In 1950 the town was completely restored; it was then donated to San Bernardino County and today has a reputation for being the best-restored "ghost town" in the United States (one-third of the town's buildings are original constructions).

In Calico you can watch gunfight shows, do some hiking, go horseback riding, even take a stagecoach ride. The Maggie Silver Mine is open for tours, and you might want to check out the Mystery Shack while you're in town. (What's in the Mystery Shack? Guess what—it's a mystery. Find out for yourself.) You can pan for gold too, and literally put yourself in the shoes of those who built Calico in the first place. Calico is a side trip well worth taking, one that will perfectly complement the dirt kicking you did in Mojave.

If you have a 4WD vehicle that you haven't used for anything tougher than picking up groceries, the Mojave Road is a perfect place to break it in. Just do your homework, be careful, and respect the creatures you see, and you'll have yourself a backcountry adventure you won't soon forget.

Price: $25–$100

(gas and food, mostly)

(Fall, Medium)

DRIVING DIRECTIONS

The Mojave National Preserve is easily reached via I–15 or I–40. It is located east of Barstow and west of Needles. There are six freeway exits that provide visitor access. Calico is also easy to reach; located midway between Los Angeles and Las Vegas, the town is 10 miles north of Barstow. Exit I–15 at Ghost Town Road.

In between off-road jaunts, give your feet a workout at Calico. ROBERT HOLMES/CALTOUR

FOR MORE INFORMATION

Outfitters/Providers

CALICO GHOST TOWN REGIONAL PARK
Yermo
(800) 862–2542 or (760) 254–2122
www.calicotown.com

MOJAVE NATIONAL PRESERVE
(760) 255–8800 (headquarters)
www.nps.gov/moja

Other

CALIFORNIA ASSOCIATION OF FOUR
WHEEL DRIVE CLUBS
(800) 494–3866
www.cal4wheel.com

TREAD LIGHTLY!
(organization dedicated to
responsible offroading)
www.treadlightly.org

RECOMMENDED READING

Casebier, Dennis. *The Mojave Road Guide.* Norco, Calif.: Tales of the
Mojave Road Publishing Co., 1987.

Foster, Lynne. *Adventuring in the California Desert: The Sierra Club
Travel Guide to the Great Basin, Mojave, and Colorado Desert Regions of
California.* San Francisco: Sierra Club Books, 1987.

McKinney, John, and Cheri Rae. *Mojave National Preserve: A Visitor's
Guide.* Santa Barbara, Calif.: Olympus Press, 1999.

SLEEP CHEAP

Your best bet for cheap lodging is to camp at the roadside as you
make your way through Mojave. Stick to areas that have been tradi-
tionally used for this purpose, as careless camping tramples vegetation and disturbs wildlife. Here are a few suggestions: Rainy Day
Mine Site, 15.2 miles south of Baker on Kelbaker Road, then 0.3 mile
northeast of the road to the Rainy Day Mine; Black Canyon Road, 5.2
miles south of Hole-in-the-Wall Ranger Station on the east side of
Black Canyon Road; Granite Pass, 6.1 miles north of I–40 on Kelbaker
Road, just north of Granite Pass, then west on one of several access
roads (campsites are located just north of the granite spires); and
Caruthers Canyon, 5.5 miles west of Ivanpah Road on New York
Mountains Road, then 1.5 to 2.7 miles north of New York Mountains
Road to campsites. You should use 4WD to access all of these sites,
and make sure you get your map from the park headquarters before
setting out. If you want to camp at Calico, there are camping hookups
available for a fee—call the Calico numbers above for information.

Air Combat U.S.A.

Into the Danger Zone

Air Combat U.S.A. operates out of Fullerton Municipal Airport a
few minutes outside L.A., and provides one of the most exhilarating
adventures you can think of: actual dogfight training in the cockpit
of high-performance combat planes. For the price of admission, you
can actually fly the aircraft and live out all your *Top Gun* fantasies.
It is not a simulation, a ground-bound ride in a virtual reality box;
we're talking about taking the controls, hitting the sky, and maneuvering through a series of dogfights while your instructor teaches
you the ins and outs of aerial combat.

The ideal situation is to take some of your friends out with you
and finally see who's the real ace among you as you battle it out in
the clouds. Air Combat gives you the controls and lets you test your
mettle as you fly; how much more fun is it to go to war against
people you know? Plan the trip now and start saving, because the
group experience is sure to stay with all of you long after the day
has passed. Think of it as a guaranteed great story for years from
now: "Remember when I blew you out of the sky?"

These ain't no Cessnas you'll be flying, either. Air Combat uses
SIAI Marchetti SF-260s, Italian-made planes still in use around the
world and popular in NATO countries as flight trainers. Although it is
a piston single plane (i.e., it has a propeller in the front, rather than
jet engines or props on the wings), its razor-thin, perfectly tapered
wings give it a jet's feel and maneuverability. The Marchetti is capable of climbing 1,800 feet per minute, cruising at over 200 mph, and
pushing 6 Gs during maneuvers—go up in one of these beasts, and

the jets aren't too far in front of you, in terms of combat ability.

You will get about as close as civilians can get to actual fighter combat, thanks to the Marchettis. Add to that a talented, willing, and able group of instructors, and you've got all the tools you'll need to come out of Air Combat a certified graduate in aerial butt kicking. All the pilots who will be teaching you have thousands of hours' flight experience along with a willingness to teach you all they can in the time they have. Listen to what they have to say, especially when you're in the air. You're safe, of course, but even safer thanks to these guys.

This adventure is not cheap, as you might imagine. However, if you go with the right program, you will be sure to get the most bang for your buck. All you want is a little sample, nothing too fancy? Go with the Phase I Basic Air Combat program, where you'll get some ground school and a minimum of six dogfights once you get into the air. Looking for a more comprehensive adventure? Then take on the all-day Fighter Lead-In Program, where you'll get intensive ground school in a variety of tactical areas and hit the air twice, once for practice on the fundamentals, and again to apply the gunsight tracking, defensive maneuvers, and attack techniques you learned on the ground. This is also your most economical option, as it entitles you to discounts later (see below), puts you in the air for the longest time, and comes complete with a leather flight jacket. Want the whole experience, but not all at one time? Air Combat offers phases II–IV if you complete the first and are still hungry for more. All the packages come with a video of your flight (or flights), so you can review what you did right and have your moment of glory preserved for posterity.

Air Combat goes to great lengths to accommodate people who want to continue adventuring after their initial pass. If you go with the Fighter Lead-In program, you will earn yourself a major's commission in the Air Combat U.S.A. Fighter Squadron, which lets you get much cheaper rates on future flights (the discount runs $300 to $400, pretty sweet if you're thinking about accepting more missions). And completing any initial program will make you eligible for Air Combat's Advanced Fighter Tactics course, which lets you explore your aircraft's (and your own) capabilities even further. This program covers combat between dissimilar aircraft, upper-level dogfighting strategies, and more tactical flight maneuvers. It is the most intense combat flight training available to civilians, and well worth it if you fancy yourself a devil-may-care aerial gunner.

That's what Air Combat U.S.A. offers those of us who will never see the inside of an actual Navy/Air Force jet: a chance to answer our own questions about whether we can do it, whether we have

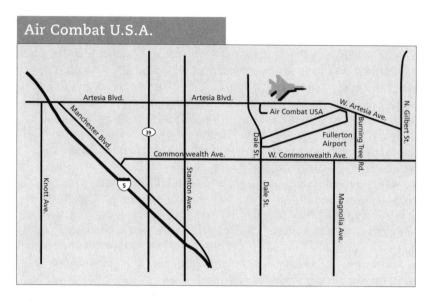

what it takes. Military flight training is both challenging and incredibly selective; Air Combat U.S.A. is challenging, but the doors are open much wider to allow all of us in. In fact, this adventure is actually a bit easier than you might think at first—most novices are surprised at their skills the first time off the tarmac and the quickness with which they pick up their dogfighting skills. It isn't every day we get to take the stick and fly our own combat missions; take advantage of this incredible opportunity to live out that dream. Jump into the cockpit and scream skyward, if you've got the guts.

Price: $900–$2000+

(Fall, Medium)

DRIVING DIRECTIONS

To Fullerton Municipal Airport: Take I–5 north from San Diego, south from L.A. Get off on the Artesia Boulevard/Knott Avenue exit, then head east on Artesia. Proceed to Dale Street, and turn right. You'll see the airport there.

FOR MORE INFORMATION

AIR COMBAT U.S.A.
Fullerton
(800) 522–7590
www.aircombatusa.com

RECOMMENDED READING

Franks, Norman. *Aircraft versus Aircraft: The Illustrated Story of Fighter Pilot Combat from 1914 to the Present Day.* London: Grub Street Press, 1999.

Shaw, Robert L. *Fighter Combat: Tactics and Maneuvering.* Annapolis, Md.: U.S. Naval Institute, 1988.

Spick, Mike. *Brassey's Modern Fighters: The Ultimate Guide to In-Flight Tactics, Technology, Weapons, and Equipment.* London: Brassey's, 2000.

SLEEP CHEAP

Featherly Canyon RV Park is located about 10 miles east of Fullerton off Highway 91, and though it is designated an RV area, tent camping is available for a reasonable price. The park offers natural riparian wilderness, wide-open spaces, and turf areas, as well as a variety of ornamental trees. The Santa Ana River also flows through the park, encouraging a variety of plant and animal life. There are a number of recreational opportunities, from campfire programs in summer evenings to guided nature walks, available through the wilderness area. Call the campground (operated by Canyon RV) at (714) 637–0210 for directions, fees, and reservations.

Flying for keeps with Air Combat U.S.A. AIR COMBAT U.S.A.

Diving the Channel Islands

No Gills Required

Your mask is secure . . . you've checked it twice. Duck-stepping your ungainly gear-loaded bulk to the edge, you take a quick look down. The landing area is clear. With one hand, you hold the mask against your face and the regulator in your mouth, while the other hand fumbles to keep track of your gauges. One more step and *whoosh*—the icy water consumes you, and you see nothing but bubbles; but your gear does what it was designed to do, and you pop safely to the surface. You look up at the divemaster and give the okay signal, smiling so hard the mouthpiece jumps from your jaw, though you don't mind at all.

Anyone who is in reasonable physical shape, can swim fairly well, and is not absolutely terrified of the water can learn to scuba dive. But be aware: Diving can get pretty taxing, no matter what kind of diver you become—getting a doctor's okay is recommended, and be sure you pay attention to the life-saving details you'll learn in your basic open water class, the first step in becoming a real-life diver. There are several certification agencies, but the Professional Association of Diving Instructors (PADI) is the largest and is globally recognized, which is important if you want to dive in exotic locales.

The quickest way to earn your basic open water certification card is in a weekend executive course. You'll spend the first weekend in the classroom and pool, learning and practicing the essential skills you'll need to dive safely in an open water environment. Even though it takes place in a pool, most people agree that their first experience breathing underwater is truly amazing and often hooks them for life. The average cost of this segment is $150 to $200, plus you will need your own mask, snorkel, fins, and booties. The dive shop providing the training will have all the other gear needed for the pool sessions.

The second weekend requires four open water certification dives out in the ocean or in a local lake. Safety is the primary concern on these jaunts; you will practice and be tested on the basic techniques you learned in class and in the pool, but now in a new, larger-scale environment. You won't complete these dives in just one day, so easy weekend trips are an inexpensive way to earn your C-card. Often, this phase is not included in the original certification cost, but most shops offer several trip options with varying prices. The Southern California coast is a perfect place to take this next step—sites like La Jolla Cove near San Diego are packed with scuba students every weekend. If you completed the classroom and pool work elsewhere and are soon heading to California for vacation, you can even receive a referral from your classroom instructor and complete your open water dives with another PADI professional. After getting certified, you can dive just about anywhere in the world and earn dozens of specialty ratings and advance certifications as you progress.

One of the more exciting weekend escapes in Southern California departs from Santa Barbara, where Truth Aquatics, considered one of the best live-aboard dive charters in the United States, takes dive enthusiasts to the Channel Islands. Truth Aquatics is a first-rate operation, where divers actually stay on one of three custom-built dive boats for the entire two- or three-day trip. The trips, which start around $400, include all air fills, gourmet meals, snacks, and beverages (except alcohol—BYOB). Compared to the cost of a hotel and dining out, the rates are very reasonable. A full-service line of high-quality rental equipment is also available, so even if you just show up in a swimsuit, you'll be set. If you have a limited time to get away, Truth Aquatics also offers various day trips for beginner through advanced divers. (Check their Web site for trip schedules.)

California's northern Channel Islands is one of the last relatively untouched and undeveloped areas in this part of the world. The islands are composed of eight land masses off the Southern

Diving the Channel Islands

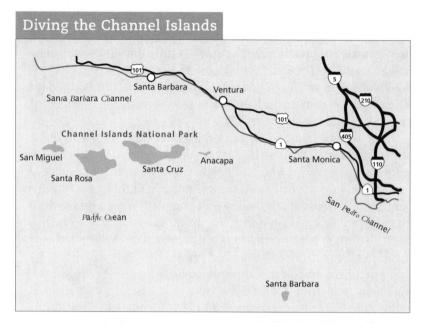

California coast and extend over 160 miles from Point Conception to San Diego. Santa Catalina Island is the most populated and best known; however, Truth Aquatics spends most of its time north, at the unspoiled paradise in and around the five islands of the National Park (San Miguel, Santa Rosa, Santa Cruz, Anacapa, and Santa Barbara). In addition to diving, sea kayaking and hiking are popular pastimes here, and for the adventurous, primitive camping is available too.

Diving the kelp forests around the Channel Islands is a truly world-class scuba experience. Neighbors to the mighty sequoias found ashore, California's kelp forests rule their ocean world. These giant plants can reach heights of more than 120 feet and help support an aquatic ecosystem that houses and protects upwards of 1,000 species of marine life. The Channel Islands offer more than just massive kelp forests, however; a variety of subsurface landscapes exist here, including rocky reefs covered with a vibrant and colorful assortment of anemones, starfish, hydrocoral, sponges, and much more. Plan a trip with Truth Aquatics in late September or October, when lobster hunting becomes a popular pastime for divers; "bugs" are common inhabitants of the rocky reef's fissures and crevices, and feasting on fresh lobster is always a treat. If spearfishing is your bag, Truth Aquatics also offers trips to large sand flats in pursuit of the mighty halibut, which, if you are lucky enough to get one, can be cleaned and grilled right on the boat.

With air compressors on board, you will get plenty of dive time whether you choose a one-day trip or a multiday live-aboard experience. On the ride back to the harbor, be sure to keep a watchful eye for migrating gray, blue, and humpback whales, as well as schools of dolphins who like to race the boat's wake. Of course, don't forget to bring plenty of film!

Some people know it right away when scuba gets into their soul: on that first jump into the water on their first certification dive, when the anticipation of a new activity—a new lifestyle, maybe—makes them giddy. For others, it happens later in that first dive, when they witness the wildlife below the surface: small schools of curious fish, the 500-pound giant black sea bass that begins to circle while they work on beginner skills, or playful sea lions trying to convince divers to join their fun. It often takes a little time to comprehend just how much there is to explore down there—and how much remains to be explored. After all, the planet is two-thirds water, and it's waiting for you.

Price: $500+
(Fall, Difficult)

DRIVING DIRECTIONS

Take the Castillo Street exit off Highway 101 in Santa Barbara. Go west toward the ocean. Take a right on Cabrillo Boulevard, and turn left on Harbor Way (this is the main harbor entrance). At the Naval Reserve Building, go left and into the parking lot. Go straight to the last parking lot to the Sea Landing Building. Be sure to validate your parking pass in the office.

FOR MORE INFORMATION

Outfitters

SEA LANDING DIVE CENTER
Santa Barbara
(805) 963–3564
www.divesantabarbara.com

TRUTH AQUATICS
Santa Barbara
(805) 962–1127
www.truthaquatics.com

Though spearfishing requires additional certification, there's nothing like freshly speared halibut, straight from the Pacific to the grill. RAY BANGS

Other

CHANNEL ISLANDS ACTIVITY AND INFO GUIDE
www.channel.islands.national-park.com

CHANNEL ISLANDS NATIONAL MARINE SANCTUARY
Santa Barbara
(805) 966–7107
www.cinms.nos.noaa.gov

CHANNEL ISLANDS NATIONAL PARK
Ventura
(805) 658–5730
Campground reservations: (800) 365–2267
www.nps.gov/chis

RECOMMENDED READING

Andersen, Cynthia, and Tim Hauf. *Channel Islands National Park.* Los Angeles: Tim Hauf Photography, 1996.

Krival, David. *Diving and Snorkeling Southern California and the Channel Islands.* Oakland: Lonely Planet Publications, 2001.

SLEEP CHEAP

You sleep right on the boat if you take a multiday charter with Truth Aquatics; however, after a one-day dive trip, many people choose to stay in the area and enjoy the relaxed yet active atmosphere of Santa Barbara. A great place to sleep cheap is Carpinteria State Beach, one of the most popular in California's state park system. Some campsites are only inches from the sandy beach, but whatever site you get, the mountain views and fresh ocean air make this the perfect place to stay on a budget. Keep in mind that this popular campground fills up quickly most of the year, so advance reservations are highly recommended (805–968–1033). To reach Carpinteria State Beach, take the Casitas Pass exit off Highway 101, and turn away from the mountains. At the end of Casitas Pass, turn right and drive until you reach Palm Street. Take a left, and the park will be at the end of Palm Street.

Survival School

Lost 'n' Bonkers

Your tent is gone, washed down the river you crossed this afternoon. It followed your food bag, cooking utensils, camp stove—and
the rest of your backpack, incidentally. All you're left with is your
trusty pocketknife, a jug of water, and your sleeping mat, which you
managed to yank out of your pack before the current swiped it.
Now the sun is taking its leave, the temperature is starting to drop,
and your stomach is growling. And did we mention your two hiking
partners got their packs washed 20 miles downriver, too?

"What are we going to do?" one of them asks in a trembling
voice.

You yawn, nonchalant and quite unconcerned. "Survive," you
say coolly as you bend down and start picking up kindling.

Of course, this situation is a little extreme; not many of us are
likely to lose everything we have during a backcountry expedition.
But accidents do happen, as do slips of the memory. Ever forget your
waterproof matches? Or the extra fuel tank for the camp stove? How
about the poles for your tent, or the food you just bought for the
trip, safe and cozy in the cabinets back home, six hours away? If
you've ever faced any of these dilemmas after four hours of hiking
away from conventional solutions, you know how nice it would be
to be able to handle them on your own. That is what survival school
is all about, and why it is an invaluable, educational adventure for
anyone who calls the outdoors their playground.

The purpose of survival school is to learn how to take care of yourself in the wild using the tools it already has available, rather than with things you might bring in with you. If you learn to build your own shelter, make your own cooking coals and fire, find the food you need, and make the utensils for eating that food, you find your pack gets a whole lot lighter. The more you know, the more pronounced this weight difference. If you make survival skills an integral part of your outdoor experience, rather than save them for when you're really in a bind, you'll travel a lot lighter, as well as keep your mental edges sharp for when you do need those skills. The name of the game in this adventure is to practice what you've learned and eventually become comfortable enough on your own in the wilderness to try a two-night survival escape.

California has some great places to practice your survival training, as it offers a multitude of environments and terrain to challenge hikers and campers. From mile-high mountains and snow to below-sea-level deserts, you could conceivably learn how to survive anywhere in the world by learning to survive in California's backcountry.

First things first: IF YOU ARE NOT ALREADY AN EXPERIENCED OUTDOORSPERSON, DO NOT HIT THE BACKCOUNTRY WITH ANYTHING LESS THAN WHAT YOU NEED. Minimalist camping can be extremely dangerous if you don't know where to go or what to do once you're there. And even if you are experienced, don't try this adventure solo or in areas lacking in natural resources (e.g., Death Valley and Joshua Tree). Don't try to go from run-of-the-mill to primitive all in one shot, either; a few survival classes do not make you the Last of the Mohicans.

So how do you lighten that heavy load and acquire the skills to compensate? Start gradually, by taking classes first. The skills you will learn vary by school and class, though they tend to fall into a few categories. Nature education—what bugs and plants are good to eat, as well as what to stay away from—is a big part of what you will learn anywhere. Primitive technology, where students learn to make snares, tools, and even bows and arrows, is another well-covered area. Rounding out the curriculum are wilderness living skills, like how to purify water, track in the wild, and build a fire. Learn everything there is to know in these three areas, and you're ready to take on the backcountry on its own terms, rather than the ones it dictates to you.

Good survival schools will teach you all of these areas, although different schools emphasize different things. They are, after all, quite versatile, and each has its own philosophy and priorities for outdoor learning. Some have a Native American style, focusing on living in harmony with the land and approaching survival from that vantage point. Others are more survival-based, providing the know-how should you be faced with an emergency. In these schools, you will see more tool construction, "what if?" scenarios, and wilderness medical training. Not far outside the L.A. area, Earth Skills has been teaching would-be survivalists for over seventeen years, in skills from tracking to traditional medicine. This school provides a nice balance between traditional, Native American skills and practical modern survival skills, making it a great place to start your outdoor survival odyssey.

Don't let the class be the end of your education, however. Step two in your quest for a lighter backpack is to practice, practice, practice until the skills you've learned are second nature. On every backcountry trip you take, concentrate on using your new abilities to do the things you used to do the "civilized" way. Instead of taking out your matches, make a bow and use friction to start your campfire. Or keep your tent in your pack, and build a lean-to out of ground timber. If you get into the habit of doing these things when you have the backup available just in case, you will start getting good enough at them to consider a trip without the safety net. And therein lies the true adventure.

First, make sure you're within a day's hike of some civilization if a real problem arises. Any of the national parks are good, as they generally provide facilities and ranger's stations throughout. State and regional parks might be OK too, but make sure you know what the ranger presence is like at the trailhead you're leaving from. Be sure to bring a reference book or two, just to verify that the little red berries you found are indeed edible. Then fill your backpack with everything you normally do, except for one *conspicuously missing item.* Maybe you're foraging for food, or building your own shelter, or cooking without a stove, bowl, plate or utensils. Whatever you decide, make sure you do so based on what you learned at your survival training, and make sure you have the mental tools and skills to provide for yourself sans the missing items. Spend your weekend living like that, and by the time it's done, you'll feel powerful, like you took on nature and won. Which, in fact, you have.

Price: $30–$250
(Fall, Difficult)

DRIVING DIRECTIONS

Earth Skills offers its classes throughout Southern California. Check out the class schedule, decide which one you'd like to attend, and ask for directions there.

FOR MORE INFORMATION

Outfitters

EARTH SKILLS
Frazier Park
(661) 245–0318
www.earthskills.org

Other

ANGELES NATIONAL FOREST
www.r5.fs.fed.us/angeles

Reading tracks in the sand. JIM LOWERY/EARTH SKILLS

District Ranger Stations

LITTLE TUJUNGA WORK CENTER
(818) 899–1900

LOS ANGELES RIVER RANGER DISTRICT
(818) 899–1900

MOUNT BALDY VISITOR CENTER
(909) 982–2829

SANTA CLARA/MOJAVE RIVER
RANGER DISTRICT
(661) 296–9710

VALYERMO WORK CENTER
(661) 944–2187

RECOMMENDED READING

U.S. Department of Defense. *U.S. Army Survival Manual.* Washington, D.C.: Apple Pie Publishers, 1992.

Nyerges, Christopher. *Guide to Wild Foods and Useful Plants.* Chicago: Chicago Review Press, 1999.

Wiseman, John. *The SAS Survival Handbook: How to Survive in the Wild, in Any Climate, on Land, or at Sea.* New York: Harper Collins, 1999.

SLEEP CHEAP

Earth Skills is near the Angeles National Forest, less than two hours north of Los Angeles. Numerous campgrounds are available. Call any of the ranger districts for more information. Most campgrounds do not require reservations and are very reasonably priced (averaging around $12 per site per night). There are both drive-in and hike-in campgrounds available, so if you want to try out some of your new survival skills away from civilization, put on your pack and light out. To reach the Buckhorn Campground and super-easy access to some of the San Gabriel Mountains' best hikes, head north from the 210 on Angeles Crest Highway for 36 miles. After hiking a little over a mile from the campground, you can find the Pacific Crest Trail, a 2,650-mile route stretching from Canada to Mexico. After pausing to dream about taking eight months off to through-hike the PCT, continue your day hike to your own private swimming hole at Cooper Canyon Falls. Call (818) 899–1900 for more information about Buckhorn Campground.

Learning to Kitesurf

Surfing Meets the Sky

If you've ever surfed before, you may have experienced the unmistakable rush of "air"—space between you and the water, or at least the illusion of it. You may have done it by accident, amazed that you kept your head and continued your run; or maybe you're an experienced, merciless wave mutilator, shredding your way up and over swells with reckless abandon.

If you're just a surfer, no matter who or how good you are, let us break the truth to you: You know nothing, absolutely *nothing* about real air. You may think you do, and within the narrow surfing definition, you very well might. But until you've strapped yourself and your surfboard to a giant mutant kite, hit the water with the kite soaring, and taken off from a crest into the wild blue, you're missing the true meaning of *air.*

This, friends, is kitesurfing, the newest extreme sport on the block. Back in 1999, there were only a few hundred kitesurfers in the world, launching themselves off the coasts of Hawaii, Australia, and California. Today, the sport has grown exponentially and is appealing to a new generation of multitasking oceanic adventurers. If you're ready for the world's newest beach challenge, give it a try.

We say "multitasking" because more than most sports, kitesurfing is a true merging of separate disciplines. Kitesurfers strap their feet to their boards on one end, indulging their inner surfer; on the other end, attached by body harnesses of various kinds, they fly huge kites to provide locomotion and lift. The result is a rare display of aerial and aquatic coordination. You have to keep yourself balanced on the board as the kite pulls you, then control yourself in the air after you launch, then come back down with the board in the right position. That launching, unlike the brief seconds of air you might catch surfing, skiing, or skateboarding, can last a good long time, and you might find yourself soaring 10 to 15 feet above the surface of the water, even as a beginner.

Interestingly enough, kiteboarding does not require big seas like surfing does, and some experienced kiteboarders even prefer calmer waters—they build up more speed and jump even higher when the water's flat. The reason: The huge kite, known as a traction kite, is capable of creating incredible force all by itself, even in somewhat tame winds. While a windsurfer is completely dependent on the force the wind generates in his sail, kitesurfers benefit from the additional energy, called apparent wind, created by the kite moving through the air. For kites, apparent wind is the vector sum of true wind (actual wind speed and direction) and the kite's velocity and direction. Don't be scared of the physics; suffice to say that once a kite is in the air, it pulls a lot harder than the force of the wind alone. Kitesurfers benefit from this additional force and harness it to fly up and off the surf.

A word of warning, however: This force is no joke. Kitesurfing is difficult, potentially dangerous, and not for just anybody. You have to take on this sport with a clear head, or you can get yourself or someone else seriously damaged. You should also have some staying power; though kitesurfing won't tax your cardiovascular system all that much, it is strenuous, and it requires a degree of physical fitness you don't get from sitting on the loveseat watching *Gilligan's Island* reruns. Have a little power of your own, and you'll be much better suited to counter and control the sail's. Also, *don't go out, buy a full rig, and head over to the nearest beach to try it out.* Seek instruction before trying to kiteboard, and save the world another moronic act resulting in broken bones, or worse.

The big problem in kitesurfing's early days was launching the kite from out in the water; no matter how good you get, you can't possibly avoid the kite touching the surf. Outfitters like Wipika and Concept Air came up with water-launchable designs in the 1980s, and the sport as we know it today was born. Now, even beginners can get a pretty good feel for kiteboarding without too many equipment concerns. The best way to get started is to take an introductory class from a licensed kitesurfing instructor and use the beginner's rig they provide. After that, if you feel the bug biting, you can go out and purchase your own gear. The kites run from around $600 new to well over $1,500 for high-end models, although you can cut your costs significantly by talking to your instructor and finding quality used gear in the area.

California's kitesurfing community is still forming, as the sport hasn't caught on with the masses until relatively recently. While the statewide kiteboarding association is not completely operational, there are a number of local organizations that can point you in the right direction for your lessons. West Coast Kiteboarding and Manta Wind and Water Sports both operate out of San Diego, a good place to head if you're going to be on that part of the coast. Both places have reasonable rates, and both will even give you private lessons for a bit more. At West Coast, your best bet financially is to take the half-day course that packs two lessons into one for about $300—big savings with maximum instruction still included. By the end of the afternoon, the goal is to have you in the water, pulling yourself behind a kite you launch yourself.

Xtreme Big Air, out of Shell Beach near San Luis Obispo, offers a five-hour beginner's class that costs a little more, but it provides the added benefit of an equipment discount when you're finished. Here, you can also learn more advanced moves, like how to increase your air, kiteboard upwind (a difficult task for beginners), and even how to be a kiteboarding instructor if you get truly obsessed. Xtreme also runs international trips—to locales where the beaches are white, the water is perfect, and the prices are extremely low. If you're interested in making an escape like this, give these guys a call—they are the real deal and will give you the knowledge you need even if you decide to stay domestic.

If you're looking for the newest sport to wow your friends with at the beach, look no further than the sky. Learn to kitesurf, and you'll be able to chuckle silently when your surfer buddies discuss their idea of "air," knowing that they haven't got a clue.

Price: $100–$250+

(Fall, Difficult)

DRIVING DIRECTIONS

Sometimes conditions dictate flying from different areas, so kitesurfers tend to move around a little. When you decide which outfitter you're going with, they will tell you on which beach to meet them.

FOR MORE INFORMATION

Outfitters

CAPTAIN KIRK'S KITEBOARDING
San Pedro, CA
(310) 833–3397
www.captainkirks.com

MALIBU KITESURFING
Malibu
(310) 430–5483
www.malibukitesurfing.net

Kitesurfing kites are mighty big—make sure you've got the muscle to handle them.
RAY BANGS

MANTA WIND AND WATER SPORTS
San Diego
(858) 270–7222
www.mantawatersports.com

WEST COAST KITEBOARDING
San Diego
(866) 994–5483
www.westcoastkiteboarding
.com

XTREME BIG AIR
Shell Beach
(805) 773–9200 or (805) 574–9200
www.xtremebigair.com

Other

**CALIFORNIA KITEBOARDING
ASSOCIATION**
www.calkite.org

**INTERNATIONAL KITEBOARDING
ORGANIZATION**
www.ikorg.com

RECOMMENDED READING

Pelham, David. *Kites.* New York: Overlook Press, 2000.

SLEEP CHEAP

If you're kitesurfing in San Diego, try camping the Sweetwater Regional Park in Bonita, just outside the city. It's beautiful, very cheap ($16 per site), and close to everything—you can be on the beach in about a half hour, or in Tijuana in about the same amount of time. Water and restrooms are available, as is electricity. Call (877) 565–3600 for reservations.

Winter

Malibu

Micro-California

Frank Sinatra sang about it. So did the Beach Boys. Even Courtney Love put in her two cents. It's inspired surf movies, served as the backdrop for TV shows of all kinds, even stood in for 1950s North Korea. It boasts 27 miles of California's most beautiful coastline and is one of the legitimate birthplaces of surfing as we know it.

Ladies and gentlemen, welcome to Malibu, jewel of the California coast, representative of the California lifestyle, and symbol for the all-around California weekend escape.

Think for a minute of every great activity and cultural resource California offers—the movie industry, Spanish missions, surf culture, hiking, biking, art museums, mellow beachcombing—and you will find it in the Malibu metro area. Not that you can really call it a metro area; even though it's a stone's throw from L.A., Malibu manages to capture a breezy, laid-back vibe you just don't get in California's more urbanized beach towns.

This is no accident, either. Malibu's city government has worked hard and carefully to preserve its rural character and atmosphere, even with all the tourism and attractions going on. The area's full-time population is only about 28,000, an amazing number considering the crush of people surrounding it. To you, the weekend escaper, all this means that only an hour outside of central L.A. lies a place where you can enjoy California's natural treasures without being stampeded by traffic, crowds, and concrete.

235

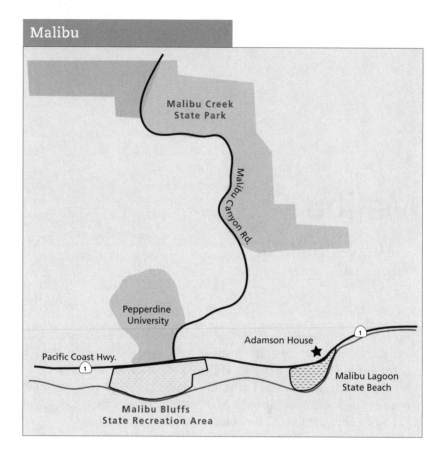

And what natural treasures they are. You can hit Surfrider Beach, right next to the Malibu Pier, and surf the same waves legendary beach denizens Frankie and Annette did back in the good ol' longboard days. It's not the place for your first ride—the waves are tough, and the pier is close—but if you're already familiar with surfing mechanics, you shouldn't have a problem.

Surfrider occupies only one part of Malibu Lagoon State Beach, however, and represents only one of the many activities available there. You can engage in pursuits both strenuous and sedentary, depending on what kind of mood overtakes you. Try bird-watching, for example, and check out the migratory species that rest here in the spring and fall en route to and from Alaska and Central America. After all, the area contains one of the California coast's few wetlands; Malibu Creek feeds them, though it often runs at only a trickle, and supplies enough water to support a small fishery and an ecosystem of tiny creatures that serve as bird food. Cultural history and nature tours dot the schedule according to season and allow visitors to observe monarch butterflies, learn about tide pools and their lives, even hunt the horizon for surfacing gray whales.

And let's not forget the area's history. A little west of Malibu Lagoon lie the million-dollar celebrity homes of Malibu Colony, a residential enclave started in 1928 as a hideaway for film stars. Residents have included Clara Bow, Ronald Colman, Bing Crosby, Jack Warner, Gary Cooper, and Gloria Swanson. (You might not know some of them, but back in the day they were the bee's knees.) Today, the Malibu area still plays host to a ton of Hollywood types, in large part because the city respects their privacy and leaves them alone. That being said, you can still satisfy your thirst for star power just by tooling around town and seeing who you see—just go with the local custom and don't harass anyone for autographs or pictures with Aunt Sally. Chances are you'll catch a glimpse of someone you last saw on a screen.

Even if you have a celebrity-free escape, however, you can still visit the places where your favorite actors played their parts. Malibu's most famous set is the *M*A*S*H* site, located in Malibu Creek State Park. Little-known fact: The famous mountain scene that opens the show wasn't Korea—it was the Malibu "skyline." You can reach the site via a short hike, and despite the fact that fire destroyed many of the sets, you'll still recognize the real estate Hawkeye Pierce and Hotlips Houlihan once occupied. In fact, Malibu Creek State Park's 4,000+ acres once belonged to 20th Century Fox Studios. Tons of movies and television shows were made in the park, including early Tarzan movies and *Planet of the Apes*, among others. The park is still a popular filming location, so you may find yourself looking in on some real Hollywood action if you happen to be moving through the park at the right time.

Even if you don't find Hollywood gold, you'll still see some beautiful country on the park's 30 miles of hiking and horseback trails. The paths run along streams, through oak and sycamore forests, an over chaparral-dense hillocks, so you'll get a nice idea of what would be growing in downtown L.A. if only there were no city there. If you're into mountain biking, the fire roads through and around Malibu Creek State Park hold some of California's most challenging routes.

Driving the PCH through Malibu first thing in the morning brings pure bliss.
CHRIS BECKER

Movie stars aren't the only people who have called Malibu home, either. Long before Tinseltown was making pictures, Chumash Indians lived on these shores and hunted in the forests nearby. You can check out Native American artifacts at the Malibu Lagoon Museum, located inside the park. You can also visit a living relic from another period in Malibu's history: the Adamson House, a national historic site and an architectural masterpiece to boot. Construction started in 1929, and the Adamson family didn't live in it full-time until 1937 (talk about your construction delays). In 1968, the state of California purchased the property, with hopes of restoring it and turning it into a museum or public site. Though nothing happened at the house immediately, the Malibu Lagoon Interpretive Association eventually formed in 1981 to determine what to do with it, and opened the house as a museum in 1983.

Adamson House is built in the Moorish-Spanish Colonial Revival style and showcases the famous tiles produced by Malibu Potteries between 1926 and 1932. One exhibit is a 20-foot-long tile replica of a Persian rug—truly beautiful, and an incredible representation of one art form by another. The pool, adjoining bathhouse, fountains, and walkways that run through the thirteen-acre beachfront grounds also are decorated with the famous tiles. (Los Angeles City Hall, incidentally, boasts twenty-three Malibu tile murals.) The house and its grounds will wow anyone with the slightest interest in history or architecture—if you've ever wondered how the other half lives, this is it in spades. Plus, you can't help but learn something new; at the very least you'll get to see examples of uniquely Californian artistry and wander the grounds remembering what brought people to the West Coast in the first place.

If you're anywhere near L.A., you've got no excuse. Hop on the freeway and head up to Malibu, where you'll get just about everything the great state of California has to give. And bring the longboard, if you're competent enough—the spirits of Surfrider will welcome you.

Price: $100–$250
(Winter, Easy)

DRIVING DIRECTIONS

Malibu is located on the Pacific Coast Highway northwest of Los Angeles. Just hop on that hallowed highway, drive north, and you'll find yourself there in no time.

FOR MORE INFORMATION

ADAMSON HOUSE
Malibu
(310) 456–8432
www.adamsonhouse.org

CITY OF MALIBU
Malibu
(310) 456–2489
www.ci.malibu.ca.us

MALIBU CHAMBER OF COMMERCE
Malibu
(310) 456–9025
www.malibu.org

MALIBU CREEK STATE PARK
Calabasas
(818) 880–0367
www.parks.ca.gov/default.asp?
page_id=614

MALIBU LAGOON STATE BEACH
Malibu
(818) 880–0350
www.parks.ca.gov/default
.asp?page_id=835

RECOMMENDED READING

Kohner, Frederick, Kathy Kohner Zuckerman, and Deanne Stillman. *Gidget*. New York: Berkeley Publishing Group, 2001.

McMillian, Elizabeth Jean. *Casa California: Spanish-Style Houses from Santa Barbara to San Clemente*. New York: Rizzoli Publications, 1996.

Rindge, Ronald L. *Ceramic Art of the Malibu Potteries, 1926–1932*. Seattle: University of Washington Press, 1994.

SLEEP CHEAP

Malibu Creek State Park's campground stays open year-round. Hiking trails and good fishing are nearby, and the price is definitely right ($13–$16 per site). The beach is only ten minutes away by car too. Showers are available for a small fee. For more information, call Malibu Creek State Park on the weekend between noon and 4:00 P.M. at (818) 880–0367.

Palm Springs Naturist Spa Getaway

Do Your Body Good

Most of the time, "treating yourself" means a candy bar after lunch or maybe a cocktail at Friday's happy hour. Very few of us take the time to truly reward ourselves for a job well done, whether that job is landing the next big account for the firm or an A on the last biology test. No, most people tend to settle for giving themselves little pats on the back, rather than the nice, gentle backrubs of self-appreciation we really deserve.

We also don't spend enough time being comfortable in our skins. Unfortunately, the superficial, TV supermodel culture we live in causes those of us with less-than-breathtakingly perfect bodies to consider ourselves somehow inferior to the gorgeous specimens that populate our popular entertainment. We avoid taking off the shirt at the beach until we're ready to run into the water, or wear the one-piece instead of the bikini to spare the world a glimpse of our midriffs. And in doing so, we slip a little farther from the idea that just being comfortable with who we are is far better than maintaining the image TV tells us to have.

We have searched long and hard and finally pulled the proverbial killing of two birds with one stone. Throw off your towels, and skimp on yourself no more. Take a trip to Palm Springs' Terra Cotta Inn, and find out just how good you can feel wearing little but your own wonderful skin.

Naturism, or nudism, is not the exotic activity some people think it is. In fact, most other countries have a fairly dismissive attitude about public nudity (under certain circumstances, of course). These folks have, fortunately for them, not picked up many of the misconceptions we Americans have about nudists and their philosophy. Nudist "colonies" are not immoral places depraved people go to have sex; nudists draw a strong line between nudity and sexuality. Naturists are also not supermodels from other planets—they are regular people like you, and part of naturism's appeal is that everybody starts from basically the same place. Nudism is not about emphasizing distinctions, but about taking them off, so to speak. The dictates of style, the economic divisions clothes can cause, and the fixation on body image are all things nudists try to eliminate in each other's company, instead embracing their bodies for what they are and, in turn, accepting others without judgment.

The Terra Cotta Inn, designed by modernist architect Albert Frey in 1960, is a perfect place to introduce yourself to this fun-loving community. In years past, the property was a celebrity retreat named the Monkey Tree, and played host to stars like Marilyn Monroe, Lucille Ball, and Spencer Tracy. Since 1995, owners Mary Clare and Tom Mulhall have created a comfortable environment that caters specifically to couples and gives both first timers and frequent nudists a chance to unwind. You can just sit around by the pool sipping cocktails or sample other activities; Palm Springs is a golfer's paradise, and Terra Cotta guests have access to many courses where the general public isn't allowed. You also have access to exclusive tennis facilities, if swinging the rackets is your game. (Clothing at the courses and courts is required, however.)

In addition, the Mulhalls have put together a first-rate spa facility, one that can finally provide that big reward you've been missing out on. If you've never had a spa treatment, you're in for a rare and unforgettable treat. People have been coming to Palm Springs for over one hundred years to cure what ails them, and today the key words are *relaxation and revitalization*. Spa personnel are professional pamperers, and the Terra Cotta's staff offers the full complement. Massage, facial treatments, pedicures, and manicures are all part of a standard spa retreat; if you want to really experiment, the spa also offers a wide range of additional services, from waxing and reflexology to more exotic treatments (salt glows, anyone?). Each of these things alone is a pleasure, but combine them all with two or three days of uninterrupted rest in beautiful Palm Springs and you have a revitalizing weekend that will leave you ready to take on your everyday routine times ten.

But don't let the Terra Cotta staff mesmerize you completely. Palm Springs is a fascinating town, one worthy of its very own book of weekend escapes. Because it is so close to the San Andreas Fault, Palm Springs sees more earthquakes over 7.0 on the Richter scale than just about anyplace else. Luckily, the town is so earthquake-proof, you might not even notice if a shaker rolls through; the highest building is only eight stories, and most every structure sits on a bed of ball bearings to allow rolling rather than collapsing. In the golden age of radio, Palm Springs hosted the top three radio shows in America; that celebrity culture continued to blossom in the 1950s and '60s, when Frank Sinatra and Bob Hope helped put Palm Springs on celebrity watchers' maps. Today, no matter how much time you spend in the city, it probably won't be enough to see everything you want to see. Have no fear—you may return on your next vacation.

If you're into incredible desert scenery, you'll find desert jeep tours (see Escape 2), helicopter tours, bike tours, and just about anything else you can think of. You can try ballooning, or stay in the city and take one of its many celebrity-focused tours. (Don't be afraid to pick Tom's brain about what's going on—he'll be glad to point you toward the best tour companies and outfitters.) If you're looking to live the good life, the Terra Cotta proprietors were restaurant critics in their previous professional lives. Just tell them what cuisine you're looking for, and they can tell you where to find it.

While there are a ton of other spas in Palm Springs, and even a few naturist facilities, none presents the balance of fun, value, and services that the Terra Cotta does. And you won't find a friendlier place to experiment with nudism anywhere; come with big smiles, ready to enjoy your natural state, and the Mulhalls will be happy to have you. Come with frowns or attitude, and they'll smile, turn you right around, and show you the door.

You may think it's a little crazy, but it works. The Terra Cotta is one of the top adventures in Palm Springs, one with something for sports buffs, spa bunnies, and lounge lizards alike. Everyone, that is, who wants to know themselves a little better and boost their self-esteem to boot. The more comfortable you are without your clothes, the better you'll feel with them; and when you are back in your workaday world, you'll be able to walk into the office comfortable in the fact that, underneath the power suits, your boss, his or her boss, and the one above them all are just as naked as you are.

Price: $200+ for two

(Winter, Easy)

DRIVING DIRECTIONS

From Los Angeles: Take I–10 East, exiting at Route 111 Palm Springs. As you come into town, the first light you see will be Tramway Station. The second light is Racquet Club Road. Turn left on Racquet Club Road. Look at your odometer and go exactly 1.75 miles (The Terra Cotta Inn has a sign that is tough to see from the street). The inn is the first building on the left past the children's day care center—2388 East Racquet Club Road.

From Arizona: Take I–10 West, exiting at Date Palm Drive in Cathedral City (Bob Hope is the previous exit). Turn left off the exit ramp onto Date Palm. The first light you will see is Vista Chino; turn right there. In about 3 miles you will see a light at Farrell Road. Turn right on Farrell. Continue past Via Escuela, as the road makes a very sharp turn left and becomes Racquet Club Road. There are a series of yellow arrows on the right that indicate the road is turning. At the end of the last arrow on your right, right on the curve, you'll see The Terra Cotta Inn.

FOR MORE INFORMATION

THE TERRA COTTA INN
Palm Springs
(800) 786–6938
www.sunnyfun.com

AMERICAN ASSOCIATION FOR NUDE RECREATION
(800) 879–6833
www.aanr.com

RECOMMENDED READING

Ableman, Paul. *Beyond Nakedness*. Topanga, Calif.: Elysium Growth Press, 1996.

Churchwell, Mary Jo. *Palm Springs: The Landscape, the History, the Lore*. Palm Springs, Calif.: Ironwood Editions, 2001.

Lange, Ed. *Family Naturism in America: A Nudist Pictorial Classic*. Newfoundland, N.J.: Events Unlimited, 1990.

SLEEP CHEAP

If you happen to be camping or lodging cheap in Palm Springs, you can still sunbathe without tan lines at the Terra Cotta for $25 per couple.

The Salton Sea

California's Strangest Treasure

Yellowstone . . . the Grand Canyon . . . the Everglades . . .
Consider any of the country's most famous natural sites, and
you'll soon come to a realization: Human development is almost
always close by. Even when nature, in all her majesty, creates
things of incredible beauty and power, the human race always
seems close behind, developing the tourist structure that will handle the flow of people coming to see the amazing sights. In most
all these cases, the human addition is much newer than the natural wonder and stands in awe of its timelessness as well as its
size, beauty, or power. Only seldom does humanity help to build
in the natural world; most often, unfortunately, our role is one of
destruction and decimation of environments and species. At best,
it is conservation—maintaining the ecological status quo.
However, creation that impacts the environment positively rather
than negatively is usually beyond our scope.

California's Salton Sea stands as a rare example of humanity's occasional ability to inadvertently help the natural world,
rather than hurt it. The Salton Sea, not even a century old, is one
of the nation's strangest, most rewarding natural sites, and as
such makes a perfect weekend escape for those willing to explore
it and reap its amazing rewards.

The Salton Sea is an inland saline lake, some 25 percent saltier
than the ocean. It sits in the Salton Basin, a remnant of prehistoric

Lake Cahuilla, one of the largest lakes in the planet's history. That body of water covered over 2,000 square miles (six times the area of the Salton Sea), stretched 100 miles by 35 miles, and filled the entire Salton Basin before drying up eons ago. The current sea formed between 1905 and 1907, when the Colorado River burst through irrigation controls south of Yuma, Arizona, and flooded the Salton Basin for a year and a half. The water flow, almost the entire volume of the Colorado River, put whole communities underwater, and also put the main line of the Southern Pacific Railroad beneath its surface. By the time this break was finally patched up, the present-day Salton Sea was covering 400 square miles of previously bone-dry basin. Today it is California's largest lake, as well as a strange oasis in the middle of the driest desert land in the state. There are activities galore, immense animal populations, and great camping, not to mention some bizarre sights to see. (Ever seen a vineyard in the middle of the desert?)

As happens so much when manmade phenomena affect the natural world, the Salton Sea is the subject of much controversy. Most of it stems from the fact that the sea is misunderstood by nearly everyone; fish and bird poisonings, unsafe salt and chemical levels, and the idea that the sea is destined to "die" in the next decade are persistent rumors that, while they are based in certain facts and possibilities, are by no means proof of some sinister, deadly quality of the sea itself. Most of the real problems the sea does face have to do with rapidly increasing salt and nutrient levels, and the fact that if these levels go much higher, the fish there won't be able to reproduce anymore. That happens, and the whole ecosystem is in trouble. The Salton Sea is not terribly polluted, nor is it unsafe for contact; indeed, hundreds of thousands of people go to the sea each year to swim and otherwise utilize it. But natural processes have taken their toll and will continue to do so unless something is done.

Unfortunately, this book doesn't give us enough room to properly deal with the sea's colorful political, ecological, and economic history and future. Suffice to say that you shouldn't be deterred from going there by any strange rumors you may hear. It is safe, lots of fun, and not going anywhere anytime soon. We definitely encourage you to check out the resources at the end of this chapter to learn more, and to make your own decisions about the Salton Sea.

But read all that stuff on the way to the sea itself, so you can see for yourself what all the fuss is about. The Salton Sea has

To Palm Springs (Indio)

Salton Sea State Recreation Area

Salton Sea Beach

Salton City

To Anza-Borrego State Park

Salton Sea NWR Headquarters

Salton Sea National Wildlife Refuge

evolved into a recreation area of incredible resources and has to be experienced to be believed. First things first: All you fish folks need to know that the Salton Sea is probably the most productive fishery in California. People catch more fish per angler hour in the Salton Sea than anywhere else in the state. And if that's not enough, get this: A 2002 study suggests that the sea might just be the most productive in the world. That's right—we're talking the whole planet here. You'll be able to catch orange mouth corvina, which can weigh upwards of 30 pounds and measure 42 inches; tilapia, a prolific breeder and nice little game fish; and gulf croaker, an important food fish that keeps the corvina population up and running. There have been striped bass caught, along with mullet and shad. Tales of strange fish taken from the sea are abundant too, and there's even a rumor that someone caught an octopus once; in the late 1990s the recreation area staff claimed to have pulled a crab out near Varner Harbor. All of these fish (along with the tilapia, corvina, and croaker) were introduced, but they have thrived in the Salton Sea, thanks to abundant food; the water in the sea is largely agricultural runoff, and is thus packed with minerals and nutrients.

This biological abundance causes the thing people misunderstand most often about the sea: the smell. Normally, it's the same as the ocean, vaguely reminiscent of decaying vegetation and salt. Sometimes, though, dying algal blooms in the water cause a sulfuric smell as microorganisms move in to "digest" the dying algae. There's no way around the fact that this is not a pleasant odor, but by avoiding the seasons during which it happens most frequently (late summer and early spring), you can minimize your chances of experiencing it. And don't get spooked by visions of watering eyes, a funny taste in your mouth, or searing pain in your nostrils; the Pacific smells funny sometimes too, and people pay millions to live right on top of it. Think of beautiful Venice, Italy, in the summer, and you see what we mean.

Birders have almost as much to do as anglers here. The Salton Sea is one of the most vital migration stopping points in California, and as 90 percent of the state's inland wetlands have disappeared, it is an important resting place for millions of birds on their long haul. Bird-watching, as a result, is one of the biggest pastimes at the Salton Sea State Recreation Area, and people come from around the country to fill their birding journals with rare avians. You can see migrating birds as early as October, but by January they are filling the sky and enjoying the lake as much as the people watching them. Head to Salton with your camera anytime from November to May, and you won't be disappointed with the shots you take.

The bird and fish populations are symbolic of the Salton Sea's importance, regardless of its origins or problems; the birds come here because they need a body of water to rest at, and the sea fits the bill. The fish, though introduced, have thrived, and should continue to do so with a little help from their human friends. As for us, we get to enjoy the sea on our boats and Jet Skis, with our fishing rods, binoculars, and hiking boots. Learn about and enjoy the Salton Sea, and you'll feel like you're one of the few who truly understand this gigantic, complicated, ultimately beautiful natural resource.

Price: $20–$40

(Winter, Easy)

The Salton Sea area is frozen in time; taking in the still-standing buildings is a great way to spend an afternoon. CHRIS BECKER

DRIVING DIRECTIONS

The Salton Sea State Recreation Area is 30 miles south of Indio (near I–10), on Highway 111. It is about three hours from both Los Angeles and San Diego, and only a short distance from Palm Springs via I–10.

FOR MORE INFORMATION

SALTON SEA AUTHORITY
(760) 564–4888
www.saltonsea.ca.gov

SALTON SEA STATE RECREATION AREA
North Shore
(760) 393–3052
www.saltonsea.statepark.org

SALTON SEA INTERNATIONAL BIRD FESTIVAL
www.newriverwetlands.com/Saltonsea.html

RECOMMENDED READING

DeBuys, William. *Salt Dreams: Land and Water in Low-Down California*. Albuquerque: University of New Mexico Press, 1999.

Local Birds of the Salton Sea. Woodside, Calif.: Local Birds, 1997.

Pepper, Choral. *Desert Lore of Southern California*. El Cajon, Calif.: Sunbelt Publications, 1998.

SLEEP CHEAP

The Salton Sea State Recreation Area has over 1,400 campsites in five campgrounds. Three campgrounds are primitive, two are developed, and one offers full hookups for RV campers. Camping is best from October through May, as temperatures can get extremely hot in the summer (though the park is still open then). Reservations are not taken for the primitive campgrounds, but you should get them if you're planning to stay in the hookup area. Call (800) 444–7275 for reservations.

SeaWorld and Aquarium of the Pacific

Welcome Underwater

Southern California rises from the Pacific, the largest ocean in the world. The abundance of sea life here is extraordinary—whether you fish or kayak, scuba dive or snorkel, or even just walk the beach's fringe with waves lapping foam onto your toes, you are certain to run into interesting marine life. Plants galore, fish and crabs, birds and bugs, and even larger mammals like sea lions and dolphins are sure to show themselves on occasion. However, even if you don't step one foot into the saltwater, the sea still surrounds life in much of Southern California.

The Pacific Ocean's scenery alone may take top honors, but the Pacific gives us a lot more than beautiful sunsets. Ocean kelp is used to manufacture cosmetics, human food, animal food, fertilizers, and nutritional supplements. Restaurants serve countless varieties of cuisine from the sea, while shipping and industry find much use in the ocean as well. The familiar salty breeze offers its palette of smells, helps keep things cool, and instigates rust on cars found parked near the ocean. The sea somehow gets into everything. Vacationers and residents will find incredibly fun and interesting great weekend escapes by venturing to one of Southern California's marine educational facilities.

One excellent option is to head to Long Beach and spend a day at the Aquarium of the Pacific. Featuring over 12,000 animals representing more than 550 species, this facility's primary purpose is to educate and enlighten visitors about the coastal regions and underwater world of the Pacific Ocean. Three main exhibit galleries showcase the three major regions of the Pacific Ocean, including the local waters of Southern California and Baja, the cold ocean of the Northern Pacific, and the warm clear sea of the Tropical Pacific. The aquarium is large enough for hours and hours of wandering—you'll need some time to check out the numerous hands-on exhibits. The stingray tanks are always a favorite with the kids, while in the outside aviary, hand-feeding the small colorful lorikeets is fun for everyone.

A popular highlight of the Aquarium of the Pacific is a large exhibit called Shark Lagoon, which features more than 150 sharks and interactive exhibits showcasing information about shark species, size, teeth, life cycle, and their importance in the ocean's food chain. Standing around the shallow shark pools, visitors can gently touch the zebra, epaulette, bamboo, and nurse sharks swimming by. Don't worry about losing any fingers here—these sharks are very docile. In other tanks, however, daily feedings and presentations showcase the beautiful power and ferocious grace of the tiger, whitetip, and sandbar sharks. As the feeding frenzy ensues, you'll see exactly why the aquarium doesn't let you wiggle your hands around in this tank.

A great supplement to the basic Aquarium of the Pacific ticket, the Ocean Experience is a fun and instructional excursion out into the harbor on the 90-foot *Conqueror* research vessel. On this ninety-minute tour, your guide gives an interesting presentation, then everyone heads out onto the boat's stern deck for the hands-on portion of the cruise. Everybody is excited when the Peterson's grab and plankton tow are opened, and you see the catch. You divide the different bounties into different bins, and use ID flip cards to identify the different species. Finally, the boat ride back gives you plenty of opportunity for scenic gazing toward Long Beach's shore. Although well suited for kids, adults are sure to have fun too. Behind-the-scenes tours, field trips, more programs for children, and other optional excursions are offered as well, even a sleepover that highlights some species that are most active at night.

The Aquarium of the Pacific is especially interesting to scuba divers, as they can start putting names to all the underwater life they have seen during Southern California dive trips. A trip to the aquarium is also the perfect instructional primer before rounding out your weekend on Catalina Island, where you can experience more of the underwater world firsthand by snorkeling, diving, or taking a

SeaWorld and Aquarium

To Long Beach and Aquarium of the Pacific

SeaWorld

submarine tour. Ferries to Catalina Island depart various ports in Long Beach regularly.

If you prefer, you can hang out in Long Beach and take in the sights. The *Queen Mary* is docked permanently and is always great for dinner and dancing; be sure to ask about a package ticket with the aquarium to save a few bucks. Of course, there are plenty of other wonderful distractions in the area. Thanks to continued renovation and upkeep, Long Beach has become one of the more interesting cities in the Los Angeles area, not to mention one of Southern California's trendiest nightlife spots.

If you really have the itch to learn more about the ocean (always a good itch to have), you could even combine your visit to the Aquarium of the Pacific with a stop at Southern California's most famous marine park, SeaWorld San Diego. Just ten minutes north of downtown San Diego, SeaWorld is famous for its incredible lineup of animal encounters, thrill rides, amazing shows, and educational programs. The park has been in operation since 1964, and since then, over 100 million guests have enjoyed countless once-in-a-lifetime fun experiences.

SeaWorld continues to develop its programs and enhance its facilities, making the park better every year. One recently added exhibit is the R. L. Stine Haunted Lighthouse, an exhilarating 4-D film that combines state-of-the-art visual effects and multisensory surprises. Another exciting recent addition is the completion of the Adventure Camp San Diego Campus, which will allow SeaWorld to accommodate five times as many students in its educational camp program. Since opening, SeaWorld has played an instrumental part in enhancing the ocean awareness and education of children, while offering a lot of fun at the same time.

Of course, SeaWorld is most famous for killer whales, namely Shamu, who performs brilliantly for cheering audiences in an often-packed stadium that seats 5,500 people. Go ahead and sit close— Shamu will welcome you personally with a whale-sized bellyflop. Although these orcas certainly give a great act, that is only one tid-bit of SeaWorld's smorgasbord of shows. Fools with Tools is a hilari-ous program featuring California sea lions Clyde and Seamore, along with several mischievous otters, all vying for the spotlight, to be the star of the show and to get the most applause. Another of SeaWorld's most popular attractions starts with visitors boarding a simulated jet helicopter off to the Wild Arctic exhibit, where beluga whales, polar bears, walruses, and other arctic animals await. The Penguin Encounter is an entertaining, close-up look at over 350 penguins featuring six Antarctic and sub-Antarctic species, as they waddle and frolic about the 25°F snow-filled habitat. SeaWorld has something for everyone.

If you're looking for splashy thrills, try Shipwreck Rapids, where you and eight other castaways jump into a huge inner tube to brave roaring rapids, raging waterfalls, a near collision, a classic dark tun-nel of terror, and much more excitement—if anything, it's a great way to cool off if you don't mind getting drenched. Other shows and exhibits include the Dolphin Discovery, the Shark Encounter, several aquariums, and additional educational opportunities. SeaWorld Sleepovers are popular overnight excursions for children in second through eighth grades.

SeaWorld San Diego also offers numerous programs designed to educate visitors about environmental concerns related to marine wildlife and ecology. The Manatee Rescue is one of only three U.S. locations outside Florida hosting several rescued and rehabilitated endangered West Indian manatees; underwater viewing provides an interesting perspective of the sea cows as they swim, eat, and interact.

Shamu and his buddies get vertical. SEAWORLD SAN DIEGO

Likewise, SeaWorld's Oiled Wildlife Care Center is a wonderful example of environmental stewardship, as the facility is used not only for crisis oil spill response, but also for housing ill and injured animals in SeaWorld's Animal Rescue and Rehabilitation Program. Of course, there are numerous behind-the-scenes opportunities available if you desire, as well as many other ways to volunteer and get involved.

With all that the Aquarium of the Pacific and SeaWorld San Diego offer, plan for more than one great weekend escape to experience the most you can. However, even a daytrip is a perfect way to have a lot of fun while doing some good. We are all stewards of the sea, and therefore we all have to play a hand in preserving it. The best first step is education. So, with your ticket purchase, feel good about supporting these marine parks and all that they do. The more you know about our oceans, the more you will want to protect them.

Price: $50–$250

(Winter, Easy)

DRIVING DIRECTIONS

To reach the Aquarium of the Pacific, from Los Angeles take the 405 freeway south to the 710 freeway south. Follow the signs to downtown Long Beach and the aquarium exit. The aquarium exit leads right to the aquarium parking lot. In San Diego, to reach SeaWorld from I–8, exit on I–5 North, exit at SeaWorld Drive, and turn west, following the signs toward the park entrance.

FOR MORE INFORMATION

AQUARIUM OF THE PACIFIC
Long Beach
(562) 590–3100
www.aquariumofpacific.org

LONG BEACH CONVENTION AND VISITORS BUREAU
(800) 452–7829
www.visitlongbeach.com

SEAWORLD
San Diego
www.seaworld.com
www.shamu.com

SAN DIEGO CONVENTION AND VISITORS BUREAU
(619) 236–1212
www.sandiego.org

RECOMMENDED READING

Love, Milton. *Probably More Than You Want to Know about the Fishes of the Pacific Coast*. Santa Barbara, Calif.: Really Big Press, 2003.

Ricketts, Edward, and Jack Calvin. *Between Pacific Tides*. Palo Alto, Calif.: Stanford University Press, 1992.

Rosenfeld, Anne, and Robert Paine. *The Intertidal Wilderness: A Photographic Journey through Pacific Coast Tidepools*. Berkeley: University of California Press, 2002.

SLEEP CHEAP

The stretch of coast between San Diego and Long Beach has a number of excellent campgrounds; however, another way to sleep cheap is to try out a hostel, especially if you do not want to rough it quite so much or cannot bring camping gear with you. Hostels are basically just inexpensive hotels, offering clean, safe, comfortable, and environmentally sensitive lodging for budget-minded travelers, small groups, and families at a considerable discount over regular hotel rates.

San Diego has two Hostelling International (HI) hostels. HI-Point Loma is located just minutes from SeaWorld and Mission Bay Park. The outdoor courtyard at the hostel is a very friendly and comfortable place to enjoy San Diego's year-round sunshine, perhaps play Ping-Pong or chitchat with new friends, or just relax with a good book. A short walk finds you at the People's Market, a co-op grocery that specializes in hormone-free, organic, and vegetarian food, perfect to bring back to HI-Point Loma's very functional hostel kitchen. Call (619) 223-4778 for current rates and reservations.

HI-San Diego is located only a short ride from SeaWorld in the heart of the historic Gaslamp Quarter. Here visitors will find 16 blocks of cafes and restaurants, art galleries and boutiques, bars and nightclubs, movie theaters, and other attractions. This fun and chic section of downtown San Diego is also famous for its seasonal celebrations such as Mardi Gras, Street Scene, Halloween, and New Year's Eve. The HI-San Diego Hostel offers a free breakfast, plus dining and lounge areas to kick back in after a long day of sightseeing. Call (619) 525-1531 for current rates and reservations.

For more information on Hostelling International, including hostels in other parts of California, please visit www.hiayh.org.

Touring Hearst Castle

Your Weekend of Dreams

Technology zips along faster every second. These days, you can get headlines, stock tickers, game scores, and even e-mail on your cell phone. The rapid advances in technology have allowed easier access to more news sources, as well as presented more platforms for more news providers. But take yourself back less than a hundred years, before this overinformed age, when there wasn't a television in almost every room and when everyone didn't have computer access, or even computers. As far as "the media" went, newspapers and magazines were CNN, Fox, and Yahoo all rolled up in one.

Next, imagine that one person owned and controlled twenty-eight major newspapers and eighteen magazines, along with several radio stations and movie companies. Needless to say, with this more than significant chunk of media, this man would have been incredibly rich and powerful, so much so that a young filmmaker named Orson Welles tried to dethrone him in what is generally considered the best American movie ever, *Citizen Kane*. Some say that this man was the single most influential person in early-twentieth-century America, even going so far as to start the Spanish-American War in order to provide some paper-selling news. Think about all that, and then take a trip to the man's actual digs—a real, honest-to-goodness castle.

As you approach San Simeon, look for zebras grazing alongside cattle in the pastures. (If anything, having a private zoo surely says something about the level of wealth we're talking about.) Keep

Touring Hearst Castle

Big Sur

5

101

198

99

1

San Simeon
(Hearst Castle)

46

San Luis Obispo

5

166

101

1

Santa Barbara

To Los Angeles

scanning the hilly horizon, and you're bound to see the shimmering
Moorish castle resting regally atop La Cuesta Encantada (The
Enchanted Hill). In 1922, media magnate William Randolph Hearst,
known as "The Chief," broke ground for the "little something" he
wanted built on his land by the sea. Architect Julia Morgan and an
army of laborers toiled nearly twenty-eight years to create Hearst
Castle, California's most royal residence.

Today, Hearst Castle is a State Historical Monument, run by the
California Park Service. In the span of a great weekend escape, you
can actually step through this romantic history and get a glimpse of
an opulent lifestyle that has lived on in many ways well past
Hearst's heyday. Unfortunately, you cannot stay there and hang out
by the Neptune pool with Clark Gable, Winston Churchill, Charlie
Chaplin, or any of the other famous guests Hearst welcomed to his
not-quite-humble abode; however, with all the far-reaching
grandiosity and lavish splendor, it does not take much stretch of the

imagination to conjure up the scenes as they might have played out years ago—starring you, of course.

Four regular year-round tours and one seasonal evening tour (available in the spring, autumn, and Christmas seasons) are available, but for your first trip stick to Tour One, a wonderful introduction and excellent overview. By all means, take the evening tour if you have the opportunity, around Christmas if possible, so you can enjoy the festive lights and decorations. However, keep in mind that this special tour means climbing quite a few stairs. Although you will still have some stairs, Tour One is the least strenuous and lasts almost two hours, including the bus ride to and from the castle. Whatever tour you decide on, be sure to make reservations as far in advance as possible; you may get lucky with a last-minute stop, but this popular excursion sells out regularly.

At the visitor center, look around a little at the artifacts on display, including an impressive collection of seventeenth-century tapestries in the lobby of the National Geographic Theater. Be sure to get a good seat for the movie, *Hearst Castle: Building the Dream*, which starts every forty-five minutes and is presented on a five-story screen. The vintage clips from the 1920s and '30s, combined with breathtaking cinematography, provide visitors with an exciting and interesting overview of the buildings and background of Hearst Castle. (Movie admission is included with Tour One.)

On the bus ride up the hill from the visitor center, you'll enjoy an audio introduction to the area, the people, and the colorful history, as well as tremendous views of Hearst's front yard. However, the 5-mile scenic ride is over almost too quickly, making it easy to underappreciate the fact that, at the time of construction, unpaved roads and the vehicles of the age often made trucking supplies up the hill an all-day struggle.

After filing off the bus, the guides introduce themselves, establish a few ground rules, and the tour begins with a bang. Both swimming pools attract top billing from most visitors and are featured stops on all tours. The first pool you'll see is the magnificent outdoor Neptune pool, 104 feet long and 95 feet wide at the alcove. Four seventeenth-century Italian bas-reliefs adorn the sides of Vermont marble colonnades, and sapphire water glows even in the most ominous weather. The majestic views of the Pacific Ocean are spectacular, but one can only imagine the same view while floating around the pool on an inflatable lounge chair, hobnobbing with the stars. For a period of time, however, even Hearst and his children

The Hearst Castle grounds are heavily adorned with art. RAY BANGS

had to use their imaginations—this giant pool took twelve years to build. And, of course, the water was even heated, almost unheard of then. For Hearst, it was nothing but the best.

The focal stop on Tour One is Casa Grande, the main residence. Your informative tour guides will delight you with the history of the Enchanted Hill, their vivid descriptions and interesting anecdotes allowing your imagination to work wonders. The first attention-grabbing aspect of the tour is the walk through the largest of the four sitting rooms known as the Assembly Room, the gathering place for Hearst's guests. The Chief threw lavish parties here, and a veritable who's who of the world, especially from Hollywood, would kill to be there. After the initial festivities, they would move to enjoy a meal in the enormous Refectory, or dining room. One of the more entertaining stories holds that Hearst would often seat the most recently arrived guests closest to him, and as time went on, they moved their way farther down the seating chart; although the table was enormous, guests would still know when they had, so to speak, worn out their welcome. After dinner, visitors were encouraged toward the private movie theater showing the latest films, probably the first place Hearst caught a glimpse of *Citizen Kane*.

The eighteen-room Casa Del Sol guesthouse is yet another tour highlight, as is the scenic stroll through the esplanade and gardens with all their stunning sculptures and meticulous landscaping. Heading indoors to the last stop (of this and all tours), the Roman pool will surely surpass anyone's expectations of luxury living; the room is covered from floor to ceiling with 1-inch-square mosaic tiles made of Venetian glass, mostly blue and orange or infused with gold. The tour guides hint of juicy gossip and wild times had by Hearst and his guests, but one can only envision how really raucous it must have been.

The tour ends with a little time for scenic contemplation on the ride back down the hill. If you take a look at the others in the bus, at least half are still in a state of shock. Some chatter on nonsensically, trying to verbalize their awe, but look closely at the quieter ones staring out the windows—their wrinkled foreheads and faraway gazes are good indicators that they are cooking up get-rich-quick ideas and planning out how to live life on their terms. Undoubtedly, as some of the splendid central coast panoramas hit you, your mental gears will be grinding away as well. Hearst Castle is all about big dreams.

Price: $15–$30

(Winter, Easy)

DRIVING DIRECTIONS

Hearst Castle is located 40 miles north of San Luis Obispo on California Highway 1, approximately halfway between San Francisco and Los Angeles, a four- to five-hour drive (230 miles) from both.

FOR MORE INFORMATION

HEARST CASTLE
San Simeon
(800) 444–4445
www.hearstcastle.com

RECOMMENDED READING

Kastner, Victoria, and Victoria Garagliano. *Hearst Castle: The Biography of a Country House.* New York: Harry N. Abrams, 2000.

Leon, Vicki. *Hearst Castle Photo Tour Guidebook.* San Luis Obispo, Calif.: Blake Publishing, 1984.

Nasaw, David. *The Chief: The Life of William Randolph Hearst.* Boston: Houghton Mifflin, 2001.

SLEEP CHEAP

The San Simeon Creek Campground is located 5 miles south of Hearst Castle on Highway 1 and offers 115 campsites for tents or RV (maximum length is 35 feet). A fire ring and picnic table are at each site. There are no RV hook-ups. The campground offers flush toilets, coin-operated showers, a dump station, water spigots, and pay phones. Firewood is for sale from the campground host.

The Washburn Primitive Campground is also accessed through the San Simeon Creek Campground entrance station. It is located 1 mile inland on a plateau overlooking the Santa Lucia Mountains and the Pacific Ocean. A fire ring and picnic table are at each site. The campground offers water spigots and chemical flush toilets.

Reservations are required at both campgrounds from March 15 to September 30 (800–444–7275); the rest of the year they are first come, first served. Two miles south, Cambria offers gas stations and grocery stores. For more information, contact San Simeon State Park (805–927–2020).

SoCal Snowriding

Dreaming of a White Christmas Adventure

Sun bounces off the sand and casts a wonderfully warm glow over your beach-bumming body, and a delightful ocean breeze gives you a noseful of reasons why living in Southern California was your choice in the first place. "Jeez," you sigh. "Wish I wasn't here right now."

Huh?

If you are like most people, the riddle of life is why you always want to be somewhere other than where you actually are, no matter how good it is. The grass inevitably seems greener else-where; spending a lazy December Sunday on the beach is always a great option, but sometimes your lounging might turn into long-ing for cooler climes and a healthy dose of knee-deep powder. Luckily, that dream is not too far off when you're in California. In fact, you could jump in your car, and about two hours later, you'll have all the snow you could ask for—hard to fathom as you apply another basting of sunscreen.

Big Bear Lake is a quick and easy escape from the sometimes too-perfect winter weather of the San Diego and Los Angeles areas. Not that sunny and mild days are appalling or unpleasant, but as they say, variety is the spice of life. For those of you who live in Southern California, it may have been a while since your last white Christmas. For others, snow is a phenomenon yet to be experienced. Throw in the thrills available at Snow Summit and Big Bear Mountain resorts, and your holiday season will quickly approach perfection.

Big Bear Mountain provides the perfect way to get your powder fix with an average snowfall of 120 inches, plus 3 to 5 feet of the slippery stuff thanks to the largest snowmaking system per developed acre this side of the Mississippi. Just down the street, Snow Summit is another option for great skiing and snowboarding, as they also utilize Big Bear Lake as a natural water supply for serious snowmaking. Artificial snow is essential to keep the area slopes white and helps ensure a prompt season opening in November and continued operations through April. Surfing on Saturday, snowriding on Sunday—you gotta love California!

Snow Summit offers over thirty trails serviced by a dozen lifts, including two high-speed quads, all of which combine to tote over 18,500 people up the mountain every hour. By limiting the number of lift ticket sales, lift lines are kept short, with waits rarely exceeding five minutes. Before most rides, you have just enough time to make sure your friends all made it back in one piece after that wild ride down. Then it's up the lift and getting ready to tackle the mountain all over again. Intermediates and advanced skiers will be happy to discover that 65 percent of the terrain is suited for their skill levels, although beginners have plenty of runs just for them too.

Snow Summit's biggest claim to fame is the way it caters to the hordes of snowboarders who make the seasonal migration every year. Snow Summit has stood proudly on the cutting edge of boarding since the sport really boomed in the late 1980s, and today the snowboard parks are generally and consistently considered the best in North America. Skiers are certainly not forgotten; however, if you want to give boarding a try, head to Snow Summit. By the end of the first day, the Snowboard School's GuaranRide program will have you comfortably cruising down from the top of the mountain. If you aren't quite ready by then, they will provide free lessons and beginner lift tickets until you are.

For experienced riders, Snow Summit brims with serious shredding potential. The Westridge and Ego Trip parks feature rails, hips, tables, boxes, and enough jumps to thoroughly thrash even the best set of knees. Entering the East Why SuperPark and enjoying its incredible, pro-quality terrain requires an additional SuperPark Pass ($5.00 and liability release, good for a year). Snow Summit also provides two huge half-pipes if you are looking for monster aerials, or for you wimpier (and probably saner) types, if you want to watch others perform those monster aerials. Just try to forget when you drop in that the higher you go, the harder you fall!

Big Bear Mountain Resort is better suited for those new to skiing and snowboarding, as the majority of the groomed runs are classified as green (beginner) and blue (intermediate). With over thirty runs served by a dozen lifts, including two high-speed quads, riders don't have to worry about long lift lines, even on the busiest days. If this is your first time out, the excellent ski school will quickly get you up on your feet and swooshing down the slopes in no time. After a couple weekends, your skills sharpening with every linked Christie turn, you'll be able to confidently master much of the easier terrain. For experts who like deep powder, Deer, Goldmine, and Bow Canyons are ideal choices for getting away from the crowds and testing your skills against 550 acres of undeveloped terrain. If that's not enough, hundreds of additional acres of pristine backcountry are available as well; just be sure to check in with mountain patrol before leaving the resort's boundaries. And for all you strong intermediates who still stick to the groomers, remember this: Backcountry skiing is tough, but falling in powder hurts a lot less than falling on hardpack.

Snowboarder at Big Bear. BIG BEAR MOUNTAIN RESORTS

Perhaps the most unique aspect of Big Bear Mountain Resort is the availability of alternative sliding options, any of which will more than likely drop at least ten years from the age you feel. When's the last time you went sledding? It's probably been a while, so the resort offers sledding and tubing as ideal ways to play like a kid again. Whipping down the hill in a rubber inner tube with your body only inches from the ground is exhilarating to say the least. You've probably forgotten how loud you can scream—but while tubing, there's no shame in finding out! If you are feeling extra adventurous, rent one of the other available snow toys, and you'll quickly discover just how coordinated (or klutzy) you are. The Snowscoot is part snowboard, part scooter, and all fun; the Snowfox and Snow Bike both feature seats and shock absorbers, making for wacky and wild adventures all the way down the hill. Riders of all three out-of-the-ordinary contraptions wear short skis to provide a bit of balance and control, and the snow toys can be safely loaded on the chairlifts for use all over the mountain. If you are convinced this sounds like too much excitement, snowshoes are available to explore some of the quieter backcountry winter wilderness.

Whatever way you decide to slip and slide down the mountains, you are sure to find the option that suits you at Snow Summit and Big Bear Mountain resorts. Make reservations in advance, because there are plenty of people who have already discovered these winter hideaways on their own. Before you know it, you may be trading in your beach blanket for good and chasing the snow around on a more permanent basis. But even if it's just for a weekend, the mountains are always intoxicating, and being a two-day ski bum is fun, simple, and rewarding. As you cruise back to your coastal quarters, don't be surprised if you find yourself saying, "This is the life!"

Price: $50–$250

(Winter, Medium)

DRIVING DIRECTIONS

Located in the San Bernardino Mountains, Big Bear Lake is approximately two hours or less from most areas of Southern California. Three main highway routes provide access: Highway 38 through Redlands, Highway 30/330 through Running Springs, and Highway 18 through Lucerne Valley. Big Bear Mountain is approximately 100 miles east of Los Angeles, 120 miles northeast of San Diego, and 70 miles north of Palm Springs.

FOR MORE INFORMATION

BIG BEAR MOUNTAIN RESORT
Big Bear Lake
(909) 585–2519
Snow report: (800) 232–7686
www.bearmtn.com

SNOW SUMMIT MOUNTAIN RESORT
Big Bear Lake
(909) 866–5766
Snow report: (888) 786–6481
www.snowsummit.com

BIG BEAR LAKE ADVENTURE HOSTEL
Big Bear Lake
(866) 866–5255
www.adventurehostel.com

BIG BEAR LAKE CHAMBER OF COMMERCE
(909) 866–4607
www.bigbearchamber.com

BIG BEAR LAKE RESORT ASSOCIATION
(800) 424–4232
www.bigbearinfo.com

RECOMMENDED READING

Clifford, Hal. *Downhill Slide: Why the Corporate Ski Industry Is Bad for Skiing, Ski Towns, and the Environment.* Berkeley: University of California Press, 2002.

Densmore, Lisa Feinberg. *Ski Faster: Lisa Feinberg Densmore's Guide to High Performance Skiing and Racing.* New York: McGraw-Hill, 1999.

Wilson, Mike. *Right on the Edge of Crazy: On Tour with the U.S. Downhill Ski Team.* New York: Vintage Books, 1994.

SLEEP CHEAP

Hostels aren't only for recent college grads backpacking Europe, or Aussies and Brits traveling the United States on the cheap. The Big Bear Lake Adventure Hostel is a great place to sleep cheap for outdoor enthusiasts, snowboarders, skiers, and any other easygoing, open-minded people who enjoy meeting others, often from all over the world, and don't mind sharing a kitchen and bathroom. Dormitory-style rooms are the cheapest way to go, starting around $20 per night. Private rooms are also available. Call (866) 866–5255 for more information and to make reservations.

ATV Adventures in Glamis

Got Sand?

As the setting sun dances light through the waves of heat, rippling mirages draw your eye all the way to Mexico. From your vantage point, it's easy to see great distances, maybe 20 miles or even farther. Scale and perspective lose all meaning, however, as the open space swallows all frame of reference. The dunes are a barren land, which holds little more than seemingly endless sand, but in this vast nothingness, a certain breed of fun-seekers have found the perfect distraction. Along the horizon, beyond three dozen or so monstrous mounds, maybe 3 miles away, you see what look like ants scurrying across anthills, and they look as if they are playing follow the leader. But of course, you know they're not ants because ants couldn't possibly be having this much fun.

The characteristic orange and red flags pop up and down in the sandy expanse, speed-curved antennas attached to machines that are even more difficult to see as they stay hidden below your line of sight. Frequently but unpredictably, they erupt airborne off some pointed crest or another, leaving a maelstrom of sandy chaos from fast spinning tires striving toward the sky. As they grow closer, you start to hear the whiny churn of the engines, and with the sun dropping even lower and glowing even warmer, the overall effect is soothing and hypnotic. To the south, you see a band of paddle-tired sandrails scooting along a ridge before dropping out of sight once again. Their rumbles fade, slowly, muffled by the infinite grains of sand. For a moment, you Zen into total peace.

You adjust your helmet and goggles, shrug and stretch your shoulders a few times, and swirl the kinks from your neck. An easy push of the ignition button, and your ATV roars to life. After a quick survey of the surroundings and turning the handlebars in the general direction you want to go, you jam the thumb throttle. The quad bucks and you drop in. Suddenly, you're flying.

California has plenty of "best of" contenders in numerous activities, and the same holds true for places to drive off-road recreational vehicles. If you've ever wanted to ride quads or sandrails, the Glamis Imperial Dunes is the best place in Southern California to do it.

There are basically three ways to get out onto the sand, and unfortunately, none of them is inexpensive. Of course, as we always say, since your fun budget should be at least half of your disposable income, going to Glamis is a great enough reason to save or splurge. Your first option is to simply head down to your local Yamaha, Honda, Kawasaki, or other ATV dealer and drop about $5,000 on a new quad. The shop can show you exactly what you need to ride the dunes, and, of course, it always helps to do some research to find the best equipment for you. Alternatively, try searching classified ads to find a used machine for considerably less. (Remember, it's a good idea to have a mechanic look it over.) New or used, owning and maintaining an ATV is a responsibility and expense, but the fun factor is definitely worth it.

Your second option is using someone else's machine, but unless you have a friend with a spare quad sitting around, you're going to have to rent one. If it is just two of you, you may want to rent two quads, but larger groups can share the machines and still have a great time. If you have ridden before and feel confident that you can handle the four-wheeler by yourself, then by all means, just check your yellow pages for a local rental shop, or call one of the outfitters mentioned later in this section. Be sure to say that you are going to Glamis so they can set you up on a high-quality machine with paddle tires and a whip. The whip is a tall antenna with an orange or red flag at the top to help others see you, and it is required at the dunes. Renting paddle tires may cost extra but is highly recommended because these special tires add traction, meaning more fun for you.

Since the Glamis Dunes are somewhat isolated, you'll have to transport your rental ATV in a pickup truck or by trailer, so you'll need a tow-hitch. A helmet and goggles are mandatory equipment as well, while a long-sleeved shirt, durable pants, boots, and gloves round out the clothing ensemble. Professional jerseys and riding pants are certainly not required, but with built-in padding, protection, and ventilation, they are very functional if you decide to make riding quads a regular pursuit. Check with the rental shop to see if professional gear is also available for rent. Don't forget the spare fuel cans!

The third option is to let someone else take care of all the details of your great weekend escape ATV adventure. California Motorsport Adventours and Recreation Unlimited are two excellent companies that offer packaged tours to the Glamis Dunes, as well as other areas such as Baja and Lake Havasu. Although these multiday trips carry a heftier price tag than renting, the pro-quality action and excitement are worth every penny. Better yet, everything is included so you can just show up with your personal

Powering a buggy through the dunes in Glamis. JAMES GRAVES

basics. Get ready for some great barbecue grilling and other hearty meals. The best reason to go with the tour, however, is simply that these crews consist of professional fun experts who are fully capable of showing you the best time on the sand. They are familiar with the area, which will maximize your playtime.

Ranging from 3 to 5 miles wide, the Imperial Sand Dunes Recreation Area spans roughly 16 miles from Highway 78 to Highway 8. Generally, the area encompasses, from north to south, the public lands from 1 mile north of Mammoth Wash to the Mexican border, and east to west, from the Southern Pacific Railroad, Ogilby Road, and the Boardmanville area, to the old Coachella Canal. With all this wide-open space, there's ample room to really open up the throttle in your quest to conquer hundreds of hills, not to mention sand moguls galore for you to test out your turning skills and countless bumps to catch air on. The immense dunes provide a playground for all types of vehicles, ranging from ATVs and quads to sandrails and dune buggies to 4WD trucks and motocross bikes. You might even see some hang gliders and sandboarders.

Glamis is an incredible opportunity for off-highway vehicle (OHV) enthusiasts, a perfect spot for a great weekend escape. Upon arrival, first-timers should scout the area to get a better idea of the boundaries and make friends who have been there before. Maps and information boards can be found along the roadside, but contact the Bureau of Land Management (BLM) for specific information and any pressing pretrip questions. The most important rule of Glamis is that, with the number and variety of vehicles using the area, keep a careful watch for others. Be especially careful when crossing over dune mounds and drop-offs. Zooming off a ridge can be a lot of fun, but crashing into or onto someone on the other side isn't.

Whatever way you end up pounding the dunes, whether you buy or rent an ATV or take a tour, once you get out on the sand, be ready for some serious fun and more than a little craziness. While the summer season sees a significant decline in dune-running enthusiasts, these folks come out in full force during the cooler months, especially on weekends. Holiday crowds can reach upwards of 100,000 people. There is plenty of room for everyone, but keep in mind that those with families may want to ask around to find a quieter area if trying to stay away from the beer-guzzling, bonfire-building, party campers. Dune riders are a fun group, often a little too much fun. And do expect to be awakened by engines running what often seems like all night long, so put earplugs on your packing list. Evening rides are great fun, but take it slow, and stay well away from the campers. As the old saying at Glamis goes, dune unto others as you'd have them dune unto you.

Price: $250+

(Winter, Medium)

DRIVING DIRECTIONS

From San Diego, follow I–8 East toward El Centro, your best place to refuel before driving into the dunes. Along Interstate 8 on the south side of the dunes, the Midway and Buttercup Campgrounds and staging areas are easy yet crowded options. To reach the north side, exit and drive north on Ogilby Road (S34). Turn west (left) on Highway 78. Past the Glamis Store, head south (left) on Gecko Road to the Roadrunner Campground.

FOR MORE INFORMATION

Outfitters

ACADEMY RENTALS
San Diego
(619) 294–2227
www.academyrentals.com

CALIFORNIA MOTORSPORT
ADVENTOURS
Santee
(619) 262–1026
www.letsatv.com

RECREATION UNLIMITED
Placentia
(714) 288–8100 or (714) 237–7000
www.recunlimited.com

AMERICAN SAND ASSOCIATION
La Verne
www.americansand
association.org

CALIFORNIA DEPARTMENT OF PARKS
AND RECREATION
Off-Highway Motor Vehicle
Program
(916) 324–4442
http://ohv.parks.ca.gov

For questions or comments regarding Glamis Dunes, call the BLM at (760) 337–4400. Alternatively, write to the El Centro Field Office at

BUREAU OF LAND MANAGEMENT
1661 South Fourth Street
El Centro, CA 92243

RECOMMENDED READING

Burch, Monte. *The Field and Stream All-Terrain Vehicle Handbook: The Complete Guide to Owning and Maintaining an ATV.* Guilford, Conn.: The Lyons Press, 2001.

Duty, Earl. *How to Build a Dune Buggy.* Sidney, Ohio: Cars & Parts Magazine, 2002.

Stambler, Irwin. *Off-Roading: Racing and Riding.* New York: Putnam, 1984.

SLEEP CHEAP

The only way to enjoy Glamis is to spend the night in a tent or RV, though keep in mind that camping here is known as "dry camping"—no water and no RV hookups. You must be self-sufficient. There are, however, a few pit toilets, a few portable toilets, a picnic table here and there, and all the soft sand you could ask for. Camping is allowed anywhere in the area as long as you are more than 10 feet from the road. (Don't drive too far unless you have a four-wheel drive.) Fees are inexpensive, costing $25 per week per vehicle. An annual pass is available. There are roughly two dozen permit vending machines that accept cash and credit cards. Permits can also be purchased at local shops, gas stations, and convenience stores. Don't forget to bring plenty of water, some means of artificial shade (such as a tarp), and earplugs for sleeping through the not-quite gentle engine purring of the nightriders.

Motorcycle Touring the PCH

Get Your Motor Runnin'

If Route 66 is the road through America's heart, California's Route 1 is the tour through its sublime soul. The Pacific Coast Highway winds down the coast between Seattle and L.A. like a fuzzy, fantastic dream, opening up into vast ocean vistas beyond towering cliffs. The sun, far from beating down, seems to cascade around you, keeping you warm and comfortable as you glide down the highway in search of your next adventure.

A good old-fashioned scenic drive is probably the best way to see this bastion of America's roadways. It's no secret, either; every year, thousands of tourists and locals pack up their families and take off on the PCH, gathering in sunsets and vistas and consuming mass quantities of film in the process. However, these car-bound masses do miss out on some things. There's no salt-tinged wind whipping their jackets; no chance to feel the sun on their backs; and—let's face it—"cruising the PCH in my kickin' Toyota" just doesn't have much romance to it. To truly experience this road, to feel it as it deserves to be felt, you need to mount the nearest hog and light out.

Motorcycle touring obviously requires that you know how to ride, but past this qualification it is a very relaxing escape—a good way to see a lot of countryside up close and personal without taking on difficult adventures that might be a little more work than play. And the PCH is built for good motorcycling; it boasts a ton of diversions to check out, not to mention soft, sweet curves and some of the best oceanside scenery you could hope for. Even if you didn't come to California on your bike, you will have no problem finding one—there are plenty of rental companies eager to not only get you a bike, but also take you out on a Route 1 cruising tour. Of course, you can just take the bike and go, but if you've never been to California before, you may want to set out with a guide who can show you all the best sights and secrets the PCH holds.

California, more than any other place in the world, can lay legitimate claim to the title "birthplace of the biker lifestyle." After World War II, most GIs fresh from the front came home to settle down and start their new lives. A few, however, came west to California, riding steel steeds up and down the coast in search of thrills and adventure. By 1947, the state practically hummed with Indians and Harleys, and the West Coast bike culture was born. The Hell's Angels sprung from this early group of outlaws, and like them or not, they did more to popularize the Harley Davidson motorcycle and the culture that surrounds it than anyone else. Today, thanks in large part to those hardcore aficionados and the mystique they created, Harley is the most popular motorcycle manufacturer in the country.

But they are by no means the only company in the world making quality bikes. California Motorcycle Rental, for example, specializes in BMWs, some of the finest two-wheeled machines on the road. Granted, it's a German bike you'll be riding over one of America's most famous highways, but don't feel bad—just tell yourself it's a great highway of *the world*. You'll not only feel better, you'll be telling the truth.

There are, however, a whole lot more shops that rent Harleys. EagleRider, the world's largest Harley rental company, has its headquarters in Los Angeles and rental shops all over the state. Their Love Ride, a three-day adventure through L.A., is one touring option that will keep you close to the city's party scene, roaring through Venice Beach, Santa Monica's Third Street Promenade, and the Sunset Strip. But to get out on the PCH, your best bet is to take the company's California Dreaming tour. You can take a four- or six-day ride, during which you'll cruise the highway through Santa Barbara, Big Sur, and Monterey, among other points of interest. You'll even get a chance to stop at the historic Alice's Restaurant, subject of Arlo Guthrie's folk masterpiece. These organized rides can get pricey, but you'll get a lot of bang for your buck: food and drinks, along with lodging, are often included. For what you get and the planning you won't have to do, it's not a bad way to spend your vacation bucks. Keep in mind that a lot of these tours are more like rallies than regular

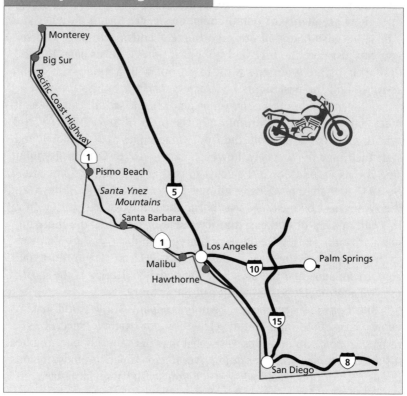

events—they only take place a couple times each year. Call ahead and find out when the tour you want is set to go, rather than just stopping in any old day to catch the tour as it pulls out of the shop.

If money is a factor, you can definitely ride on the cheap and still enjoy the PCH experience. Daily rental rates with EagleRider start at $75 a day, plus insurance and deposit. Rebel Harley Davidson Rentals is a company based in San Diego that provides much longer guided tours, but they can also help you come up with a shorter itinerary should you want one; their rental rates are roughly comparable to EagleRider's. California Motorcycle Rental is a bit more expensive, but then you're riding luxury BMW machines. Above all, make sure you have some idea what you want before you call your outfitter; they each offer bikes and packages for every budget, from "rent the bike and pack the tent" to "gimme the big one." Ask the right money questions, and you'll get what you want.

Keep in mind, too, that any security deposit you're putting down is going to be pretty hefty ($1,000 and up), as motorcycles are expensive beasts. Moral of the story: Don't wreck the thing, and you'll get your credit card back intact. Do some offroading, and your vacation gets a whole lot more expensive.

If you do it right, the Pacific Coast Highway is some of the most bike-friendly pavement around. Anyone who can ride should take the extra time to set up a rental and explore this natural and cultural treasure. Sure, you can take the car, and miss the smell of the ocean breeze whipping by or the feel of the road's curves undulating under you as you move. But why would you want to?

Price: $500+ (deposit)
(Winter, Medium)

DRIVING DIRECTIONS

Route 1 runs up the California coast from Los Angeles to beyond San Francisco. Hook up with your bike rental company, and they'll point you toward the Pacific.

FOR MORE INFORMATION

Outfitters

CALIFORNIA MOTORCYCLE RENTAL LTD.
La Jolla
(858) 456–9577
www.calif-motorcyclerental.com

EAGLERIDER MOTORCYCLE RENTALS
(This is the corporate office, as well as a rental site; other offices are located in Glendale, Palm Springs, San Diego, San Francisco, Santa Barbara, and San Jose.)
(800) 501–8687
www.eaglerider.com

REBEL HARLEY DAVIDSON RENTALS
San Diego
(858) 292–6200
www.rebelusa.com

Other

HARLEY DAVIDSON
www.harley-davidson.com

SOUTHERN CALIFORNIA MOTORCYCLING ASSOCIATION
www.sc-ma.com

RECOMMENDED READING

Hough, David. *Street Strategies: A Survival Guide for Motorcyclists.* Mission Viejo, Calif.: Bowtie Press, 2001.

Salvadori, Clement. *Motorcycle Journeys through California.* North Conway, N.H.: Whitehorse Press, 2000.

Thompson, Hunter S. *Hell's Angels: A Strange and Terrible Saga.* New York: Ballantine, 1966.

SLEEP CHEAP

The Santa Monica Mountains National Recreation Area is just north of L.A., and holds four California state parks with numerous camping facilities. Call (818) 880–0350 or visit www.nps.gov/samo to make reservations, or for more information on the options closest to your weekend escape. Of course, the ideal way to sleep cheap is just take your bedroll and lay it out on the ground next to a campfire. Watch *Easy Rider* for pointers!

Soaring and Sailplanes

Silent Sky Slicing

If you've ever been to an airshow (or within a mile or so of one), the first thing that strikes you is the incredible noise. Stunt planes, especially jet-power stars like the Blue Angels, are *loud,* and with good reason—death-defying aerial acrobatics require tons of power (and fuel) to execute, as the rules of nature and gravity do not bend easily.

Or so you might think, until you strap into the passenger seat of a glider and embark on a silent-but-thrilling aerobatic flight that packs enough Gs to make the motorized flyboys blanch. It starts out calmly enough—a few bumps here and there, as the tow plane brings you to the proper altitude. But after that motorized safety net lets go at a few thousand feet, leaving nothing between you and the earth but two wings and a tail, you'll find yourself in the middle of a stomach-knotting adventure.

Gliding, also known as soaring, involves flying in a motorless sailplane propelled by the atmospheric phenomenon known as lift. California air, unlike that around much of the world, boasts all three forms of lift energy: thermals, columns of warm, rising air; ridge lift, where air currents following the land's terrain rise over the windward side of a hill and create a brief, upward surge; and wave lift, the breathtaking result of very powerful winds deflecting off a ridge or mountain and shooting upwards with incredible force. Even without an engine, sailplanes are incredibly agile; you'll feel g-forces pull and push whenever the pilot banks sharply. Experienced pilots can bank their planes into tight circles, moving in the various lifts until high enough to fly "cross-country," or at least well beyond the launch site in search of more thermals. Wave lift is best for intense, expert-level soaring, as it is the most turbulent and powerful; wave flights can reach altitudes up to almost 50,000 feet, although the legal limit is only 18,000.

A note to adrenaline junkies: These powerful lift energies provide the fuel for gut-churning aerobatic excursions that rival any airshow stunt flight. Hitting a fierce wave of rising air can feel roughly the same as being shot from a cannon, straight into the wild blue yonder. If you enjoy the edgy, lump-in-the-throat feeling of moving just a little faster than you probably should, aerobatic flying is definitely for you. Wary first-timers, or anyone with even a passing heights problem, should probably forgo naked thrills and opt for an introductory flight without any extra spins or loops. Don't think you're missing out if you go basic, though; soaring through the atmosphere in a plane without an engine will be excitement enough for your first time. Once you know what it means to glide with the condors, think about going back to scream with the falcons.

Introductory flights are reasonably priced between $70 and $180, depending on how long you fly and what kind of flight you want. Two commercial gliding operations in Southern California, Sailplane Enterprises and Sky Sailing, stand out for their quality first-timer flights. Several introductory flights are available at both locations, as are more extreme aerobatic adventures. You will be towed up, and after release your qualified, expert instructor will explain and demonstrate basic flying techniques.

Flight length depends on flying conditions, but introductory trips are generally long enough to enjoy yourself and short enough to leave you wanting more. The cockpit, a bubble of glass allowing for incredible views, is well suited for enjoying the scenery thousands of feet below. The visuals, along with the silence, make for an almost spiritual experience on calmer flights. You may even want to share the beauty with your significant other; if your combined weight is less than 300 pounds, the two of you can enjoy a quiet mile-high together, maybe to kick off a night out (or at least down) on the town.

When you finally land, your pilot will enter the flight information in a logbook, which works well as a souvenir or as the first completed checkmark on your glider pilot training. You can book additional training flights to fit your schedule. If you're relaxed while flying during the lessons, take instructions well, and have the time, you could be certified to fly solo after only twenty to thirty flights.

But if you get the gliding bug, the wait is worth it. And novice fliers are no worse off than seasoned power pilots seeking their glider rating; just getting used to the quiet thrill of soaring takes some time. Silently cruising off a thermal can be a weird, disconcerting experience, especially for someone used to an engine's purr. Nearly everyone will have a tendency to be extra careful, especially at first, but all pilots and passengers are required to wear a parachute just in case of problems.

So the next time you are driving along some flat ground and notice the wind whipping forward and up, imagine flying on it. And don't be intimidated; you will not be flying solo at first, so soaring is within everyone's skill set. The instructors and pilots at Sky Sailing and Sailplane Enterprises are top-notch, and most have logged thousands of hours in the air—you'll be in very accomplished,

Gliding might seem a little intimidating at first, but have no fear—great pilots make the experience a breeze. CHRIS BECKER

professional hands. The toughest part is convincing yourself you really can fly with the birds.

Price: $70–$180 (more for lessons)
(Winter, Medium)

DRIVING DIRECTIONS

To Warner Springs, home of Sky Sailing, from San Diego: Take Interstate 15 to Scripps Poway Parkway (East) to Highway 67. Then go north on Highway 67 through Ramona; in Ramona, Highway 67 turns into Highway 78. Continue to Santa Ysabel. In Santa Ysabel, just past Dudley's Bakery, turn left onto Highway 79. Continue on Highway 79 into Warner Springs. Warner Springs Airport is 2 miles past the Warner Springs Ranch entrance. Hemet, where Sailplane Enterprises is based, is north on Route 79 to Route 74; then head east. Sailplane Enterprises is at Hemet-Ryan Airport; turn right at Warren Road, then left on Whittier Avenue. Adventure Flights also flies out of Hemet-Ryan; call for detailed directions.

FOR MORE INFORMATION

Outfitters

ADVENTURE FLIGHTS (flying out of
Lake Elsinore and Hemet)
(800) 404–6359
www.advflights.com

SAILPLANE ENTERPRISES
Hemet
(909) 658–6577
www.members.aol.com/soar
socal/

SKY SAILING
Warner Springs
(760) 782–0404
www.skysailing.com

Other

ASSOCIATED GLIDER CLUBS OF
SOUTHERN CALIFORNIA
San Diego
www.agcsc.org

RECOMMENDED READING

Piggot, Derek. *Understanding Gliding: The Principles of Soaring Flight.*
London: A&C Black, 1998.

Thomas, Fred. *Fundamentals of Sailplane Design.* College Park, Md.:
College Park Press, 1999.

SLEEP CHEAP

Anza-Borrego Desert State Park is located very close to Warner
Springs, with Highway S2 entering the park from the north off
Route 79. It is the largest desert state park in the contiguous forty-
eight states and has two developed campgrounds, at Borrego Palm
Canyon and Tamarisk Grove; the Borrego Palm Canyon facility has
electricity hookups. You can make reservations by calling Reserve
America at (800) 444–7275. There is also a small campground at
Bow Willow and, for those wishing to camp with horses, an equestrian camp located at the mouth of Coyote Canyon. Elsewhere in the
park, backcountry camping is permitted with the purchase of a
$5.00 daily park use permit. Rates for the campgrounds range from
$7.00 to $22.00. For more information, call the park at (760)
767–5311.

Snow Camping Mount San Jacinto

Snowshoes Off in the Igloo, Please

In 1935, an electrical engineer named Francis Crocker went to Banning, California, on a very hot day. As the sun soared into the sky and baked the ground below, young Francis, wiping the sweat from his forehead, happened to glance skyward, at the majestic white peak of Mount San Jacinto, 10,804 feet above sea level. We do not know what Crocker's actual words were when he began to stare longingly at the cool, snowy expanse above him; we do know, however, that on this day, the kernel of an idea hatched in his engineer's head, and we know we have him to thank for the Palm Springs Aerial Tramway, the vehicle that in this day and age can take us up to those blinding white heights.

Construction of the tramway was an engineering challenge of massive proportions. Building roads in the region was next to impossible, yet the huge support towers had to go up at intervals all the way up the mountain. The engineers conquered the problem with some relatively new flight technology—helicopters were used to erect four of the five towers. The helicopters flew some 23,000 missions without any problems during the twenty-six months of construction, bringing the men and materials necessary to erect four of the towers and the 35,000-square-foot mountain station. Even today, you can reach only one of the towers by road. Twenty years after its completion in 1963, the tramway was designated a historical civil engineering landmark.

Riding the tram in the winter brings you up to a snowy white paradise, one complete with loads of fun activities and landscape to explore. In order to make the most of your escape, may we suggest that you bring your camping gear, and make a go of it on the top of ol' San Jacinto (for one night, anyway)?

Snow camping is a different beast than the run-of-the-mill variety. It requires many of the same skills but uses a different set of equipment, and some things that are a matter of course for summertime camping are either no-nos or impossible when there's white stuff on the ground. Building a fire, for example, becomes more trouble than it's often worth in the snow. First you have to find the wood (and busting limbs off trees is not allowed, remember); then you have to find some solid ground to build it on. Your fingers could be black from frostbite by the time you'd get things up and running, *if* you were relying on the flames for warmth.

But as a snow camper, you won't be doing that. You will stay warm by stoking your body's furnace and holding that heat, rather than relying on outside sources. First off, eat lots of good-for-you food, starting and ending your day with hot meals (and dress in layers). Your body will process the nighttime fuel while you sleep, creating warmth that is then trapped within your sleeping bag (and your layers of clothing). Make sure your bag is the right size too; your body will waste energy trying to warm empty space by your feet if it is too long. And did we mention bringing lots of layers, rather than one goliath parka and a thermal shirt? You have more control over your temperature with five different pieces than you do with one—dress smart, and you won't even miss the fire.

Unfortunately, following these bits of advice will not ensure that you will stay warm or have a good time. Living outdoors in snow is a complicated endeavor, and we wouldn't presume to tell you everything you should know in these few pages. Nor will we even get into the fine art of snow cave building, an activity you should try if you have an adequate snow base. Pick up some of the recommended reading listed below; each book is a cornucopia of information and will tell you just about everything you need to know in order to stay safe and warm on the snow-capped summits. You may also need some more high-speed gear; if your tent is good for three seasons rather than four, or if you have a sleeping bag with a higher temperature rating (warm to 20° instead of 0°F), you may want to visit your local equipment outfitter. The conditions at

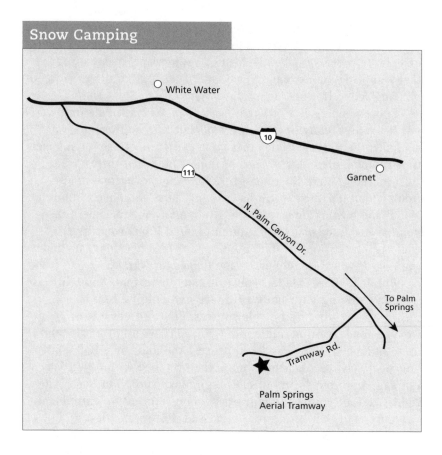

the top of the tram aren't terribly extreme as high mountains go, but they certainly get that way often enough to require being careful. Again, consult the recommended reading below to get a feel for what you don't already know.

You'll have no trouble staying occupied at the top of the tram, even after you've dug your own snow cave. If you're into cross-country skiing, by all means bring yours; the area boasts miles of beautiful trails, some of which are quite challenging. If you do not have skis of your own, never fear—the tramway's Adventure Center can rent them to you, along with snowshoes and snow tubes if you should want them. The center also provides refreshments, in case you want to chow a little before setting off to your campsite. Since you'll be walking around a bit while you're up there, you will have a perfect chance to try out snowshoes and find out just how much easier alpine life can be with a pair strapped to your feet. They're fun when you're just messing around, but they get mighty necessary (if you're not skiing) on longer expeditions into deeper snow. Learn to use them at the tram, where the environment is more controlled, and you'll be ready to take on more difficult snow camping adventures in the future.

Snow camping, unlike conventional camping, is an escape all by itself. Rather than simply bedding down between days of activity, you will feel like a true adventurer, defeating the elements with skill and know-how. Be sure to take pictures of your alpine igloo so you can show everyone back home just how hard core you have become.

Price: $25–$100
(Winter, Medium)

DRIVING DIRECTIONS

From Los Angeles, take I–10 East toward Palm Springs. Exit on Highway 111 to Palm Springs, and turn right when you reach Tramway Road. The Valley Station is located approximately 4 miles up Tramway Road.

FOR MORE INFORMATION

MOUNT SAN JACINTO STATE PARK
P.O. Box 308 (25905 Highway 243)
Idyllwild, CA 92549
(909) 659–2607
www.sanjac.statepark.org

PALM SPRINGS AERIAL TRAMWAY
Palm Springs
(888) 515–8726
www.pstramway.com

Cars depart at least every half hour from 10:00 A.M., Monday to Friday, 8:00 A.M. weekends and holiday periods. Last car up is 8:00 P.M. with the last car down at 9:45 P.M.

PALM SPRINGS DEPARTMENT OF TOURISM
(800) 927–7256
www.palm-springs.org

Cross-country skiing is only one of the activities worth taking on during your winter camping escape. ROBERT HOLMES/CALTOUR

RECOMMENDED READING

Clelland, Mike, and Allen O'Bannon. *Allen and Mike's Really Cool Backcountry Ski Book*. Evergreen, Colo.: Chockstone Press, 1996.

Gorman, Stephen. *Winter Camping* (2nd ed.). Boston: Appalachian Mountain Club, 1999.

Wilkinson, Ernest. *Snow Caves for Fun and Survival*. Boulder, Colo.: Johnson Books, 1992.

SLEEP CHEAP

Sleeping at the top of the mountain is very economical, and there are campsites close to the tram (2 miles) and a good distance farther (over 10 miles). Campsite reservations can be made by calling (800) 444-7275 between 8:00 A.M. and 5:00 P.M. seven days a week. Wilderness permits are also required for any backpacking, hiking, or camping in the wilderness; contact the state park in person or by written request (phone or fax queries are not accepted). Keep in mind this is a pristine, fragile, high-country wilderness, and the state deals out permits to ensure it stays that way—they don't do it to inconvenience people. Wilderness permits are free.

Jumping the Border

The Classic Baja Sojourn

Years ago Southern California was a wild, rowdy territory, but soon after explorers told of the vast riches and glorious climate bordered by the beauty and bounty of the Pacific Ocean, people flocked west. Throughout the past century, the dazzle of Southern California has led to massive population growth and continued development, eventually evolving into the huge expanding metropolitan areas of Los Angeles and San Diego that residents and visitors experience today. This once rugged territory is now notorious for congested traffic and ever-growing crowds. Sometimes, you just want to get as far away from the hustle and bustle as possible. Sometimes, you have to escape.

South of the border lies Baja California, Mexico, a unique opportunity to step back in time and see what SoCal was like before the mammoth influx of people. Not too far south of Tijuana, the land opens up to wild red-hued desert country relatively void of settlement. Cruising south on Highway 1, you'll see side roads leading west to the Pacific or east to the Sea of Cortez, offering plenty of options to hop off the beaten path whenever whim calls. At countless points on both sides of the peninsula, the sea kayaking and snorkeling is especially spectacular, thanks to the sparkling clear, deep azure sea. In addition to the coastal desert habitat, several regions of Baja are more mountainous, good for rock climbers, while hikers can find a number of trails.

There are just as many wild areas where wandering is better suited and, in certain places, may be the only option. When playtime is over for the day, you'll find numerous campgrounds and RV sites scattered throughout the Baja peninsula; keep in mind that there are just as many deserted beaches perfect for pitching a tent or hanging a hammock off the truck.

The quiet tranquility, however, once and still to some degree one of the region's biggest draws, is now harder to find. Time is starting to catch up in Baja. While there is still plenty of untamed land and coastline, the more popular cities and regions are seeing much of the same elaborate development as Southern California. In the tourist hotspots, visitors can find every imaginable type of accommodation, ranging from towering oceanfront hotels with breezy balconies to quaint palapas to posh bed-and-breakfast villas. Baja's rise in popularity has made it easier to get there, however. For a long time, driving was a tough option, but roadway conditions have improved. Don't drive into Baja expecting to race around on freshly paved interstate freeway, as the roads aren't quite that spiffy, but the point anyway is to take your time and explore along the drive. Also remember that insurance coverage for Mexico is required before you bring a car across the border. If you're really in a hurry or simply don't want to drive, various flights to the bigger cities are offered daily through a number of carriers.

One of the more popular great weekend escapes to Baja is to jump on a plane to Cabo San Lucas, where the party always starts soon following the afternoon siesta and rolls strong all night long. After dinner—often a Mexican smorgasbord of huge lobsters and other amazing fresh seafood—you could likely find one of your hands gripping a Corona bottle, while the other hand waves about wildly while you salsa and shake your thang barhopping down the streets of Cabo. The nightlife is always spirited, with plenty of live bands and good DJs found at a variety of clubs. The "casual beach bar in paradise" is an underlying theme, so dress accordingly. Thrown into the mix is a bottomless cooler of frosty Mexican cervezas, priced cheap and sure to be topped with a fat wedge of lime. Don't worry too much about bad water or ice in the tourist areas; the service establishments don't want their clientele getting sick, and thus have taken appropriate precautions. If you have concerns, ask. Frankly, there's a better chance Montezuma will get revenge by starting you out with a gut-popping meal of too much rich seafood and Mexican fare, all washed

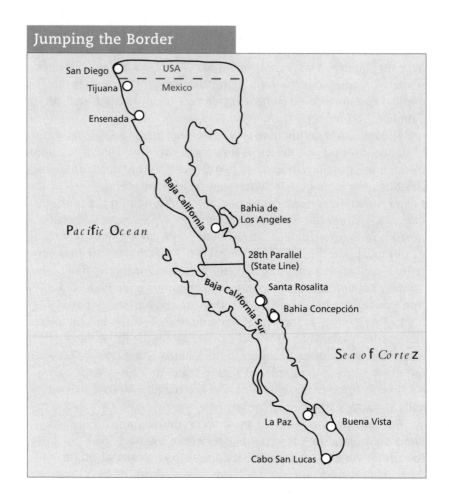

down with way too many beers. Have fun, but take it easy, especially with the tequila shots—the fiesta will still be waiting for you tomorrow. Of course, if the nightclub scene in Cabo isn't your preferred party, there's plenty of ocean fun awaiting. For starters, the fishing is as good as it gets.

All you have to do is head out on the water and slather on the sunscreen. Then don your favorite fishing hat, crack open a frosty beverage, and get your line in the water. The crew will even bait your hook, sissy, though we agree sliced sardines and squid are slimy baits to be sure. Of course, you won't be worrying about a little slime on your hands after that first 500-pound tug on your fishing rod. Strap in, partner, because that's a heck of a billfish you've just hooked—it could take an hour or more to reel in this pig. You may even get lucky and hook a few more beauties on the day, but on the other hand, so what if the fishing was so slow that all you saw was a single nibble that didn't amount to anything but a stolen chunk of squid—the memories of the day on the water will last a lifetime. Most captains and crews turn out to be great fishing guides and fun companions who look after your every need and do their best to ensure you have a great time. They make it pretty easy to catch fish. And, of course, if you land a huge marlin or the crew simply hosts a marvelous trip for you, tip them well.

If you're considering half-day and single-day trips, check out the Los Cabos Fishing Center, Picante Bluewater Sportfishing, Solmar Sportfishing, or the Pisces Fleet—there's a whole slew of other outfitters as well. Prices usually start around $100 per person and vary based on the number of people in your group, the size of the boat, how long you want to fish, and several other charter options like lunch, drinks, and fish freezing. While certain times of the year are better for different species of fish, anglers out of Cabo generally enjoy great fishing all year long with good populations of black, blue and striped marlin, sailfish, swordfish, mahi mahi, and yellowtail.

No matter how you like to have your fun on weekends, one of the best things about Baja is the quality and variety of outdoor activities available. In addition to the kayaking, hiking, camping, and fishing, many people enjoy riding ATVs, dune buggies, and other off-road vehicles in the huge stretches of sand. The famous Baja 500 and other rally races are popular spectator and participant sports. Or, if you've done the training, the scuba diving is incredible, while sailing and surfing are other common water sports. Adventurers of almost every cloth can find a place to play. First-timers to Baja may want to keep it simple and forgo trying to plan too much more than the basics—grab a couple of guidebooks or peruse a great Web site, like www.baja.com. From there, pick a few places to explore, then just hop the border. There are so many options that you're basically limited only if the weather diverts from beautiful, warm, and sunny. Whatever you decide to do, take into consideration that heading to these different areas of Mexico presents an increased risk, so be sure to keep the trip safe, and, as a result, you'll keep it fun too. Before you return to the United States, be sure you have checked the latest import and export regulations, and, of course, don't try to bring any prohibited items back into the country. If you're driving, allow adequate time to get back across the border, and be patient. Heavy traffic from Mexico, combined with the U.S. Customs inspections, makes for a hellacious waiting game, but really, the only thing you can do is wait and hope your car doesn't get selected for a more thorough search.

Before you return north, be sure to stroll your fill of empty beaches, enjoy enough time with yourself and your companions, and take the opportunity to meet the locals. Stop in at as many of the small shops, restaurants, and cantinas as you can, always smile, and give it your *mejor intento* at speaking Spanish. You'll quickly discover a colorful culture of friendly, easy-going people who like to laugh and have fun, and are quick to tell you of a potential adventure the guidebooks may have not yet uncovered. Of course, you've only got a weekend, so despite Baja's relaxed, almost lazy, pace of life, you'll find yourself in the last night of the weekend too soon enough. Under the gentle glow of a rising moon hanging huge over the horizon, snug in your sleeping bag, you look up to billions and billions of stars burning the night sky. It's hard to believe such a light show. Life sure sounds good as the dying embers of the campfire crackle, and you listen out to the waves lapping the shore, calming you toward sleep with a most hypnotic cadence. Who knows after this, you ask yourself as you drift off to dreamland— maybe this weekend escape will be the big one, the weekend that never ends. We'll see. Adios from Baja.

Price: $150–$500+

(Winter, Difficult)

DRIVING DIRECTIONS

Rugged mountains rising out of this unlikely desert nestled between the Pacific Ocean and the Sea of Cortez make the thousand-mile road trip following Highway 1 from San Diego to Cabo San Lucas one of the most beautiful drives in the world. Fly to Cabo unless you have time to spare, however, because the journey is too far and too strenuous for a single weekend. Driving south for shorter trips is much more feasible. Before heading across the border, though, purchase the most up-to-date and detailed road map you can find, and don't forget about auto insurance. With only one lane going in each direction, most roads are narrow by U.S. standards, and many don't even have a painted centerline. Despite a few scattered towns, most of the drive down the Baja peninsula is desolate, with very few gas stations, and the ones you do see might be closed or dry. Bring a spare fuel can, and fill up whenever possible. A second spare tire is also a good idea. Due to cattle and wildlife on the roads, avoid driving at night.

FOR MORE INFORMATION

Outfitters

ADVENTOURS OUTDOOR EXCURSIONS
Santa Barbara
(805) 899–2929
www.adventours.com

BAJA EXPEDITIONS
(858) 581–3311
www.bajaex.com

LOS CABOS FISHING CENTER
(011) 52–114–33736 (from U.S.)

PICANTE BLUEWATER SPORTFISHING
(714) 572–6693
www.picantesportfishing.com

PISCES SPORTFISHING FLEET
(011) 52–624–143–1288 (from U.S.)
www.piscessportfishing.com

SOLMAR SPORTFISHING, HOTEL, AND SCUBA
(800) 344–3349
www.solmar.com

TOFINO EXPEDITIONS LTD.
(800) 677–0877
www.tofino.com

TOUR BAJA
(800) 398–6200
www.tourbaja.com

Other

BAJA ONLINE
www.baja.com

BAJA QUEST ONLINE
www.bajaquest.com

BAJA TOURIST GUIDE
www.bajatouristguide.com

RECOMMENDED READING

Cummings, Joe. *Moon Handbooks: Baja— Tijuana to Cabo San Lucas* (4th ed.). Emeryville, Calif.: Avalon Travel Publishing, 2000.

Harris, Richard. *Hidden Baja: Including Tijuana, Ensenada, Mulege, La Paz, and Los Cabos* (3rd ed.). Berkeley, Calif.: Ulysses Press, 2002.

Salvadori, Clement. *Motorcycle Journeys through Baja*. Plano, Tex.: Whitehorse Press, 1997.

Steinbeck, John. *The Log from the Sea of Cortez*. New York: Penguin, 1941.

Willams, Jack. *The Magnificent Peninsula—Baja* (7th ed.). Sausalito, Calif.: H.J. Publications, 2002.

SLEEP CHEAP

Cabo San Lucas offers the whole gamut of lodging accommodations. The Los Milagros Hotel is an excellent option for those wanting to keep the price low. Rates start at $65 per night (including tax); kitchenettes and other options are also available. The hotel is clean and comfortable, but its major draw is its central location. Both beaches (Pacific and Sea of Cortez) are fifteen-minute walks, while famous party stops Cabo Wabo and Squid Roe are only blocks away. All rooms feature cable television, telephones, private baths, and air-conditioning. Reservations are necessary, as Los Milagros has only twelve rooms. For more information, call (718) 928–6647 (from U.S.), (624) 143-4566 (in Baja), or check www.losmilagros.com.mx.

Camping is another inexpensive option for Cabo visitors. Camping at Club Cabo, however, isn't exactly "roughing it," with its pool, Jacuzzi, and Internet access. Campsites run $12 to16 per night. Cabanas, RV sites, and palapa suites are also available. Club Cabo is conveniently located just a short walk from Cabo's best beaches, bars, the marina, and other downtown areas. Club Cabo's well-manicured grounds showcase a number of exotic fruits and colorful flowers including mangos, bananas, star fruit, coconuts, roses, bougainvillea, and hibiscus. Birding is very popular. For more information or reservations, call (011) 52-624-143-3348, or visit www.clubcabo.com.

Coastal Pavement Pounding

Running the Carlsbad Marathon

Runners are dedicated—and, sometimes, a little crazy. It takes an uncommon amount of personal commitment to run a marathon. For all but the most masochistic, the run is agony, and the agony lasts 26.2 miles. An average jogger may need four or five hours to complete the course. Even if it takes a little more time, maybe less, the distance is the same. Buy comfy running shoes, preferably two or three pairs of the same kind, and rotate wearing the different pairs. You're going to war with the pavement. Training starts now.

The air is crisp early. Start slow. Warm up. Do a little stretching. Start walking. Yell "double-time" if you have to. And just start running. Make your running an easy, effortless thing. Breathe in cadence, challenge yourself often. Train hard. Train consistently. Be fair to yourself. Several months in, you'll be ready if you trust you will be. Respect yourself. Get up early every morning you've scheduled for runs, and go run. If you haven't done this sort of thing before, or even if you have, training for and completing a marathon will be one of the toughest things you'll ever voluntarily put yourself through. Just as long as you know and act like you're braver than some stinking alarm clock, tougher than some stinking piece of pavement, smarter than some stinking uphill that seems to go on forever, and stronger than any stinking breeze in your face, you'll make it. Just start running.

Before you know it, you'll be cruising around the block a couple times, so why not start cruising through parks, and eventually to the other side of town. Take a weekend drive or bicycle ride to find and "clock" quiet roads and interesting running routes. Have fun. Pretend you're Forrest Gump if you want to. Be Rocky. Be who you are and run strong. Drink plenty of water. The training will get easier as you start getting into your rhythm and finding your own stride. Don't worry about pace so much if your pace is slow. You're going faster than walking anyway. If you keep going, you'll get there eventually. Buy a good book, or three, written by people who make sense to and for you, authors who outline different marathon training strategies based on what your marathon goals are—we recommend several inspiring books full of first-timer information. There are others, so browse at your local bookstore. Run inspired.

Running is also fun with partners, but you'll need to find some-one with a similar pace, although sometimes it helps to run with a stronger runner. Go faster, go slower, and make it a workout for both of you. Maybe you're the stronger runner, so have fun and slow down a bit. Or maybe you'll need to run alone. Running can be that kind of thing and that's okay. As you're running, you'll have a chance to think, or not to think, and time goes by. Miles go by. You'll hit walls—hopefully not of the reinforced concrete variety—and you'll find incredible bursts of energy and powerful second winds. Before you know it, two miles turns into ten, ten into fifteen, fifteen into a marathon. You've crossed the finish line.

Take the photo finish and compare it to your picture taken on the first day of training. Keep a running journal. Don't forget to send in your race registration early, or register online. The Carlsbad Marathon is limited to 3,000 participants. There's a chance you'll be able to register on race day, but don't count on it, thanks to the popularity of the run. The spectacular weather alone is a big factor in its fame. Late January, when the marathon is held, while much of the country is swallowed in snow and covered in cold, San Diego is breezy and bordering on tropical. The weather will likely be perfect, running conditions are incredibly ideal, and the course is ridiculously scenic.

There's history too. The annual Carlsbad Marathon (formerly the San Diego Marathon) is the second-oldest marathon on the West Coast. The very first marathon in San Diego was run from Oceanside to Mission Bay, and for years, the race was held here, but in 1978, a new race started, the Heart of San Diego Marathon, which crossed the Coronado Bridge and finished at Qualcomm Stadium. Then in 1985, the two marathons merged, and in 1990, the event was moved to North San Diego County, where now over 10,000 people participate in the runs, the golf tournament, and the other festivities.

If you're feeling strong and kicking well out at the front of the pack, go for it. Run your race. The Carlsbad Marathon is a certified course and therefore is considered a qualifier for the Boston Marathon. However, unless you've run a few of these runs before, you probably won't be worried about that. Of course, you might just happen to qualify anyway—a significant segment of the course stretches out along the beautiful coast, allowing runners to marvel away many miles of muscle aches or pains. For many people it feels like a fast course, and it often turns out to be. The marathon (and half-marathon) out-and-back route gently rolls along the Pacific Ocean while a section even winds past the LEGOLAND California amusement park. The road is closed to traffic, while the Carlsbad Police Department and thousands of volunteers ensure everything goes smoothly.

For those interested in finding run partners or receiving training advice, the Carlsbad Marathon also offers a unique six-month program. These USA Fit programs (see sdmarathon.com) are held in San Diego, North County, Temecula, North County Inland, and South Bay. Otherwise, train by yourself, by the book, and always remember to have fun. If you happen to miss the Carlsbad Marathon, or if you really get into it and decide to run several more marathons, there are plenty more held in Southern California in the cooler winter months. The Catalina Island Buffalo Run is a popular off-road trail run, held in late February, or hop the ferry instead in late March for the annual Catalina Island Marathon. Beware of the lung-busting hills making for a 3,700-foot elevation gain, and keep in mind that hotel space on the island is limited. The popular Los Angeles Marathon is an option for early March. On the other hand, you may discover you want to branch out into other endurance sports such as triathlons or ultra-distance events. Whatever the case, and however far you end up going, it all begins or continues at the Carlsbad Marathon. Every run and every new adventure start with just that single step.

Price: Less than $100
(Winter, Difficult)

DRIVING DIRECTIONS

The Carlsbad Marathon is held in North San Diego County, approximately thirty minutes north of San Diego and ninety minutes south of Los Angeles in the charming coastal community of Carlsbad. From San Diego, take the 5 Freeway north (from Los Angeles and Orange County, follow 5 Freeway south) to Highway 78 East. Exit El Camino Real, and you will find the run start point on the right at the Plaza Camino Real. There will be a big tent located behind Sears. Follow the signs to free and plentiful parking, but be sure to arrive early on race day to avoid delays. LEGOLAND California is located just north of Carlsbad. From the 5 Freeway South, exit on Cannon Road East, and follow signs to park.

FOR MORE INFORMATION

CARLSBAD MARATHON
(760) 692–2900
www.sdmarathon.com

CARLSBAD CONVENTION AND
VISITORS BUREAU
(760) 434–6093
www.carlsbadca.org

LEGOLAND CALIFORNIA
(760) 918–5346
www.legoland.com

SAN DIEGO CONVENTION AND
VISITORS BUREAU
(619) 236–1212
www.sandiego.org

RECOMMENDED READING

Galloway, Jeff. *Marathon: You Can Do It!* Bolinas, Calif.: Shelter
Publications, 2001.

Kislevitz, Gail. *First Marathons.* Halcottsville, N.Y.: Breakaway Books,
1999.

Whitsett, David, et al. *The Non-Runner's Marathon Trainer.* New York:
McGraw-Hill/Contemporary Books, 1998.

SLEEP CHEAP

The stretch of coast near Carlsbad is one of Southern California's
most beautiful. The Carlsbad Marathon's host hotel is the Carlsbad
Holiday Inn; when reserving a room, be sure to ask for special runner rates (760–438–7880; www.holidayinn.com). Another fun lodging option for your marathon weekend is to camp at South Carlsbad
State Beach. The campground is located atop a large bluff and
offers incredible ocean views. Not far away, stairs lead down to the
sand. The beach here is known for excellent surfing and swimming,
fishing, scuba diving, and picnicking. Showers and restroom facilities are available. The campground is quite popular for race weekend (and also during the summer or for holidays), so reservations
are recommended. Campsites have no shade. The beach and campground are located 3 miles south of Carlsbad on Carlsbad
Boulevard. Call (760) 438–3143 for more information. And, of
course, since you just ran 26.2 miles, don't forget the air mattress!

Swimming with Sharks

My, What Pretty Teeth

Thanks to ruthless media playing on fears thousands of years old, most people will break a sweat just from the mention of sharks. Going one step further in the conversation, talking about swimming with sharks—shark diving—is regarded as absolute lunacy, crazy talk that can only lead to getting munched by mouthfuls of razor-sharp teeth. Most people have no interest whatsoever in even seeing a shark, let alone purposely jumping into waters where these sleek, ballistic-bodied ocean predators are likely to cruise by, and sometimes even take a swipe at your arm. Granted, sharks can be every bit as dangerous as the flesh-ripping accounts told in books and movies, but only if they attack. In reality, being attacked by a shark is less likely than your car losing its brakes and driving off a cliff on your way to the harbor. Still, there's nothing like getting in harm's way.

San Diego Shark Diving Expeditions offers one-day trips to the deep blue water 10 to 20 miles off the Southern California coast. Encounters are not guaranteed but very likely, as buckets full of bloody chum help ensure you will be swimming front row for a ferocious feeding frenzy. Of course, even getting your fins wet in water with worked up sharks, despite protection from a steel cage, takes a particular level of commitment—some might say the straitjacket variety. Although you only need an open-water scuba certification, the reality is that shark diving is not for everyone. Ironically, the biggest concern is not being eaten alive, but rather that riding in a 32-foot sea vessel this far off shore means enduring some boat-rocking, stomach-churning surface swells. If you get seasick, you're stuck on board until the end of the day, so bring Dramamine or whatever works for you. Oh, and since the bottom to all this blue water sits more than 3,000 feet below your feet, the conditions can be a little intimidating.

Once the boat arrives on site, the cage is dropped, and divers get a quick practice dive to dial in their equipment and get accustomed to the cage; nonessential gear such as snorkels and dive computers that could tangle in the cage are secured aboard the boat. To allow you to stand comfortably in the cage without bouncing up and down with each wave, 4 or 5 pounds of extra lead is added to your weightbelt. Then, after the practice dive, the water is chummed, and lunch is served. The waiting game is on, but it's usually over before you finish your sandwich, when someone spots a distinct fin breaking the water's surface. Soon enough, the thrashing attacks on fish chunks ensue. And before we forget to mention it, you'll soon be surface swimming 20 feet or so from the boat to reach the cage after the sharks arrive.

Many experts insist that sharks can sense fear, so hopefully your wetsuit mutes the pounding of your heart and other telltale signs; however, as an extra safety precaution, a divemaster clad in chainmail escorts each student to the cage. Very aware of the sharks coming a little too close for comfort despite your overadrenalined daze, you'll probably find yourself wishing you were wearing shark-proof steel mesh too. Reaching the cage is a huge psychological relief. Depending on the cooperation of the sharks, mostly blues and the occasional mako, divers usually get two trips to the cage, each lasting about an hour. Chance sightings of mola mola, ocean sunfish, or pelagic stingrays can add a special touch to the trip, so an underwater video or still camera is a highly recommended, if not a required, accessory. Inquire about rental equipment.

The shark diving lasts until just before dark, so the boat usually gets back to shore between 7:00 and 9:00 P.M. When you are soaking in the hotel tub, sobbing from the realization that you were cavorting with the top predators of the underwater food chain only hours ago, don't worry about it much—the reaction is normal. You dove, you conquered. However, on the odd chance this isn't enough excitement for you, San Diego Shark Diving Expeditions also offers multiday adventures where you have a chance of diving with a great white shark, the sea's apex predator. The day trip is reasonably priced at around $275, but the multiday trips cost more, depending on how far and how long you're out to sea.

A great way to supplement a shark-searching blue water day trip is to dive one of Southern California's greatest shipwrecks, the *H.M.C.S. Yukon*, also known as the "Wreck of the West." The *H.M.C.S. Yukon*, a 366-foot Canadian destroyer, rests in the water less than 2 miles from Mission Beach in the northern stretch of the artificial reef area called Wreck Alley. Going by the technical definition, however, the *Yukon* is not an artificial reef; although the San Diego Ocean Foundation was indeed intending to sink her in July 2000, the ship accidentally slipped below the surface the night before planned. After thorough cleaning and preparation, which included cutting over one hundred holes in the sides to allow for easy penetration and escape, then being towed to the planned site, rough seas caused the *Yukon* to take on too much water. Heading down bow first, the ship settled on her port side, and although the plan called for the *Yukon* to be positioned upright, the openings now point to the surface, which conveniently allows a lot more light into the interior. Whether you call it a wreck or an artificial reef, diving the *Yukon* is an incredible experience and perfect way to maximize your San Diego dive trip.

The *Yukon* is exciting and can be as easy or as challenging as you desire, whether this is your first wreck dive or your fiftieth. With a maximum bottom depth of around 100 feet, the ship staggers beginners with her immensity, and most will find that much of the wreck's outside can be explored while staying shallower than 75 feet. More experienced divers will appreciate the *Yukon* as a great introduction to or training ground for wreck penetration and nitrox diving. Wherever this puts you, be sure to pick up the dive slate (available at most San Diego scuba shops) that provides a detailed diagram of the wreck, including numbers to correspond with the holes on the ship, which are also marked with numbers. Some of the bigger holes even have matching diagrams marked with YOU ARE HERE to make sure you don't get lost. Diver safety is the primary concern.

The best way to get yourself down to the *Yukon* is to book a trip with Blue Escape; two-tank dives are available almost every day of the year and cost about $75. Blue Escape's extensive experience bringing divers to the *Yukon* prominently shows as they point out some of the more interesting nooks and crannies—apparently, the barrels of the forward guns are fake. Also, be sure to keep watch for the giant black sea bass that has claimed the area under the bow as his territory. Probably the most fun part of diving the *Yukon*, however, is overcoming your mental predisposition of which way is up; because of the 70 degree tilt, the walls are now the floor and ceiling, and vice versa. Even experienced divers often orientate their bodies to the ship rather than reality. Of course, this is nothing to worry about, but instead, is rather amusing as you watch the bubbles veer off sideways.

If you want to boost your dive experience by facing your fears of sharks, and then as an option, do some easier wreck diving to cap off the weekend escape, San Diego is your best bet in Southern California. The folks at San Diego Shark Diving Expeditions and Blue Escape will help ensure that your bottom time is maximized,

Don't worry—you'll have a cage to protect you. DIVERSMAG.COM

your fun levels reach new depths, and you keep all your fingers and limbs right where they should be.

Price: $250+
(Winter, Difficult)

DRIVING DIRECTIONS

To reach the Blue Escape Dive Center, take I–8 West to the Sports Arena Boulevard exit. Stay to the right, and turn right at the end of the off-ramp. Drive over the bridge and past SeaWorld Drive, keep to the right onto West Mission Bay Drive. Go through the traffic loop to the first stoplight. Turn left twice onto Quivira Road. The shop is located 100 feet on your right at Sportsman's Seafood Restaurant.

San Diego Shark Diving Expeditions is located past Blue Escape, at the end of Quivira Road. Turn right into the parking lot just before entering the loop at Hospitality Point.

FOR MORE INFORMATION

Outfitters

BLUE ESCAPE
(619) 223–3483
www.blueescape.com

**SAN DIEGO SHARK DIVING
EXPEDITIONS**
www.sdsharkdiving.com
(619) 299–8560

Other

**PELAGIC SHARK RESEARCH
FOUNDATION**
Capitola
www.pelagic.org

RECOMMENDED READING

Carwardine, Mark, Ken Watterson, and Clive James. *The Shark-Watcher's Handbook: A Guide to Sharks and Where to See Them.* Princeton, N.J.: Princeton University Press, 2002.

Jackson, Jack. *Diving with Sharks: And Other Adventure Dives.* New York: McGraw-Hill/Contemporary Books, 2001.

SLEEP CHEAP

Visitors to the San Diego area will find a wealth of available lodging options, including high-rise hotels, budget motels, cozy bed-and-breakfasts by the sea, hostels (see Escape 43), and plenty of campgrounds (see Escape 15). Numerous other San Diego camping parks are available. For more information, call San Diego County Parks and Recreation (858–694–3049).

For larger groups or those seeking low-key independence, San Diego offers a slew of vacation rental houses and condominiums. Options vary greatly, as do prices. Split between several couples or a group of friends or family, a rental is often the most economical way to stay indoors. For more information, contact Accommodations Online (619–741–1158; sandiego.bookarental.com), Sandy Beach Rentals (619–224–1500; www.sandybeachrentals.com), Beach and Bayside Vacations (858–488–8827; www.beachnbayside.com), or San Diego Vacation Cottages (619–291–9091; www.sandiegocottages.com).

About the Authors

Ray Bangs includes bicycle touring, mountaineering, powder skiing, and diving among his favorite outdoor activities. Working as a writer and photographer, Ray makes his home in Tempe, Arizona, though he spends at least five months of the year traveling. In researching this book, he spent well over a year on vacation.

Chris Becker works as a freelance editor and travel writer in Phoenix, Arizona. He has written dozens of feature articles on travel, both regional and abroad, and is the coauthor of *52 Great Weekend Escapes in Arizona*. He is currently working on more books, learning to fly fish, and figuring out a way to move to Malibu.